ENTER THE World of MASS MEDIA

PRINT MEDIA TELEVISION INTERNET RADIO

Barun Roy

PUSTAK MAHAL®

Delhi • Mumbai • Patna • Hyderabad • Bengaluru

Publishers
Pustak Mahal®

J-3/16 , Daryaganj, New Delhi-110002
☎ 23276539, 23272783, 23272784 • *Fax:* 011-23260518
E-mail: info@pustakmahal.com • *Website:* www.pustakmahal.com

Sales Centre

- 10-B, Netaji Subhash Marg, Daryaganj, New Delhi-110002
☎ 23268292, 23268293, 23279900 • *Fax:* 011-23280567
E-mail: rapidexdelhi@indiatimes.com
- **Hind Pustak Bhawan**
6686, Khari Baoli, Delhi-110006
☎ 23944314, 23911979

Branches

Bengaluru: ☎ 080-22234025 • *Telefax:* 080-22240209
E-mail: pustak@airtelmail.in • pustak@sancharnet.in
Mumbai: ☎ 022-22010941, 022-22053387
E-mail: rapidex@bom5.vsnl.net.in
Patna: ☎ 0612-3294193 • *Telefax:* 0612-2302719
E-mail: rapidexptn@rediffmail.com
Hyderabad: *Telefax:* 040-24737290
E-mail: pustakmahalhyd@yahoo.co.in

ISBN 978-81-223-1080-1

Edition: 2010

Printed at : Glorious Printers, Delhi

Dedicated to my Heroes

Raghubir Rawat and Jiten Roy

Contents

Preface

IN 2007, I decided to give myself a much needed holiday from my professional endeavours. I had been travelling for too long. While my work and research took me to places, the call of the mountains back home was too strong to resist. On my return thence, I immediately settled down to write a couple of books and blog[1] . *Gorkhas and Gorkhaland* and *Enter The World of Mass Media* are the fruit of this year's writing.

The need for this book spelt out itself in the numerous interactions that I had with my readers and Mass Communication enthusiasts all over the nation. "Why don't you write a resource book on Mass Communication?" they frequently asked. Truly, there was a great need of an all-encompassing book on Mass Communication – one that did not merely go through the different aspects of Mass Communication but also set standards for the future. Technology has always had the role of redefining Mass Communication. Similarly today, Internet has transformed Mass Communication. Yet a great deal of standardisation in form and set of norms needs to be worked upon and unanimously accepted for the Internet to be established as a respected medium of Mass Communication.

This book with the help of some of the best known minds in the field of Mass Communication, Marketing and Information Technologies seeks to set forward, for the first time in India, a germinating set of standards, norms and ethics to be followed on the Internet. Chapters on "Internet Ethics" among others are believed to go a long way in helping Online Mass Communication gain respectability that it deserves. This book also sets out to lay grounds for the future of Mass Communication. A reader, I hope after going through this book, will not just have an understanding of the subject, but coupled with his or her own added insights, he or she will in fact, become a transforming force in the field.

1 The Himalayan Beacon also popularly known as Beacon Online is one of the fastest growing blogs in India. It can be reached at http://www.beacononline.wordpress.com

Acknowledgements

This work would not have been possible if Journalists, Researchers, Scholars, Professors, Editors, Newscasters, Policy Makers, Web Publishers, and Bloggers from all around the world had not come to my aid and helped me with their insights and experiences. Indeed, all the photographs, statistics and the rest have been contributed by them. I have acknowledged their contribution individually as and when I have used them. However, let me also take this instance to begin to offer my heartfelt gratitude to all my friends, peers and support groups who granted me permission to reproduce and examine their works.

I am particularly grateful to William Heifer, Peter Scribner and R. Raju[2] who offered their insights on Internet Laws. I am also particularly grateful to the fellow bloggers at *The Himalayan Beacon* that helped me set up the Bloggers' Code of Ethics which was a result of a popular consensus[3] , a practice inherent to the Internet. I am also grateful to my muse, Sanjana, for her love and support. She has been with me through thick and thin.

I, most definitely, would not have been able to complete this work without the support of my parents, whose love, blessings and prayers have been the foundation of my life and work. I must also thank my readers who have since my first book been my inspiration and my patrons. Without the readers, no author can exist. Thank you all and Thank you God! I am indebted to you all.

Thursday, September 18, 2008

Clarke Road, Darjeeling

Barun Roy

---

2. William Heifer, Peter Scribner and R. Raju are some of the best known Internet Lawyers operating in the world. While William Heifer is a Bonn-based Lawyer, Peter Scribner and R. Raju operate from New York and United States, and have handled cases involving Microsoft, Google, Yahoo etc.

3. This proves beyond doubt that Internet is perhaps the most democratic of technologies.

BRIEF HISTORY oF MASS MEDIA

"If Mass Media were to ever fail,

humanity would be thrust back to its primitive oblivion."

A Brief History of Print Media

For centuries human civilisation has utilised the printed media to spread news and information about political and social happenings to the masses. The *Roman Acta Diurna*, appearing around 59 B.C., is the earliest recorded newspaper. Julius Caesar, wanting to inform the public about important social and political happenings, ordered upcoming events posted in major cities. Written on large white boards and displayed in popular places like the Baths, the *Acta Diurna* kept citizens informed about government scandals, military campaigns, trials and executions. In the 8th century in China, the first newspapers appeared as handwritten news sheets in Beijing. However, it was only with the invention of the printing press in 14th century Europe[4] , that the spread of news and

4. In fact, a Chinese would be invariably surprised to hear that Johannes Gutenberg in Germany invented printing approximately 550 years ago. Why? Because the art of printing is much older. It was first developed in Eastern Asia, and centuries before Gutenberg's birth around 1400, the Chinese knew the system of 'movable characters' which Gutenberg is supposed to have 'invented'. Characters on bones, bronze, ceramic and stone slabs give evidence of the use of writing in China already in the 5th millennium before Christ. Writing became reproducible in larger quantities when the Chinese succeeded in inventing paper approximately 2200 years ago. In the beginning, paper consisted largely of hemp fibres, then silk rags or mulberry bark and similarly exotic raw materials. But it worked! Suddenly, large writing surfaces were available that could be easily produced.

Soon, the question of reproducing the characters also arose. Chinese abrasions and simple printing of stone inscriptions on paper are considered to be early forms of printing. They enabled a direct spreading of texts. In the 2nd century AD, at about the same time when in the western world the Roman emperor Marc Aurel recorded his philosophical thought on papyrus roles and for the duplication was dependent on scribes, in China since the year 175, the main works of the classical Chinese literature were carved in stone slabs. Thousands of copies were made by simple printing. Moistened paper was pressed onto the inscription stones, and when brushing the paper with ink, the cut characters stood out white against the blackened paper. The next level was the so-called woodblock printing in the 7th century. Each character was cut in reverse into a piece of wood by removing all surrounding wood. These raised lines were dyed and abraded on paper, thus producing a positive print of the desired text.

This method remained over centuries the primary means for printing religious and everyday books, from playing cards, calendars, paper money and pictures in China. The sophisticated Chinese administrative and education system of the Song dynasty (960-1269) caused a printing boom. Thus, encyclopaedias, manuals and literature collections of all kinds were produced. The method of printing from wood was used in China until the end of the 19th century. But around 1040 A.D., when in Europe William the Conqueror still spent his childhood days in Normandy, a Chinese called Bi Sheng already experimented with movable, individual printing types made of ceramic. He arranged them on an iron plate as whole texts and fixed them with a layer of wax and resin.

information on paper increased dramatically. Short pamphlets reported on a news event and were circulated around the community.

The First Modern Newspapers

Johannes Guttenberg

The first modern newspapers, or publications that would appear regularly and frequently, were a European invention. The first half of the 17th century saw weekly news publications popping up in Germany, Italy, France, England, and many other European nations. These newspaper featured items from all over Europe and occasionally from America or Asia. However, they rarely, if ever, reported any news about the country in which they were being printed. English papers reported on French military blunders, while French papers reported on the latest royal scandal from across the channel. In most countries, the government required print shops to obtain a licence to print. This gave governments the power to quickly halt the printing of anything that seemed detrimental to the current administration. The newspapers were allowed to be published as long as they did not discuss any local issues or events that might disturb or invite opposition from citizens. Crime and violence was of little concern in those early days of newspaper printing.

During the English Civil War, it was the first time when events within England began to be reported to the English population. As the grip of King Charles I on the media began to loosen, the newspapers found themselves able to report on

---

These were then printed. If the characters were to be used again, one heated the iron plate until melting wax and resin released the forms again. 300 years later, the first wooden characters appeared.

From there, it was only a small step to manufacture the individual wood characters in uniform size to be able to always assemble them in standardised blocks. Soon successful experiments were carried out with characters of copper, lead or brass. But printing with movable characters never really established itself in China until the end of the last century. The reason was obvious. While traditional printing with whole wooden plates required enormous storage space, the thousands and thousands of Chinese characters prevented a simple and above all fast composition of printing plates from movable letters.

In comparison, it was much simpler for Gutenberg, with 26 characters and a handful of auxiliary characters to set all words! In Asia only the Koreans reached the crucial step. They developed an alphabetical script called "Han'gul", almost at the time of Gutenberg's invention in Germany. This script consisted initially of 28 and later 24 characters and was presented officially in Korea in the year 1444 – almost at the same time (i.e. from 1452 to 1455) that Gutenberg printed his famous Bible in Mainz.

national issues without fear of being shut down or repressed. Issues of violence were reported more frequently as the country struggled to find a leader. One of the first times, a headline used on any newspaper came towards the end of the English Civil War with the beheading of Charles I. A short respite in this newfound freedom came under the Parliamentary rule of Oliver Cromwell.

However, with the Glorious Revolution of 1688, and the Licensing Act of 1695, the belief that the Press needed to be free from censorship and had the right to criticise government eventually took root.

The Americana's

The Ideal of Freedom of the Press made its way slowly to the American Colonies during the 1600's and 1700's. England's tight control over the colonies made it extremely difficult for news publication to be produced without being scrutinised by the English Governors. On September 25, 1690, the Boston-based '*Publick Occurrences Both Forreign and Domestick*'[5] became the first American newspaper to be published. One of its stories attacked a group of Indians[6] who had been allied with the English against the French. With authorities expressing "High Resentment and Disallowance" towards the publication, they immediately barred further printing. It would not be until the *Boston Newsletter* printed in 1704 that the colonies would have a newspaper again. The new generation of newspapers tried to avoid political confrontations with colonial authorities. However, when James Franklin, publisher of the *New England Courant,* accused the colonial government of failing to adequately protect the area from pirate attacks in the 1720's, he was thrown in jail and banned from

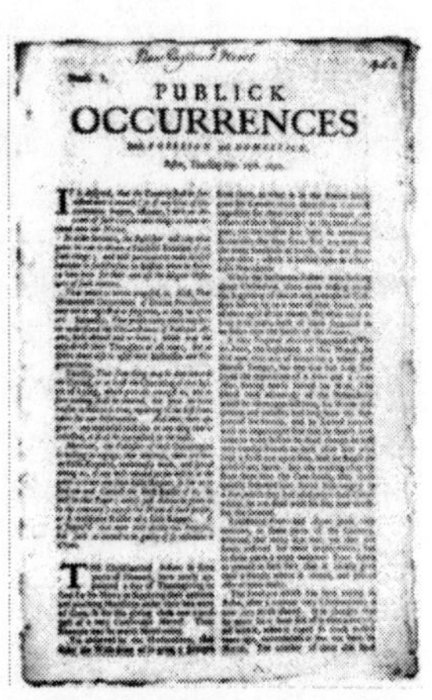
PUBLICK
OCCURRENCES

The Front page of Publick Occurrences Both Forreign and Domestick

5. Published by Benjamin Harris, Publick Occurrences was hardly quality journalism by modern standards. According to leading Mass Communication Historian John Tebbel – "Harris was a bigot and an anti-Catholic. It is safe to say, no major American institution has been launched by so unworthy a pioneer." John may have been a bit overwhelmed by his hate for Harris but this much was unanimous – it contained no news less than a month old, and its intentions, at least as Harris explained them, were honourable. His paper, the publisher told his readers in a front-page notice, would print "Memorable Occurrents of Divine Providence" as well as "Circumstances of Publique Affairs... which may not only direct their thoughts at all times, but at some times also to assist their Businesses and Negotiations."

6. Native Americans

running the publication. His younger brother, the famous Benjamin Franklin, soon took over the newspaper, and went on to begin publication of the *Pennsylvania Gazette* in 1729.

Newspapers soon began to play a huge role in inciting patriotic feelings throughout the colonies in the years preceding the American Revolution. John Peter Zenger was arrested in 1734 for publishing seditious libel (disloyal slander) against the Governor of New York[7] . However, the jury in his trial found him innocent, and from that moment on, it became increasingly difficult for British authorities to convict publishers who spoke out against governmental decisions. When the British Parliament tried to pass the Stamp Act in 1765 to tax publications within the colonies, the newspapers reported massive protests by civilians, and the Act was soon repealed. The Boston Tea Party was planned in the house of a local newspaper editor. For the first time in the history of printed media, mainstream newspapers began to lead the call for an overthrow of a governing body. They played a huge part in inspiring the American Revolution.

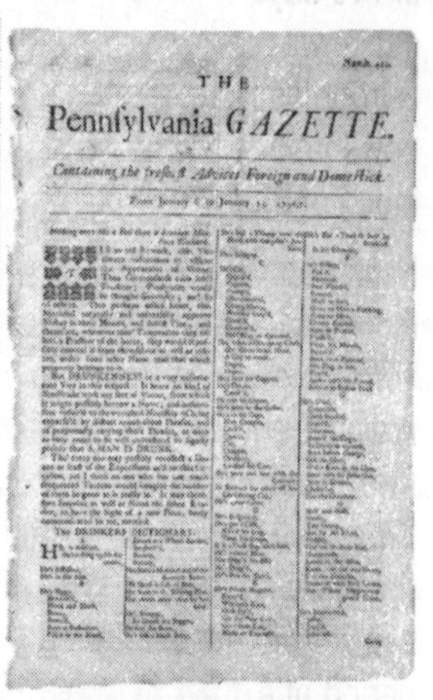
THE
Pennsylvania GAZETTE.

Pennsylvania Gazette.
Courtesy Bill Collins

In the years after the Revolutionary War, newspapers began to take on many partisan-specific points of view in their publications. They took a step back from focusing on the crime and violence that they reported during the Revolutionary War and became puppets of the political parties. Newspapers began to be financed, sponsored, and run directly by Federalist and Republican Party leaders. Publishers who supported one political party would criticise the actions of its opposition. Many times people needed to buy competing newspapers to obtain each side of a particular argument. In 1787, the Bill of Rights guaranteed Freedom of Speech for newspapers and other media under the first amendment. A direct challenge to this freedom came in 1798 when Federalist leaders passed the Sedition Act. The Sedition Act stated that "any false, scandalous and malicious writing... against the Government of

7. The Governor of colonial New York had in fact stood before his council, angrily waving Zenger's newspaper (New York Weekly Journal) and said, "This Journal... it's making me the laughing stock of the whole colony! We must suppress the paper! Burn every copy! This man Zenger... he's broken the Law by publishing scandalous libels about me, the King's personal representative in this miserable town!"

the United States, the Congress or the President with intent to... bring them... into contempt or disrepute" was illegal. It was an attempt by Federalists to stop Republican newspapers from printing papers that criticised their actions. This act was repealed though with the election of Thomas Jefferson, after which political influence over the nations newspapers began to fall.

The Advent of Telegraph

The invention of the telegraph in 1844 revolutionised the print media industry. For the first time, information could be transferred within a matter of minutes from all parts of the world. Publications were reporting events that were now only one or two days old, rather than one or two weeks. In 1866, a transatlantic telegraph cable was completed, and American newspapers were receiving news from Europe as fast as they were from other parts of the US. By the mid-19th century, newspapers had evolved to become the prime means of getting information for much of the United States and Europe.

Newspaper reporting may have come of age in terms of coverage during the American Civil War. Reporters had to overcome horrible conditions, and sometimes even government attempts to censor their reports. And when they crossed enemy lines to get detailed accounts of issues and battles, they faced the threat of being labelled as a spy. Albert D. Richardson of the *New York Tribune*, Henry Villard of the *New York Herald*, Felix Gregory de Fontaine of the *Charlotte Courier* and Peter W. Alexander of the *Savannah Republican* are considered among the best Civil War reporters of the time. The Civil War was a period of extreme growth in the field of newspapers in the United States. There were 3,000 newspapers in 1860, 4,500 in 1870 and 7,000 in 1880.

However, newspapers in the 18th and the first half of the 19th century were not very objective. Typically they only reflected the point of view of one person, their publisher. In 1841, a man named Horace Greeley, who was one of the most talented American journalists of the time, started the *New York Tribune* as a penny paper. He used it to express his abolitionist, Whig and then Republican views, while Bennett's *Herald* reflected his support of the Democratic Party. Henry J. Raymond, founder of the *New York Daily Times,* which has been shortened to the *New York Times,* became a major player in the Republican Party in 1851. Weekly editions of these New York papers, the *Tribune* in particular, were read throughout the United States, spreading the views of their publishers around the country.

In 1831, abolitionist advocate William Lloyd Garrison started *The Liberator* with the purpose of changing people's minds. In 1827, John B. Russwurm and Reverend Samuel Cornish brought out *Freedom's Journal*, the first newspaper published by blacks[8] in the United States; their paper had a goal similar to that of Garrison's paper. They wrote, "We wish to plead our own cause, too long have others spoken for us." Frederick Douglas, a great Afro-American writer, started *The North Star* in 1847 solely as he put it, "to attack slavery in all its forms and aspects".

As newspapers began to go into mass circulation, they became valuable businesses with large staffs. They started to be less of a vehicle for one person's opinion and more of a provider of information. The rise of wire services also helped to reduce the emphasis on personal opinions, because now news stories could be distributed to many different papers of many different political persuasions. The rise of science as well as the development of realism in literature during the 19th century gave new respect to the way facts were treated.

After the Civil War, the *'inverted pyramid'* writing style became more popular and helped give more respect to the facts. In the inverted pyramid style, the facts are detached from the narrative structures in which they were formally imbedded and arrayed in order of importance with the most important facts such as who, what, when, where, and why, in the 'lead' at the top of the story. Journalism was beginning to be thought of as a profession and with that came its own professional standards. In 1904, the University of Missouri became the home of the first school of journalism in the United States. The American Society of Newspaper Editors drafted the '*Canons of Journalism*[9]' in 1923, which included this dictum: "News reports should be free from opinion or bias of any kind."

But, of course, it is impossible for any human writing to be completely unbiased. True objectivity is an unreachable goal; there are just too many different sides to issues and too many different ways of viewing events for them all to be treated fairly in a news story. However, the new emphasis on facts above opinions did not stop certain journalists, such as Lincoln Steffens, Ida Tarbell, and Jacob Riis from using newspapers, magazines and books to crusade against the injustices they saw in American society in the late 19th and early 20th century. Nor did it prevent publishers like William Allen White, who purchased the *Emporia Gazette* in 1895, from using their newspapers to make a personal mark on American

8. African Americans or Afro-Americans

9. Canons of Journalism were revised and renamed "Statements of Principles" in 1975.

politics. Nevertheless, in the second half of the 19th century and the early 20th century, newspapers slowly began to try to keep their opinions restricted to the editorial columns and out of the news stories.

Some news stories have focused on crime, violence, and sex for as long as news has been exchanged. A few of such stories could be found in the first American newspaper, *Publick Occurrences*. However, there have been certain periods in the history of American journalism, especially when new audiences were being pursued and competition for circulation was intense, that sensationalism seemed to play an unusually large role in the news coverage. During these times, cries of outrage over a decline in seriousness and good taste could be heard. One of these periods occurred in the era of the Penny Press in the beginning of the 1830's and 1840's. Crime news and human-interest stories occupied a large portion of the newspaper columns. In 1840, James Gordon Bennett became the object of a 'moral war', led by other newspapers, with his eagerness to cover the details of bloody murders and pass on rumours of sex scandals. Nevertheless, Bennett's *Herald* became the best-selling newspaper in the United States.

The second period of sensationalism came when Joseph Pulitzer[10] introduced his 'new journalism'. Pulitzer, who created the *St Louis Post-Dispatch* in 1878 and then took over the '*New York World*' in 1883, was an unusually aggressive, demanding and intelligent editor. He fought important crusades on behalf of workers, immigrants and the poor. He was a major innovator, particularly in his Sunday paper to which he added expanded women's and sports pages and the first colour comics in a newspaper. Pulitzer also knew how to use reports tinged with violence and sex to sell his newspapers. Such as is seen in the headlines from his **World**: 'CORNETTI'S LAST NIGHT' and 'LITTLE LOTTA'S LOVERS.'

A style of journalism similar to Pulitzer's was beginning to be practised with some success in London by Alfred Harmsworth, who started the *Daily Mail* in 1896. Harmsworth created the first modern, small-sized 'tabloid'[11] newspaper, the *Daily Mirror*, in 1903. Joseph Medill Patterson and Robert R. McCormick

10. Joseph Pulitzer, the son of a grain dealer, was born in Budapest, in the Austro-Hungarian Empire in April, 1847. He emigrated to the United States in 1864 and settled in St. Louis. He worked as a mule tender, waiter and hack driver before studying English at the Mercantile Library. In 1868, Pulitzer was recruited by Carl Schurz for his German language daily, the Westliche Post. Pulitzer later became the first media tycoon of the world. Today, Pulitzer Prize is the highest prize given to US nationals who excel in newspaper journalism, literary works and musical compositions. The prize is administered by Columbia University.

11. The term 'Tabloid' was actually borrowed from the drug industry.

meanwhile, seeing how well Harmsworth's *Mirror* was selling[12] , decided to start tabloid journalism in the United States. They created the *Illustrated Daily News*,

A cartoon showing Joseph Pulitzer, as the self-proclaimed caretaker of the Universe. Cartoon Courtesy Spartacus Educational

which appeared in New York in 1919, heralding the third period of sensationalism in American Journalism.

Tabloids, like the *Daily News* and its competitors, Bernard McFadden's *Daily Graphic* and Hearst's *Daily Mirror* were easy to read on the city's new subway trains and they were filled with sensational crime and scandal stories. Other tabloid newspapers started during this time period were the *Los Angeles News*, the *Philadelphia Daily News*, the *Detroit Daily* and the more serious *Chicago*

12. In fact, over a million copies per day!

Times. By 1940, the *New York Daily* News had a circulation of almost two million.

After World War II, anti-Vietnam war protests and severe changes in cultures throughout the world produced various alternative newspapers. These alternative newspapers were more 'adventurous' in regard to culture than newspapers prior to this time. They were also considered controversial due to the anti-war sentiments of the time. An example of the more successful of these papers was 1955's New York's *Village Voice*.

Despite this new strain of newspapers, the numbers continued to decline over time. The remaining newspapers usually fell into control of large corporations. The limitations brought forth by the small amount of newspapers in circulation led to an increase in Press criticism, since news coverage in mainstream society was so limited. This first became an issue in 1940 courtesy of AJ Liebling. In 1961, Liebling argued that the United States was advancing towards a monopolistic Press. His basis for this argument was the fact that only 61 US cities had competing newspaper companies. He stated that the lack of newspapers indicated a lack of variety in objectivity and perspective.

Nine Eras of the American Press

(Adapted from Emery and Emery – The Press and America)

1. Colonial Press (up through 1776)
2. Revolutionary Press (1765-1788)
3. Political Press (1788-1833)
4. Penny Press (1833-1883)
5. Personal Editors (1840-1890)
6. Yellow Journalism (1890-1917)
7. Jazz Journalism (1914-1933)
8. Age of Consolidation (1929-till date)
9. Electronic Journalism (1960-till date)

The British Indian Empire

William Bolts, a former employee turned private businessman of the British East India Company[13] was the first individual to attempt to start the first newspaper in India in 1776. Bolts, however, had to give up due to the disapproval of the Court of Directors of the Company. The subsequent misappreciation by the Board of Directors stayed on for about four years and it was only in 1780 that the first newspaper in India *The Bengal Gazette* was started by James Augustus Hicky. *The Bengal Gazette*, a two-sheet newspaper, however, concentrated itself in writing on the private lives of the elites of the Company, which in turn, in due time, led Hicky to much trouble with the Company. For instance, in one of his issues, Augustus Hicky is said to have mounted a 'mocking attack' on the then Governor-General Sir Warren Hastings' wife. The British East India Company did not take Hicky's words lightly. Hicky was sentenced to four months of imprisonment and a fine of Rs. 500 was imposed on him. However, this did not

---

13. The British East India Company, originally two very similarly named companies, and popularly known as John Company, founded by the Royal Charter of Queen Elizabeth I on December 31, 1600, became one of the most powerful commercial enterprises in its time. The original company, The Governor and Company of Merchants of London Trading into the East Indies, merged in 1702 with The English Company Trading to the East Indies (which had been formed in 1698), to become The United Company of Merchants of England Trading to the East Indies.

The Company was founded by a coterie of enterprising and influential businessmen, who obtained the Crown's charter for exclusive permissions to trade in the East Indies. Initially, however, it made little impression on the Dutch control of the spice trade and could not establish a lasting outpost in the East Indies in the early years. Ships belonging to the company arrived in India, docking at Surat in 1608, and established a trade transit point and a factory. In 1615, Sir Thomas Roe represented the British interests at the Court of the Mughal Emperor Jehangir, who ruled over nearly 70 per cent of the Indian subcontinent and obtained his permission for exclusive trade in Surat. The company managed to eclipse the Portuguese, who had established their bases in Bombay (which was later acceded to the British as dowry of Catherine de Braganza) and Goa. It managed to create strongholds in Surat, Bombay (1668), Madras (1639) and Calcutta. By 1647, the Company had 23 factories and 90 employees in India. The major factories became the walled forts of Fort William in Bengal, Fort St George in Madras and the Bombay Castle. In 1717, the company was also waived of its custom duty for trading in Bengal by the Mughal emperor. The company's mainstay businesses were by now, in cotton, silk, indigo, saltpeter and tea, all the while making inroads into the Dutch monopoly of the spice trade in the Malaccan straits. In 1711, the Company established a trading post in Canton (Guangzhou), in China to trade tea for silver.

The efforts of company in administering India was the model for the civil service system in Britain. Deprived of its trade monopoly in 1813 and wound up as a trading enterprise twenty years later, the Company lost its administrative functions to the British government in 1858 following the Sepoy Mutiny of the previous year. When the Company finally reverted to the Crown in 1874, The Times reported, "it accomplished a work such as in the whole history of the human race no other company ever attempted and as such is ever likely to attempt in the years to come."

seem to deter Hicky. As soon as he came out of the prison, Hicky led a seething attack on the Governor-General and the Chief Justice. Hicky was subsequently sentenced to one year in prison and a fine of Rs. 5,000 was further imposed. This time, however, there was no fight left in Hicky, as he was now a broken and a bankrupt man. One can really describe this as the first step towards the evolution of journalism in India.

After Augustus Hicky's *The Bengal Gazette*, a new newspaper was brought out by B. Messink and Peter Reed. Their publication was known as *The India Gazette*. However, both B. Messink and Peter Reed were nothing like James Augustus Hicky as they were 'men of rather sublime nerves and attitudes'. The *Indian Gazette* hence, did not follow the path led by *The Bengal Gazette*. Meanwhile, the colonial establishment started *The Calcutta Gazette* also known as the *Oriental Advertiser* which was followed by another private initiative the *Bengal Journal*. *The Oriental Magazine of Calcutta Amusement*, a monthly magazine made a tally of four weekly newspapers and one monthly magazine published from Calcutta.

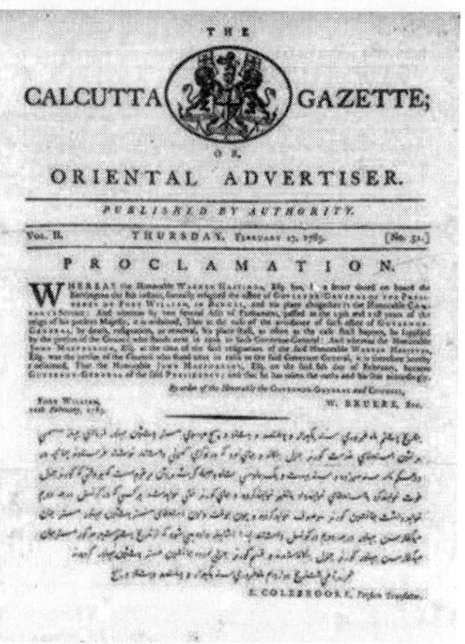
THE
CALCUTTA GAZETTE;
OR,
ORIENTAL ADVERTISER.
PUBLISHED BY AUTHORITY.
Vol. II. THURSDAY, February 17, 1785. [No. 31.]
PROCLAMATION.
W. BRUERE, Sec.

The Calcutta Gazette also known as the Oriental Advertiser.
Courtesy: Kolkata Museum

In Madras, meanwhile, *The Madras Courier* was started in 1785. Richard Johnson, who was a government printer was its founder and Hugh Boyd was its editor. In 1791, however, Hugh resigned from *The Madras Courier* and started his own paper named *Hurkaru*. It was another thing that Hugh died soon after, ceasing the publication of the paper.

In 1875, *Madras Gazette* was founded followed by *India Herald* which became an instant competitor of the *Courier*. However, *Indian Herald* was banned on account of it being an unauthorised publication and its publisher Humphrey deported back to England. *Madras Courier* meanwhile became the 'official purveyor of the official information' of Madras.

The *Bombay Herald* founded in 1789[14] became the first newspaper to be published from Bombay[15] . In 1790, *Courier* was founded. It started carrying advertisements in Gujarati. The first media merger in British India was that of *Bombay Gazette* (founded in 1791) and *Bombay Herald* (founded in 1792).

The first regional language newspaper in Bombay was the Gujarati daily *Mumbai Samachar*[16] , published in 1822 by Fardoonjee Marzban. And remarkably, *Mumbai Samachar* is still going strong being regularly published even today as India's oldest newspaper.

Meanwhile, the first Marathi daily to be published was *Dig Dursan*. The first issue of *Dig Dursan* came out in 1837. Similarly, the first Gujarati newspaper, *Vartaman* was founded in 1849 in Ahmedabad.

These regional language newspapers were all targeted towards educating the Indian masses on social issues, hence it was not a surprise that all of the pioneering Indian regional language newspapers concentrated on various social issues.

It was only in the year 1851 when Dadabhai Naoroji founded the first political newspaper named *Rast Goftar*[17] that regional newspapers began to fuel the freedom movement.

In 1878, the Government of India passed the Censorship Act. Protests from the press had no effect. Four years later, in 1882, the newspaper *Kaiser-i-Hind* was founded by Framjee Cowasji Mehta. This became a platform for the fledgling Congress from its inception in 1885. The leading British newspaper of this time was *The Times of India*.

---

14. Although the first printing Press was imported into Bombay as early as 1670 by a Parsi businessman named Bhimjee Parikh, it was only after a passage of almost a hundred years that newspaper was first published from Bombay.

15. There is some controversy regarding this surmise especially on our Indian side. While it is true that the first newspapers in Bombay were owned and printed by Parsis, we cannot yet prove that the first English newspaper in Bombay was printed by Rustomji Keshaspathi in 1777.

16. While Mumbai Samachar was the first regional language newspaper in Bombay, Sangbad Kaumudi, a Bengali newspaper was the first regional language newspaper to be published from India

17. Interestingly, when K. N. Kabraji took over as the publisher of the paper, he stopped all political commentary. This lead to much distress on the part of Naoroji who accused Kabraji from deviating from the original agenda of the paper.

Facts

- *PTI* [18] (Press Trust of India) and *UNI* (United News of India) are the two primary Indian news agencies. The former was formed after it took over the operations of the Associated Press of India and the Indian Operations of Reuters soon after independence on August 27, 1947. UNI on the other hand began its operations on March 21, 1961, though it was registered as a company in 1959 itself.

Pages From History

1. The Athenian Mercury – (Saturday, February 13, 1692)

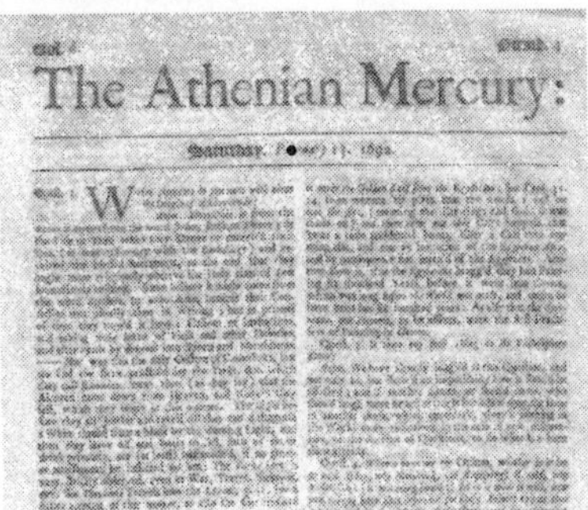

The Athenian Mercury:

2. The Asiatic Mirror and Commercial Advertiser – (Wednesday, October 9, 1793)

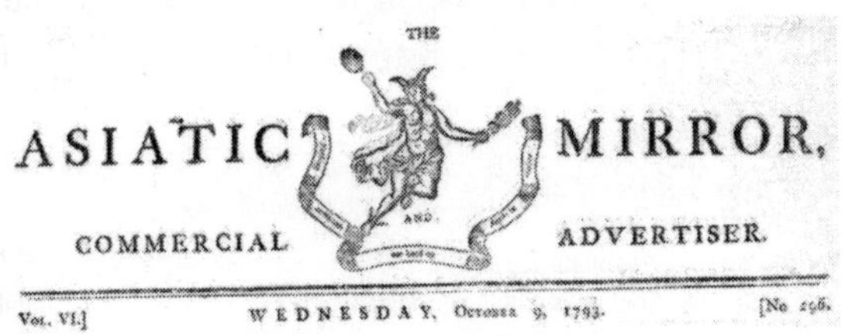

THE
ASIATIC MIRROR,
AND
COMMERCIAL ADVERTISER.

Vol. VI.] WEDNESDAY, October 9, 1793. [No 296.

18. Press Trust of India is the largest news agency in India. It is a non-profit cooperative sharing news among more than 450 Indian newspapers and has a staff of more than 1,300. It exchanges information with several other news agencies including 100 news agencies based outside India, such as Associated Press, Agence France-Presse, The New York Times Company and Bloomberg. Major Indian subscribers of PTI include Times of India and Hindustan Times.

3. Hicky's *Bengal Gazette* or the original *Calcutta General Advertiser* – (From Saturday March 3rd to Saturday March 19th, 1781)

HICKY's
BENGAL GAZETTE;
OR THE ORIGINAL
Calcutta General Advertiſer.

A Weekly Political and Commercial Paper, Open to all Parties, but influenced by None,

59 From Saturday March 3d to Saturday March 10th 1781. No. VII

A Brief History of Radio Broadcasting

Lee de Forest [21]

The birth of the 20th century saw radio as the most powerful medium of Mass Communication. Such was the power of the radio waves carrying audio throughout the world with a speed that could only be termed 'magical', that experiments[19] were immediately carried out to carry public messages through it.

The first public radio broadcasting is credited to Lee de Forest[20] . In 1907, Lee de Forest advertised the beginning of a wonderful era of radio broadcasting

19. The very first transmission of music by radio is credited to Dr Nussbaumer of the University of Graz in 1904, however, it was not to the general public. He yodelled an Austrian folk song into an experimental transmitter, which was received in the next room at the university where he worked. He does not show in any standard reference works of science.

20. Lee de Forest, (August 26, 1873-June 30, 1961) was an American inventor with over 300 patents to his credit. de Forest invented the Audion, a vacuum tube that takes relatively weak electrical signals and amplifies them. de Forest is one of the pioneers of the 'electronic age', as the Audion helped usher in the widespread use of electronics. He was involved in several patent lawsuits and he spent a fortune from his inventions on the legal bills. He had four marriages and several failed companies; he was defrauded by business partners, and was once even indicted for mail fraud, but was later acquitted.

21. This image is in public dominion due to its age.

thus: "It will soon be possible to distribute grand opera music from transmitters placed on the stage of the Metropolitan Opera House by a Radio Telephone Station on the roof to almost any dwelling in Greater New York and vicinity.... The same applies to large cities, church music, lectures, etc., which can be spread abroad by the Radio Telephone...."

The above Lee de Forest advertisement best surmises the excitement and prospect that radio broadcasting was set to herald.

On January 13, 1910 the first public radio broadcast was an experimental transmission of a live Metropolitan Opera House performance of several famous opera singers. The first to perform on radio were Cavalleria Rusticana and Pagliacci. Riccardo Martin performed as Turridu, Emmy Destinn as Santuzza, and Enrico Caruso as Canio. This wireless radio transmission event of the Italian tenor Enrico Caruso of a concert from the Metropolitan Opera House in New York City is regarded as the birth of public radio broadcasting.

On its January 14, 1910 issue *The New York Times* reported, "Opera broadcast in part from the stage of the New York City Metropolitan Opera Company was heard on January 13, 1910, when Enrico Caruso and Emmy Destinn sang arias from Cavalleria Rusticana and I Pagliacci, which were 'trapped and magnified' by the dictograph directly from the stage and borne by wireless Hertzian waves over the turbulent waters of the sea to transcontinental and coastwise ships and over the mountainous peaks and undulating valleys of the country." The microphone was connected by telephone wire to the laboratory of Dr Lee de Forest. Truly, this was the beginning of one of the most fascinating eras of Radio Broadcasting.

In 1916, de Forest, from experimental radio station 2XG in New York City, broadcast the first radio advertisements (for his own products) and the first Presidential election report by radio in November 1916 for Charles Evans Hughes and Woodrow Wilson. A few months later, de Forest moved his tube transmitter to High Bridge, New York. Like Charles Herrold in San Jose, California – who had been broadcasting since 1912 with call letters 'FN', 'SJN', and then '6XF' – de Forest had a licence from the Department of Commerce for an experimental radio station, but, like Herrold, had to cease all broadcasting when the US entered World War I in April 1917.

Just like Pittsburgh's KDKA three years later in November 1920, de Forest used the Hughes/Wilson presidential election returns for his broadcast. The New York American installed a private wire and bulletins were sent out every hour. About

2000 listeners heard 'The Star-Spangled Banner' and other anthems, songs, and hymns. de Forest went on to sponsor radio broadcasts of music featuring opera star Enrico Caruso and many other events even though he received little financial backing.

Types of Radio Broadcasting

The best known types of radio stations are the ones that broadcast via radio waves. These include the foremost AM and FM stations. There are several subtypes, namely commercial, public and non-profit varieties as well as student-run campus radio stations and hospital radio stations that can be found throughout the developed world.

Although now being eclipsed by Internet-distributed radio, there are many stations that broadcast on shortwave bands using AM technology that can be received over thousands of miles (especially at night). For example, the BBC has a full schedule transmitted via shortwave. These broadcasts are very sensitive to atmospheric conditions and sunspots.

Also, many other non-broadcast types of radio stations exist. These include:

- Base stations for police, fire and ambulance networks
- Military base stations
- Dispatch base stations for taxis, trucks, and couriers, especially in the United States
- Emergency broadcast systems
- Amateur radio stations

AM Broadcasting

AM broadcasting is the process of radio broadcasting using Amplitude Modulation.

AM was the dominant method of broadcasting during the first eighty years of the 20th century and remains widely used into the 21st.

AM radio began with the first, experimental broadcast in 1906 by Reginald Fessenden[22] , and was used for small-scale voice and music broadcasts until

22. Reginald Aubrey Fessenden (October 6, 1866-July 22, 1932), born in East Bolton, Quebec, Canada, was a Canadian inventor, best known for his work in early radio. At the age of fourteen, Bishop's College School in Lennoxville, Quebec granted Fessenden a mathematics mastership. In late 1886, Fessenden began working directly for Thomas Edison at the inventor's new Laboratory in West Orange, New Jersey. Fessenden quickly made major advances, especially in receiver design, as he worked to develop audio reception of signals.

World War I. The great increase in the use of AM radio came the following decade. The first licensed commercial radio services began on AM in the 1920s. XWA of Montreal, Quebec (later CFCF) was the first commercial broadcaster in the world, with regular broadcasts commencing on May 20, 1920. The first licensed American radio station was started by Frank Conrad, KDKA in Pittsburgh, Pennsylvania. Radio programming boomed during the 'Golden Age of Radio' (1920s-1950s). Dramas, comedy and all other forms of entertainment were produced, as well as broadcasts of news and music.

Reginald Fessenden. Source: FARC

AM radio technology is simpler than FM radio and DAB[23]. An AM receiver detects amplitude variations in the radio waves at a particular frequency. It then amplifies changes in the signal voltage to drive a loudspeaker or earphones. The earliest crystal radio receivers used a crystal diode detector with no amplification.

In North American broadcasting practice, transmitter power input to the antenna for commercial AM stations ranges from about 250 watts to 50,000 watts. Experimental licenses were issued for up to 500,000 watts radiated power, for stations intended for wide-area communication during disasters, but no current commercial broadcaster in the US or Canada is authorised for such power levels. Other countries authorise higher power operation (for example, the Mexican station XERF formerly operated at 250,000 watts). Antenna design must consider the coverage desired and must direct the transmitted signal so as not to interfere with other stations operating on the same or adjacent frequencies.

Medium wave and short wave radio signals act differently during daytime and night time. During the day, AM signals travel by ground wave, diffracting around the curve of the earth over a distance up to a few hundred miles (or kilometres) from the signal transmitter. However, after sunset, changes in the ionosphere

---

23. Digital Audio Broadcasting (DAB), also known as Eureka 147, is a digital radio technology for broadcasting radio stations, used in several countries, particularly in Europe. As of 2007, approximately 1,000 stations worldwide broadcast in the DAB format.

cause AM signals to travel by sky wave, enabling AM radio stations to be heard much farther from their point of origin than is normal during the day. This phenomenon can be easily observed by scanning an AM radio dial at night. As a result, many broadcast stations are required as a condition of licence to reduce their broadcasting power significantly (or use directional antennas) after sunset, or even to suspend broadcasting entirely during night time hours. Such stations are commonly referred to as 'day-timers'.

In the United States, some AM radio stations are granted clear channel status, meaning that they broadcast on frequencies with few other stations allocated, allowing an extended coverage area. Nowadays relatively few stations enjoy clear channel status. Commercial broadcasters generally rely on the ground-wave coverage only as their target market for advertising.

The hobby of listening to long distance signals is known as DX or DXing, from an old telegraph abbreviation for 'distance'. Several non-profit hobbyist clubs are devoted exclusively to DXing the AM broadcast band, including the National Radio Club and International Radio Club of America. Similarly, people listening to short wave transmissions are SWLing.

Frequency Bands

AM radio is broadcast on several frequency bands. The allocation of these bands is governed by the ITU's[24] Radio Regulations and, on the national level, by each country's telecommunications administration (the FCC[25] in the US, for example and TRAI[26] in India) subject to international agreements.

Long wave is 148.5 kHz-283.5 kHz, with 9 kHz channel spacing generally used. Long wave is used for radio broadcasting in Europe, Africa and parts of Asia (ITU region 1), and is not allocated in the Western Hemisphere. In the United States and Canada, Bermuda and US territories, this band is mainly reserved for aeronautics navigational aids, though a small section of the band could theoretically be used for micro-broadcasting under the United States

24. The International Telecommunication Union is an international organisation established to standardise and regulate international radio and telecommunications. It was founded as the International Telegraph Union in Paris on May 17, 1865. Its main tasks include standardisation, allocation of the radio spectrum, and organising interconnection arrangements between different countries to allow international phone calls — in which regard it performs for telecommunications a similar function to what the UPU performs for postal services. It is one of the specialised agencies of the United Nations, and has its headquarters in Geneva, Switzerland, next to the main United Nations campus.

25. Federal Communications Commission

26. Telecom Regulatory Authority of India

Part 15 rules. Due to the propagation characteristics of long wave signals, the frequencies are used most effectively in latitudes north of 50°.

Medium wave is 520 kHz-1,610 kHz. In the Americas (ITU region 2), 10 kHz spacing is used, elsewhere it is 9 kHz. ITU region 2 also authorises the Extended AM broadcast band between 1610 kHz and 1710 kHz. Medium wave is by far the most heavily used band for commercial broadcasting. This is the 'AM radio' that most people are familiar with.

Short wave is 2.3 MHz-26.1 MHz, divided into 15 broadcast bands. Shortwave broadcasts generally use a narrow 5 kHz channel spacing. Short wave is used by audio services intended to be heard at great distances from the transmitting station. The long range of short wave broadcasts comes at the expense of lower audio fidelity. The mode of propagation for short wave is different . AM is used mostly by broadcast services—other shortwave users may use a modified version of AM such as SSB or an AM-compatible version of SSB such as SSB with carrier reinserted.

Frequencies between the broadcast bands are used for other forms of radio communication, and are not broadcast services intended for reception by the general public.

Limitations

Because of its susceptibility to atmospheric and electrical interference, AM broadcasting now attracts mainly talk radio and news programming, while music radio and public radio mostly shifted to FM broadcasting in the late 1970s. However, in the late 1960s and 1970s, top 40 rock-and-roll stations in the US and Canada, such as WABC and CHUM transmitted highly processed and extended audio to 11 kHz, successfully attracting huge audiences. In the UK, during the 1980s, BBC Radio 4 (a largely speech channel) had an FM location, whereas BBC Radio 1, a music channel, was confined to AM broadcasts over much of the UK. Frequency response is typically 40 Hz-5 kHz with a 50 dB S/N ratio.

The limitation on AM fidelity comes from current receiver design. Moreover, to fit more transmitters on the AM broadcast band, in the United States maximum transmitted audio bandwidth is limited to 10 kHz by an NRSC standard adopted by the FCC, resulting in a channel occupied bandwidth of 20 kHz.

AM radio signals can be severely disrupted in large urban centres by metal structures, tall buildings and sources of radio frequency interference (RFI) and electrical noise, such as electrical motors, fluorescent lights, or lightning. As a result, AM radio in many countries has lost its dominance as a music broadcasting service, and in many cities is now relegated to news, sports, religious and talk radio stations. Some musical genres – particularly country, oldies, nostalgia and ethnic/world music – survive on AM, especially in areas where FM frequencies are in short supply or in thinly populated or mountainous areas, where FM coverage is poor.

Other Distribution Methods

Stereo transmissions are possible, and hybrid digital broadcast systems are now being used around the world. In the United States, iBiquity's proprietary HD Radio has been adopted and approved by the FCC for medium wave transmissions; while Digital Radio Mondiale is a more open effort often used on the shortwave bands, and can be used alongside many AM broadcasts. Both these standards are capable of broadcasting audio of significantly greater fidelity than that of standard AM, and a theoretical frequency response of 0 kHz-16 kHz, in addition to stereo sound and text data.

While FM radio can also be received by cable, AM radio generally cannot, although an AM station can be converted into an FM cable signal. In Canada, cable operators that offer FM cable services are required by the CRTC (Canadian Radio-television and Telecommunications Commission) to distribute all locally available AM stations in this manner. In Switzerland, a system known as 'wire broadcasting' transmits AM signals over telephone lines in the long-wave band.

Micro-broadcasting

Some micro-broadcasters and pirate radio broadcasters, especially those in the United States under the FCC's Part 15 rules, broadcast on AM to achieve greater range than is possible on the FM band. On medium-wave (AM), such radio stations are often found between 1610 kHz and 1710 kHz. Hobbyists also use low-power AM transmitters to provide local programming for antique radio equipment in areas where AM programming is not widely available or is of questionable quality; in such cases the transmitter, which is designed to cover only the immediate property and perhaps nearby areas, is hooked up to a computer or music player.

The Evolution of FM Broadcasting

Edwin Howard Armstrong

FM broadcasting is a broadcast technology invented by Edwin Howard Armstrong[27] that uses frequency modulation (FM) to provide high-fidelity sound over broadcast radio.

Terminology

The term 'FM band' is effectively shorthand for 'frequency modulation band in which FM is used for broadcasting'. It can upset purists, because it conflates a modulation scheme with a range of frequencies[28] .

The term 'VHF' was previously in common use in Europe. 'UKW', which stands for Ultrakurzwellen in German, meaning 'ultra short wave', is still widely used in Germany.

Broadcast Bands

Throughout the world, the broadcast band falls within the VHF part of the radio spectrum. Usually 87.5 MHz-108.0 MHz is used, or some portion thereof, with few exceptions:

In the former Soviet republics, and some Eastern Bloc nations, an older band from 65.9 MHz-74 MHz is also used. Assigned frequencies are at intervals of 30 kHz. This band, sometimes referred to as the OIRT band, is slowly being phased out in many countries. In Japan, the band 76 MHz-90 MHz is used.

The frequency of an FM broadcast station (more strictly its assigned nominal centre frequency) is usually an exact multiple of 100 kHz. In most of the Americas and the Caribbean, only odd multiples are used. In some parts of Europe, Greenland and Africa, only even multiples are used. In Italy, multiples of 50 kHz are used. There are other unusual and obsolete standards in some countries, including 0.001, 0.01, 0.03, 0.074, 0.5, and 0.3 MHz.

---

27. Edwin Howard Armstrong (December 18, 1890-January 31, 1954) was an American electrical engineer and inventor. Armstrong was the inventor of frequency modulation (FM) radio.

28. FM band did to Radio Broadcasting in 1930s what MP3 did to music uploading and downloading on Internet in 1990s. Both essentially resorted to compromising quality for better and easier transmission.

Distance Covered by an FM Stereo Transmission

The range of an FM mono transmission is related to the transmitter RF (Radio Frequency) power, the antenna gain and antenna height. The FCC[29] publishes curves that aid in calculation of this maximum distance as a function of signal strength at the receiving location.

For FM stereo, the maximum distance covered is significantly reduced. This is due to the presence of the 38 kHz sub-carrier modulation. Vigorous audio processing improves the coverage area of an FM stereo station.

Adoption of FM Broadcasting Worldwide

Despite having been developed in 1933, FM broadcasting took a long time to be adopted by the majority of radio listeners.

The first FM broadcasting stations were in the United States, but initially they were primarily used to broadcast classical music to up-market listeners in urban areas and for educational programming. By the late 1960s, FM had been adopted by fans of 'alternative rock' music, but it wasn't until 1978 that listeners to FM stations exceeded those of AM stations. During the 1980s and 1990s, top 40 music stations and later even country music stations largely abandoned AM for FM. Today AM is mainly the preserve of talk radio, news, sports, religious programming, ethnic (minority language) broadcasting and some types of minority interest music. Ironically, this shift has transformed AM into the 'alternative band' that FM once was.

Belgium, the Netherlands, Denmark and particularly West Germany were among the first countries to adopt FM on a widespread scale. Among the reasons for this were:

The medium wave band in Western Europe is heavily overcrowded, leading to severe interference problems and, as a result, most MW (Medium Wave) frequencies are suitable only for speech broadcasting. Particularly in Germany after World War II, the best available medium wave frequencies were used by the Allied occupation forces both for broadcasting entertainment to their troops and for broadcasting cold war propaganda across the iron curtain.

---

29. The Federal Communications Commission (FCC) is a United States government agency. The FCC was established by the Communications Act of 1934 as the successor to the Federal Radio Commission and was charged with regulating all non-Federal Government use of the radio spectrum (including radio and television broadcasting), and all interstate telecommunications (wire, satellite and cable) as well as all international communications that originated or terminated in the United States. It is an important factor in US telecommunication policy. The FCC took over wire communication regulation from the Interstate Commerce Commission.

The regional structure of German broadcasting meant that the few remaining AM frequencies available for civilian domestic broadcasting fell far short of the number required and the broadcasters looked to FM as an alternative.

Public service broadcasters in Ireland and Australia were far slower at adopting FM radio than those in either North America or continental Europe. However, in Ireland, several unlicensed commercial FM stations were on air by the mid-1980s. These generally were simulcast[30] on AM and FM.

In the United Kingdom, the BBC began FM broadcasting in 1955, with three national networks carrying the Light Programme, Third Programme and Home Service (renamed Radio 2, Radio 3 and Radio 4 respectively in 1967). These three networks used the sub-band 88.0 MHz-94.6 MHz. The sub-band 94.6 MHz-97.6 MHz was later used for BBC and local commercial services. Only when commercial broadcasting was introduced to the UK in 1973 did the use of FM pick up in Britain. With the gradual clearance of other users (notably Public Services, such as the police, fire and ambulance) and the extension of the FM band to 108.0 MHz between 1980 and 1995, FM expanded rapidly throughout the British Isles and effectively took over from LW[31] and MW[32] as the delivery platform of choice for fixed and portable domestic and vehicle-based receivers.

In addition, Ofcom (previously the Radio Authority) in the UK issues on demand Restricted Service Licences on FM and also on AM (MW) for short-term local-coverage broadcasting, which is open to anyone who does not carry a prohibition and can put up the appropriate licensing and royalty fees. In 2006, almost 500 such licenses were issued.

FM started in Australia in 1947, but did not catch on and was shut down in 1961 to expand the television band. It was not reopened until 1975. Subsequently, it developed steadily until in the 1980s many AM stations were transferred to FM because of its superior sound quality. Today, as elsewhere in the developed world, most Australian broadcasting is on FM – although AM talk stations are still very popular.

Most other countries expanded their use of FM through the 1990s. Because it takes a large number of FM transmitting stations to cover a geographically large

---

30. Simultaneously broadcasted

31. Long Wave

32. Medium Wave

country, particularly where there are terrain difficulties, FM is more suited to local broadcasting than national networks. In such countries, particularly where there are economic or infrastructural problems, 'rolling out' a national FM broadcast network to reach the majority of the population can be a slow and expensive process.

ITU Conferences About FM

The frequencies available for FM were decided by some important conferences of ITU. The milestone of those conferences is the Stockholm agreement of 1961 among 38 countries.

Micro-broadcasting

Low-power transmitters such as those mentioned above are also sometimes used for neighbourhood or campus radio stations, though campus radio stations are often run over carrier current. This is generally considered a form of microbroadcasting. As a general rule, enforcement towards low-power FM stations is stricter than AM stations due to issues such as the capture effect, and as a result, FM microbroadcasters generally do not reach as far as their AM competitors.

Clandestine Use of FM Transmitters

FM transmitters have been used to construct miniature wireless microphones for espionage and surveillance purposes (covert listening devices or so-called 'bugs'); the advantage to using the FM broadcast band for such operations is that the receiving equipment would not be considered particularly suspect. Common practice is to tune the bug's transmitter off the ends of the broadcast band, into what in the United States would be TV channel 6 (<87.9 MHz) or aviation navigation frequencies (>107.9); most FM radios with analog tuners have sufficient over-coverage to pick up these beyond-outermost frequencies, although many digitally-tuned radios do not.

Constructing a 'bug' is a common early project for electronics hobbyists, and project kits to do so are available from a wide variety of sources. The devices constructed, however, are often too large and poorly shielded for use in clandestine activity.

In addition, much pirate radio activity is broadcast in the FM range, due to the band's greater clarity and number of listeners, and the lower size and cost of equipment.

FM Broadcasting in India

In the mid-nineties, when India first experimented with private FM broadcasts, the small tourist destination of Goa was the fifth place in this country of one billion where private players got FM slots. The other four centres were the big metropolitan cities: Delhi, Mumbai, Kolkata and Chennai. These were followed by stations in Hyderabad, Jaipur and Lucknow.

Indian policy currently states that these broadcasters are assessed a One Time Entry Fee (OTEF[33]) , for the entire licence period of 10 years. Under the Indian accounting system, this amount is amortised over the 10-year period at 10% per annum. Annual licence fee for private players is either 4% of revenue share or 10% of Reserve Price, whichever is higher.

Earlier, India's attempts to privatise its FM channels ran into rough weather when private players bid heavily and most could not meet their commitments to pay the government the amounts they owed.

Content

News in not permitted on private FM, although the Information and Broadcasting Minister has stated that[34] this may be reconsidered in two to three years. Nationally, many of the current FM players, including the *Times of India*, *Hindustan Times, Mid-Day*, and BBC are essentially newspaper chains or media, and they are already making a strong pitch for news on FM.

Current Allocation Process

In FM Phase II – the latest round of the long-delayed opening up of private FM in India – some 338 frequencies were offered of which about 237 were sold. The government may go for rebidding of unsold frequencies quite soon. In Phase III of FM licensing, smaller towns and cities will be opened up for FM radio.

Reliance and South Asia FM (Sun group) bid for most of the 91 cities, although they were allowed only 15% of the total allocated frequencies. Between them, they have had to surrender over 40 licenses.

---

33. In fact, the massive One Time Entry Fee of 10 years is the greatest huddle in the growth of FM stations in India. While in the neighbouring country of Nepal, the licence fee is around 25 lakhs, OTEF crosses 1 crore in India. I (Author) had myself tried to establish an FM radio station in Darjeeling but the licence fee which crossed 1 Crore was clearly unaffordable.

34. The Telegraph, 12, September 2008

All India Radio – A Case Study

AIR Headquarters, Akashwani Bhavan, New Delhi.
Source: AIR

All India Radio (abbreviated as AIR) and officially known as Akashvani is the radio broadcaster of India and a division of Prasar Bharati[35] (Broadcasting Corporation of India), an autonomous corporation of the Ministry of Information and Broadcasting, Government of India. Established in 1936[36], today it is the sister service of Prasar Bharati's Doordarshan, the national television broadcaster.

All India Radio is one of the largest radio networks in the world. The headquarters is at the Akashwani Bhavan, New Delhi. Akashwani Bhavan houses the drama section, the FM section and the National service. The Doordarshan Kendra (Delhi) is also located on the 6th floor of Akashvani Bhavan.

Services

AIR has many different services each catering to different regions/languages across India. One of the most famous services of the AIR is the Vivídh-Bharati Seva (roughly translating to 'Multi-Indian service'). Vividh Bharati celebrated its Golden Jubilee on 3rd October, 2007. Vividh Bharati has the only comprehensive database of songs from the so termed 'Golden Era' of Hindi film music (roughly from 1940s to 1980s). This service is the most commercial of all and is popular in Mumbai and other cities of India. This service offers a wide range of programmes including news, film music, comedy shows, etc. The Vividh Bharati service

---

35. Prasar Bharati is India's largest public broadcaster. It is an autonomous corporation of the Ministry of Information and Broadcasting, Government of India and comprises Doordarshan television network and All India Radio. Prasar Bharati was established on November 23, 1997 following a demand that the government-owned broadcasters in India should be given autonomy like those in many other countries. The Parliament of India passed an Act to grant this autonomy in 1990, but it was not enacted until September 15, 1997.

36. During his regular broadcasts from the Azad Hind Radio, Netaji Subhash Chandra Bose used to refer to the pre-independence AIR as Anti Indian Radio.

operates on different MW band frequencies for each city.

External Services

The External Services Division of All India Radio broadcasts operates in 27 languages to countries outside of India, primarily by high powered short wave broadcasts, although medium wave is also used to reach neighbouring countries. In addition to broadcasts targeted at specific countries by language, there is a General Overseas Service which broadcasts in English with 81/4 hours of programming each day and is aimed at a general international audience.

News Reading at All India Radio.

Source: H Rama Krishnan[37]

Yuva Vani: The Voice of the Youth

The Yuva Vani service of AIR provides an enriching and novel radio-experience by encouraging youth participation and experimenting with varied script ideas. It is broadcast at 1017 kHz which corresponds to 294.9 metres. Its broadcast begins every evening at 7 pm. With shows like 'Mehfil', 'In the groove' and 'The Roving Microphone', which have been around for more than three decades, Yuva Vani still holds a firm ground of its own.

Some of the big names on the Indian media scene began their journey with Yuva Vani. Praful Thakkar, a well-known documentary filmmaker says, "Yuva Vani came as a breath of fresh air in our reckless college days. It was a great learning experience for me and it made me realise that radio is not all about goofy quotes and RJs[38] ."

Some of the other names that have been associated with Yuva Vani in the past include celebrity game show host Roshan Abbas, VJ[39] Gaurav Kapoor, DJ[40] Kaushal Khanna and DJ Pratham among others.

---

37. http://www.hramakrishnan.com

38. Radio Jockeys

39. Video Jockey

40. Disc Jockey

News-on-Phone Service

All India Radio, after launching the news-on-phone service on 25th February 1998 from New Delhi, is running the service from Chennai, Mumbai, Hyderabad, Patna and Bangalore also. The service is accessible through STD, ISD and local telephone calls. The service is going to be started from 9 more cities — Ahmedabad, Guwahati, Imphal, Jaipur, Kolkata, Lucknow, Raipur, Simla and Thiruvananthapuram shortly.

A Brief History of Television Broadcasting

One of the first televisions to make its appearances in the house of the rich and famous. Source: UK Science Museum.

Television is a widely used telecommunication medium for sending (broadcasting) and receiving moving images usually accompanied by sound. Television may also refer specifically to a television set, television programming or television transmission. The word is derived from mixed Latin and Greek roots, meaning 'far sight': Greek tele meaning far, and Latin visio, sight.

Commercially available since the late 1930s, the television set has become a common communications receiver in homes, businesses and institutions, particularly as a source of entertainment and news. Since the 1970s, recordings on video cassettes, and later, digital media such as DVDs, have resulted in the television frequently being used for viewing recorded as well as broadcast material.

A standard television set comprises multiple internal electronic circuits, including those for tuning and decoding broadcast signals. A display device which lacks these internal circuits is therefore properly called a monitor, rather than a television. A television set may be designed to handle other than traditional broadcast or recorded signals and formats, such as closed-circuit television (CCTV), digital television (DTV) and high-definition television (HDTV).

The Evolution

In its early stages of development, television included devices employing a combination of optical, mechanical and electronic technologies to capture, transmit and display a visual image. By the late 1920s, however, those employing only optical and electronic technologies were being explored. All modern television systems rely on the latter; however the knowledge gained from the work on mechanical-dependent systems was crucial in the development of fully electronic television.

Paul Gottlieb Nipkow in the later phase of his life.
Source: Kiev University

In 1884, Paul Gottlieb Nipkow, a 20-year-old university student in Germany patented the first electromechanical television system which employed a scanning disk, a spinning disk with a series of holes spiralling toward the centre, for 'rasterisation', that is, the process of converting a visual image into a stream of electrical pulses. The holes were spaced at equal angular intervals such that in a single rotation the disk would allow light to pass through each hole and onto a light-sensitive selenium sensor which produced the electrical pulses. As an image was focused on the rotating disk, each hole captured a horizontal 'slice' of the whole image.

Nipkow's design would not be practical until advances in amplifier tube technology became available in 1907. Even then the device was only useful for transmitting still halftone images – those represented by equally spaced dots of varying size – over telegraph or telephone lines. Later designs would use a rotating mirror-drum scanner to capture the image and a cathode ray tube (CRT) as a display device, but moving images were still not possible, due to the poor sensitivity of the selenium sensors.

Scottish inventor John Logie Baird[41] demonstrated the transmission of moving silhouette images in London in 1925, and of moving, monochromatic images in 1926. Baird's scanning disk produced an image of 30 lines resolution, barely enough to discern a human face, from a double spiral of lenses.

John Baird's Pioneering Televisor. Source: Science Museum, England

By 1927, Russian inventor Léon Theremin developed a mirror drum-based television system which used interlacing to achieve an image resolution of 100 lines.

The first known photograph of a moving image produced by Baird's Televisor in 1926. Source: Science Museum, England

Also in 1927, Herbert E. Ives of Bell Labs transmitted moving images from a 50-aperture disk producing 16 frames per minute over a cable from Washington, DC to New York City, and via radio from Whippany, New Jersey. Ives used viewing screens as large as 24 by 30 inches (60 by 75 centimetres). His subjects included Secretary of Commerce Herbert Hoover.

In 1928, Philo Farnsworth made the world's first working television system with electronic scanning of both the pickup and display devices, which he first demonstrated to news media on 1928-09-01, televising a motion picture film.

First Public Demonstrations

On January 26, 1926, John Logie Baird repeated the transmission for members of the Royal Institution and a reporter from *The Times* in his laboratory at 22, Frith Street in the Soho district of London. By this time, he had improved the

41. In his first attempts to develop a working television system, Baird experimented with the Nipkow disk, and in February 1924 demonstrated to the Radio Times that a semi-mechanical analog television system was possible by transmitting moving silhouette images, such as his fingers wiggling, in his London laboratory. Baird gave the first public demonstration of moving silhouette images by television at Selfridges department store in London in a three-week series of demonstrations beginning on March 25, 1925. In his laboratory on October 2, 1925, Baird successfully transmitted the first television picture with a greyscale image: the head of a ventriloquist's dummy nicknamed 'Stooky Bill' in a 30-line vertically scanned image, at five pictures per second. Baird went downstairs and fetched an office worker, 20-year-old William Edward Taynton, to see what a human face would look like, and Taynton became the first person to be televised in a full tonal range.

scan rate to 12.5 pictures per second. It was the world's first demonstration of a true television system, one that could broadcast live moving images with tone graduation.

He demonstrated the world's first colour transmission on July 3, 1928 using scanning discs at the transmitting and receiving ends with three spirals of apertures, each spiral with a filter of a different primary colour, and three light sources at the receiving end, with a commutator to alternate their illumination. That same year, he also demonstrated stereoscopic television. In 1932, he was the first to demonstrate ultra-short wave transmission.

First Television Broadcasting

In 1927, Baird transmitted a long-distance television signal over 438 miles (705 kilometres) of telephone line between London and Glasgow, when the world's first long-distance television pictures were transmitted to the Central Hotel at Glasgow Central Station[42] . Baird then set up the Baird Television Development Company Ltd, which in 1928 made the first transatlantic television transmission, from London to Hartsdale, New York, and the first television programme for the BBC. In November 1929, Baird and Bernard Natan established France's first television company, Télévision-Baird-Natan. He televised the first live transmission of the Epsom Derby in 1931. He demonstrated a theatre television system, with a screen 2 feet by 5 feet (60 centimetre by 150 centimetre), in 1930 at the London Coliseum, Berlin, Paris, and Stockholm[43] . By 1939, he had improved his theatre projection system to televise a boxing match on a screen 15 feet (4.6 metres) by 12 feet (4.6 metre by 3.7 metre).

From 1929 to 1932, the BBC transmitters were used to broadcast television programmes using the 30-line Baird system, and from 1932-1935, the BBC also produced the programmes in their own studio at 16, Portland Place. In November 1936, the BBC began alternating Baird 240-line transmissions with EMI's electronic scanning system, which had recently been improved to 405-lines after a merger with Marconi. The BBC ceased broadcasts with the Baird system in February 1937, due mostly to the immobility of the Baird system's cameras.

---

42. Interview with Paul Lyons, Historian and Control and Information Officer at Glasgow Central Station

43. Baird Television Limited – Growing Demand For Home Receivers – Success Of Large Screen Projections In Cinemas – etc. The Times newspaper, 03 April 1939 page 23 column A.

Baird's television systems were replaced by the Electronic Television System developed by the newly-formed company EMI-Marconi[44] under Isaac Shoenberg, which had access to patents developed by Vladimir Zworykin and RCA[45] . Similarly, Philo T. Farnsworth's electronic 'Image Dissector' camera was available to Baird's company via a patent-sharing agreement. However, the Image Dissector camera was found to be lacking in light sensitivity, requiring excessive levels of illumination.

Baird made many contributions to the field of electronic television after mechanical systems had taken a back seat. In 1939, he showed colour television using a cathode ray tube in front of which revolved a disc fitted with colour filters, a method taken up by CBS and RCA in the United States. On August 16, 1944 he gave the world's first demonstration of a fully electronic colour television display. His 600-line colour system used triple interlacing, using six scans to build each picture. In 1943, the Hankey Committee was appointed to oversee the resumption of television broadcasts after the war. Baird persuaded them to make plans to adopt his proposed 1000-line Telechrome electronic colour system as the new post-war broadcast standard. The picture quality on this system would have been comparable to today's HDTV[46] . The Hankey Committee's plan lost all momentum partly due to the challenges of post-war reconstruction. The monochrome 405-line standard remained in place until 1985 in some areas, and it was three decades until the introduction of the 625-line system in 1964 and (PAL) colour in 1967.

Content Programming

Getting TV programming shown to the public can happen in many different ways. After production, the next step is to market and deliver the product to whatever markets are open to using it. This typically happens on two levels:

Original Run or First Run – A producer creates a programme of one or multiple episodes and shows it on a station or network which has either paid for

---

44. The Marconi Company Ltd was founded by Guglielmo Marconi in 1897 as The Wireless Telegraph & Signal Company (sometimes presented as Wireless Telegraph Trading Signal Company). It was renamed Marconi's Wireless Telegraph Company in 1900 and The Marconi Company in 1963.

45. RCA, founded as Radio Corporation of America, was an electronics company in existence from 1919 to 1986. Today, the RCA trademark is owned by Thomson SA through RCA Trademark Management SA, a company owned by Thomson. The trademark is used by two companies, namely Sony BMG Music Entertainment and Thomson SA, which licenses the name to other companies, like Audiovox and TCL Corporation for products descended from that common ancestor.

46. High Density Television

the production itself or to which a licence has been granted by the producers to do the same.

Syndication – This is the terminology rather broadly used to describe secondary programming usages (beyond original run). It includes secondary runs in the country of first issue, but also international usage which may or may not be managed by the originating producer. In many cases, other companies, TV stations or individuals are engaged to do the syndication work, in other words, to sell the product into the markets, they are allowed to sell by contract from the copyright holders, in most cases, the producers.

First run programming is increasing on subscription services outside the US, but few domestically produced programmes are syndicated on domestic FTA elsewhere. This practice is increasing, however, generally on digital-only FTA channels, or with subscriber-only first run material appearing on FTA.

Unlike the US, repeat FTA[47] screenings of a FTA network programme almost only occur on that network. Also, affiliates rarely buy or produce non-network programming that is not centred on local events.

Funding

Around the globe, broadcast television is financed by government, advertising, licensing (a form of tax), subscription or any combination of these. To protect revenues, subscription TV channels are usually encrypted to ensure that only subscription payers receive the decryption codes to see the signal. Non-encrypted channels are known as Free-to-Air or FTA.

Advertising

Advertising attempts to influence people's behaviour and beliefs and television is, therefore, a powerful and attractive medium for advertisers to use. TV stations sell air time to advertisers in order to fund their programming.

---

47. Free-to-Air (FTA) television (TV) and radio broadcasts are sent unencrypted and may be received via any suitable receiver. Free-to-View (FTV) is, generally, available without subscription but is digitally encoded and may be restricted geographically. Neither of these are pay-TV, which is an encrypted subscription (or pay-per-view) service. FTA is sometimes delivered by satellite television, but in various parts of the world, Free-to-Air television channels are broadcast unencrypted on UHF or VHF bands. Although these channels are described as free, in some cases, the viewer does in fact pay for them. Some are paid directly by payment of a licence fee (as in the case of the BBC) or voluntary donation (in the case of educational broadcasters like PBS), others indirectly by paying for consumer products and services where part of the cost goes toward television advertising and sponsorship (in the case of Japanese television broadcasters, like TV Asahi and TV Tokyo, which rely on sponsorship heavily). One further variation is in Canada, where the CBC Television/Télévision de Radio-Canada network is partly funded by taxpayer dollars, and otherwise supports itself with commercial advertising revenues, as it competes with other free over-the-air commercial networks.

United States

Since its inception in the US in 1940, TV commercials have become one of the most effective, persuasive, and popular method of selling products of many sorts, especially consumer goods. US advertising rates are determined primarily by Nielsen Ratings[48] . The time of the day and popularity of the channel determine how much a television commercial can cost. For example, the highly popular American Idol can cost approximately $750,000 for a thirty second block of commercial time, while the same amount of time for the World Cup Football can cost several million dollars.

In recent years, the paid programme or infomercial has become common, usually in lengths of 30 minutes or one hour. Some drug companies and other businesses have even created 'news' items for broadcast, known in the industry as video news releases, paying programme directors to use them.

Some TV programmes also weave advertisements into their shows, a practice that began in films and came to be known as product placement. For example, a character could be drinking a certain kind of soda, going to a particular chain restaurant, or driving a certain make of car. (This is sometimes very subtle, where shows have vehicles provided by manufacturers for low cost, rather than wrangling them.) Sometimes, a specific brand or trademark, or music from a certain artist or group, is used. (This excludes guest appearances by artists, who perform on the show.)

United Kingdom[49]

The TV regulator oversees TV advertising in the United Kingdom. Its restrictions have been in application since the early days of commercially-funded TV. Despite this, an early TV mogul, Lew Grade, likened the broadcasting licence as a 'license to print money'. Restrictions mean that the big three national commercial TV channels, ITV, Channel 4, and Channel 5 can show an average of only seven minutes of advertising per hour (eight minutes in the peak period). Other broadcasters must average no more than nine minutes (twelve in the peak). This means that many imported TV shows from the US have unnatural breaks,

48. Nielsen Ratings are audience measurement systems developed by Nielsen Media Research to determine the audience size and composition of television programming. Nielsen conducts these tests by calling the locals and asking them what they are watching at the moment. Nielsen operates in over 100 countries and was founded in 1923.

49. England, Wales, Ireland and Scotland

where the UK company has edited out the breaks intended for US advertising. Advertisements must not be inserted in the course of any broadcast of news or current affairs programme of less than half an hour scheduled duration, or in a documentary of less than half an hour scheduled duration, or in a programme for children of less than half an hour scheduled duration. Nor may advertisements be carried in a programme designed and broadcast for reception in schools or in any religious service or other devotional programme, or during a formal Royal ceremony or occasion. There also must be clear demarcations in time between the programmes and the advertisements.

The BBC, being strictly non-commercial, is not allowed to show advertisements on television in the UK, although it has many advertising-funded channels abroad. The majority of its budget comes from TV licensing and the sale of content to other broadcasters.

Subscription

Some TV channels are partly funded from subscriptions and therefore the signals are encrypted before broadcast to ensure that only paying subscribers have access to the decryption codes. Most subscription services are also funded by advertising.

Television Genres

Television genres include a broad range of programming types that entertain, inform, and educate viewers. The most expensive entertainment genres to produce are usually drama and dramatic ministries. However, other genres, such as historical Western genres, may also have high production costs.

Popular entertainment genres include action-oriented shows, such as the police, crime, detective dramas, horror or thriller shows. There are also other variants of the drama genre, such as medical dramas and daytime soap operas. Science fiction shows can fall into either the drama or action category, depending on whether they emphasise philosophical questions or high adventure. Comedy is a popular genre which includes situation comedy (sitcom) and animated shows for the adult demographic such as South Park.

The least expensive forms of entertainment programming are game shows, talk shows, variety shows, and reality TV. Game shows show contestants answering questions and solving puzzles to win prizes. Talk shows feature interviews with film, television and music celebrities and public figures. Variety shows feature a range of musical performers and other entertainers such as comedians and magicians introduced by a host or Master of Ceremonies. There is some crossover between some talk shows and variety shows, because leading talk shows often feature performances by bands, singers, comedians, and other performers in between the interview segments. Reality TV shows 'regular' people (i.e., not actors) who are facing unusual challenges or experiences, ranging from arrest by police officers (COPS) to weight loss (The Biggest Loser). A variant version of reality shows depicts celebrities doing mundane activities such as going about their everyday life (The Osbournes) or doing manual labour (Simple Life).

Television in India

Television in India is a huge industry and has thousands of programmes in all the states of India. The small screen has produced numerous celebrities of their own kind some even attaining national fame. TV soaps are extremely popular with housewives as well as working women. Several small screen actors have made it big in Bollywood. Approximately half of all Indian households own a television, remarkable for a country where 77% of the population lives on less than Rs 20 (US $0.50) per day.

History

Television first came to India as the National Television Network of India. The first telecast started on September 15, 1959 in New Delhi. After a gap of about 13 years, second television station was established in Mumbai (Maharashtra) in 1972, and by 1975, there were five more television stations at Srinagar (Kashmir), Amritsar (Punjab), Kolkata (West Bengal), Chennai (Tamil Nadu) and Lucknow (Uttar Pradesh). Till 1982, transmission was in black & white, when Doordarshan introduced colour during the 1982 Asian Games.

1980s

Indian small screen programming started off in the early 1980s. At that time, there was only one national channel—Doordarshan, which was government-owned. The *Ramayana* and *Mahabharata* were the first major television series produced. These two serials notched up the world record in viewership numbers for a single programme. By the late 1980s, more and more people started to own television sets. Though there was a single channel, television programming had reached saturation. Hence, the government opened up another channel, which had part national programming and part regional. This channel was known as DD 2, and later DD Metro. Both channels were broadcast terrestrially.

Post Liberalisation Television

The central government launched a series of economic and social reforms in 1991 under Prime Minister Narasimha Rao. Under the new policies, the government allowed private and foreign broadcasters to engage in limited operations in India. This process has been pursued consistently by all subsequent federal administrations. Foreign channels like CNN, Star TV and domestic channels such as Zee TV and Sun TV started satellite broadcasts. Starting with 41 sets in 1962 and one channel (Audience Research unit, 1991), at present TV in India covers more than 70 million homes giving a viewing population more than 400 million individuals through more than 100 channels. A large relatively untapped market, easy accessibility of relevant technology and a variety of programmes are the main reasons for rapid expansion of Television in India.

It must be stressed that Television Entertainment in India is one of the cheapest in the world.

Cable Television

In 1992, the government liberated its markets, opening them up to cable television. Five new channels belonging to the Hong Kong-based STAR TV gave Indians a fresh breath of life. MTV, STAR Plus, BBC, Prime Sports and STAR Chinese Channel were the said five channels. Zee TV was the first privately owned Indian channel to be broadcast over cable. A few years later, CNN, Discovery Channel, and National Geographic Channel made their foray into India. STAR expanded its bouquet introducing STAR World, STAR Sports, ESPN and STAR Gold. Regional channels flourished along with a multitude of Hindi channels and a few English channels. By 2001, HBO and History Channel were the other international channels to enter India. By 2001-2003, other international channels such as Nickelodeon, Cartoon Network, VH1, Disney and Toon Disney came into foray. In 2003, news channels started to boom.

Audience Metrics

Television Metrics in India have gone through several phases in which it fragmented, consolidated and then fragmented again.

DART

During the days of the single channel Doordarshan monopoly, DART (Doordarshan Audience Research Team) was the only metric available. This used the notebook method of record keeping across 33 cities across India. DART continues to provide this information independent of the private agencies. DART till this date is the only rating system that still measures audience metrics in rural India.

TAM & INTAM

In 1994, claiming a heterogeneous and fragmenting television market ORG-MARG[50] introduced INTAM (Indian National Television Audience Measurement). Ex-officials of DD (Doordarshan) claimed that INTAM was introduced by vested commercial interests who only sought to break the monopoly of DD and that INTAM was significantly weaker in both sample size, rigour and the range of cities and regions covered.

In 1997, a joint industry body appointed TAM[51] (backed by AC Nielsen) as the official record keeper of audience metrics. Due to the differences in methodology and samples of TAM and INTAM, both provided differing results for the same programmes.

In 2001, a confidential list of households in Mumbai that were participating in the monitoring survey was released, calling into question the reliability of the data. This subsequently led to the merger of the two measurement systems into TAM. For several years after this, in spite of misgivings about the process, sample and other parameters, TAM was the de facto standard and monopoly in the audience metrics game.

aMap

In 2004, a rival ratings service, funded by a slew of American NRI investors, called aMAP was launched. Although initially, it faced a cautious uptake from clients, the TAM monopoly was broken.

aMap USP is that ratings are available as early as next day as compared to TAM's timeline of next week.

Broadcast Audience Research Council

An even newer industry body called Broadcast Audience Research Council seeks to set up an almost real-time audience metrics system. Plans for this was announced in March 2008 and work is said to be in progress.

---

50. Multiple Action Research Group

51. Television Audience Measurement

CAS – Conditional Access System

CAS or Conditional Access System is a digital mode of transmitting TV channels through a Set-Top Box (STB). The transmission signals are encrypted and viewers need to buy a set-top box to receive and decrypt the signal. The STB is required to watch only pay channels.

The idea of CAS was mooted in 2001, due to a furore over charge hikes by channels and subsequently by cable operators. Poor reception of certain channels, arbitrary pricing and increase in prices, bundling of channels, poor service delivery by Cable Television Operators (CTOs), monopolies in each area, lack of regulatory framework and redress avenues were some of the issues that were to be addressed by implementation of CAS.

It was decided by the government that CAS would be first introduced in the four metros. It has been in place in Chennai since September 2003, where until very recently, it had managed to attract very few subscribers. It has been rolled out recently in the other three metros of Delhi, Mumbai and Kolkata.

Benefits of CAS

All the involved players and the viewers (consumers) can benefit greatly once CAS is rolled out across the country. However, vested interests and the price of STB's have been some of the reasons for delay in implementation of CAS all over India.

Consumers: Consumers get the option to choose the channels they want to pay for and view, rather than receiving the whole set of channels that the Cable Operator makes available to them, and hence benefit by having to pay only for the channels they want to watch. Currently, in most of India, there is no segregation and subscribers pay a blanket rate for the entire service.

Cable Operators: Cable operators get the opportunity to pay a part of the subscription fees to the broadcasters only for the actual number of end users who opt for the channel, rather than all households having cable access. This will help streamline their infrastructure, operations and reduce points of dispute with the MSOs and broadcasters by being able to disclose the exact number of subscribers for each channel.

Broadcasters: Broadcasters have a long-standing complaint that the Cable Operators under-declare the actual number of subscribers, and hence pass on only a fraction of the paid subscriptions. With a system like this in place, it is possible to address the exact number of subscribers with a cable operator.

Advertisers: CAS gives a far more accurate indicator of programme popularity with only the actual subscribers of each channel being accounted for.

Government: Since the issue of addressability ensures a fair degree of transparency in accounting across the entire value chain, it minimises the loss of revenues to the government through misreporting or non-disclosure of actual revenue figures. The government also facilitates the introduction and development of consumer-friendly systems, like pay per view, interactive programming, etc. At the time of writing this chapter (August 22, 2008) only 25 per cent of the people have subscribed to the new technology. The rest watch only free-to-air channels. As mentioned above, the inhibiting factor from the viewer's perspective is the cost of the STB.

The Indian TV regulatory authority has recommended that all cable operators be given 5 years to change from the analog system to the digital platform[52].

DTH – Direct to Home

DTH is defined as the reception of satellite programmes with a personal dish in an individual home. DTH does not compete with CAS. Cable TV and DTH are two methods of delivery of television content. CAS is integral to both the systems in delivering pay channels.

Cable TV is through cable networks, and DTH is wireless, reaching direct to the consumer through a small dish and a set-top box. Although the government has ensured that free-to-air channels on cable are delivered to the consumer without a set-top box, DTH signals cannot be received without the set-top box.

India currently has 4 major DTH service providers and a total of over 5 million subscriber households. Dish TV (a ZEE TV subsidiary), Tata Sky, Reliance owned BIG TV and the public sector DD Direct. Next in the line-up are Bharati Airtel's DTH service and Videocon's DTH service, all lined up for launch within 2008. BIG TV has very recently launched India's first HDTV channels on its platform besides bringing in more niche programming. Also, beginning with BIG TV, the latest entrants in DTH business are all launching the services using the latest MPEG-4 digital compression, leading to higher number of channels and much better picture quality.

52. As of July 2008

Doordarshan – A Case Study

Doordarshan Logo

Doordarshan (literally Tele-Vision) is the public television broadcaster of India and a division of Prasar Bharati, a public service broadcaster nominated by the Government of India. It is one of the largest broadcasting organisations in the world in terms of the infrastructure of studios and transmitters. Recently, it has also started Digital Terrestrial Transmitters.

Beginning

Doordarshan had a modest beginning with the experimental telecast starting in Delhi in September 1959 with a small transmitter and a makeshift studio. The regular daily transmission started in 1965 as a part of All India Radio. The television service was extended to Mumbai (then Bombay) and Amritsar in 1972. Till 1975, seven Indian cities had television service and Doordarshan remained the only television channel in India. Television services were separated from radio in 1976. Each office of All India Radio and Doordarshan were placed under the management of two separate Director Generals in New Delhi. Finally, Doordarshan as a National Broadcaster came into existence.

Going National

National programme was introduced in 1982. In the same year, colour TV was introduced in the Indian market with the live telecast of the Independence Day speech by the then Prime Minister Indira Gandhi on 15th August 1982, followed by the 1982 Asian Games being held in Delhi. The 80s was the era of Doordarshan with soaps like *Hum Log (*1984), *Buniyaad* (1986-87), comedy shows like *Yeh Jo Hai Zindagi* (1984), as well as mythological dramas like *Ramayana* (1987-88) and *Mahabharata* (1989-90) which glued millions to Doordarshan. Other popular programmes included Hindi film songs based programmes like *Chitrahaar* and *Rangoli* and crime thrillers like *Karamchand* (starring Pankaj Kapoor), *Byomkesh Bakshi* (starring Rajit Kapur) and *Janki Jasoos*. Some children-based shows included *Fairy Tale Theatre*, *Dada Dadi ki Kahaniyan*, and *Vikram Betaal*. There was also a horror serial *Kile ka Rahasya* (1989).

Now more than 90 per cent of the Indian population can receive Doordarshan (DD National) programmes through a network of nearly 1400 terrestrial transmitters and about 46 Doordarshan studios produce TV programmes today.

Channels

Presently, Doordarshan operates 19 channels – 2 All India Channels, 11 Regional Languages Satellite Channels (RLSC), 4 State Networks (SN), an International Channel, a Sports Channel and 2 channels (DD-RS & DD-LS) for live broadcast of parliamentary proceedings.

On DD National, Regional programmes and Local programmes are carried on time-sharing basis. DD-News channel, launched on 3rd November 2003, which replaced the DD-Metro Entertainment channel, provides 24-Hour news service. The Regional Languages Satellite channels have two components – the Regional service for the particular state relayed by all terrestrial transmitters in the state and additional programmes in the Regional Language in prime time and non-prime time available only through cable operators. Sports Channel is exclusively devoted to the broadcasting of sporting events of national and international importance. This is the only Sports Channels which telecasts rural sports like Kho-Kho, Kabaddi etc, something which private broadcasters will not attempt to telecast as it will not attract any revenues.

Active Doordarshan: It is an Interactive Service of Tata Sky[53] to show 4 TV Channels of Doordarshan which are not available at Tata Sky as normal Channel. Active Doordarshan channels are Rajya Sabha TV, Gyan Darshan, DD Urdu and DD Bharati. DD has its DTH called DD Direct Plus, which is free of cost.

International Broadcasting: DD-India is being broadcast internationally through satellite. It is available in 146 countries worldwide, however, the information on picking up this channel in other countries is not easily available. In the UK, DD-India was available through the Eurobird Satellite on the Sky system on Channel 833 (the logo is shown as Rayat TV). The timing and programming of DD-India International is different from that of India. Transmissions for UK stopped in July 2008.

53. A private Direct-to-Home service in India

Internet – What It is and the Future it Holds...

The Internet is a global system of interconnected computer networks that interchange data by packet switching using the standardised Internet Protocol Suite (TCP/IP). It is a 'network of networks' that consists of millions of private and public, academic, business, and government networks of local to global scope that are linked by copper wires, fibre-optic cables, wireless connections, and other technologies.

The Internet carries various information resources and services, such as electronic mail, online chat, file transfer and file sharing, online gaming, and the interlinked hypertext documents and other resources of the World Wide Web (WWW).

Terminology

The terms 'Internet' and 'World Wide Web' are often used in everyday speech without much distinction. However, the Internet and the World Wide Web are not one and the same. The Internet is a global data communications system. It is a hardware and software infrastructure that provides connectivity between computers. In contrast, the Web is one of the services communicated via the Internet. It is a collection of interconnected documents and other resources, linked by hyperlinks and URLs.

Genesis

A 1946 comic science-fiction story, *A Logic Named Joe*, by Murray Leinster laid out the Internet and many of its strengths and weaknesses. However, it took more than a decade before reality began to catch up with this vision.

The USSR's launch of Sputnik spurred the United States to create the Advanced Research Projects Agency, known as ARPA, in February 1958 to regain a technological lead. ARPA created the Information Processing Technology Office (IPTO) to further the research of the Semi Automatic Ground Environment (SAGE) programme, which had networked countrywide radar systems together for the first time. JCR Licklider was selected to head the IPTO, who saw universal networking as a potential unifying human revolution.

Licklider moved from the Psycho-Acoustic Laboratory at Harvard University to MIT in 1950, after becoming interested in information technology. At MIT, he served on a committee that established Lincoln Laboratory and worked on the SAGE project. In 1957, he became the Vice President at BBN, where he bought the first production PDP-1 computer and conducted the first public demonstration of time-sharing.

At the IPTO, Licklider recruited Lawrence Roberts to head a project to implement a network, and Roberts based the technology on the work of Paul Baran, who had written an exhaustive study for the US Air Force that recommended packet switching (as opposed to circuit switching) to make a network highly robust and survivable. After much work, the first two nodes of what would become the ARPANET were interconnected between UCLA and SRI International in Menlo Park, California, on October 29, 1969. The ARPANET was one of the 'eve' networks of today's Internet. Following on from the demonstration that packet switching worked on the ARPANET, the British Post Office, Telenet, DATAPAC and TRANSPAC collaborated to create the first international packet-switched network service. In the UK, this was referred to as the International Packet Stream Service (IPSS), in 1978. The collection of X.25-based networks grew from Europe and the US to cover Canada, Hong Kong and Australia by 1981. The X.25 packet switching standard was developed in the CCITT (now called ITU-T) around 1976. X.25 was independent of the TCP/IP protocols that arose from the experimental work of DARPA on the ARPANET, Packet Radio Net and Packet Satellite Net during the same time period. Vinton Cerf and Robert Kahn developed the first description of the TCP protocols during 1973 and published a paper on the subject in May 1974. Use of the term 'Internet' to describe a single global TCP/IP network originated in December 1974 with the publication of RFC 675, the first full specification of TCP that was written by Vinton Cerf, Yogen Dalal and Carl Sunshine, then at Stanford University. During the next nine years, work proceeded to refine the protocols and to implement them on a wide range of operating systems.

The first TCP/IP-based wide-area network was operational by January 1, 1983 when all hosts on the ARPANET were switched over from the older NCP protocols. In 1985, the United States National Science Foundation (NSF) commissioned the construction of the NSFNET, a university 56 kilobit/second network backbone using computers called 'fuzzballs' by their inventor, David L. Mills. The following year, NSF sponsored the conversion to a higher-speed 1.5 megabit/second network. A key decision to use the DARPA TCP/IP protocols was made by Dennis Jennings, then in charge of the Supercomputer programme at NSF.

The opening of the network to commercial interests began in 1988. The US Federal Networking Council approved the interconnection of the NSFNET to the commercial MCI Mail system in that year and the link was made in the summer of 1989. Other commercial electronic email services were soon connected, including OnTyme, Telemail and Compuserve. In that same year, three commercial Internet Service Providers (ISP) were created: UUNET, PSINET and CERFNET. Important, separate networks that offered gateways into, then later merged with the Internet include Usenet and BITNET. Various other commercial and educational networks, such as Telenet, Tymnet, Compuserve and JANET were interconnected with the growing Internet. Telenet (later called Sprintnet) was a large privately funded national computer network with free dial-up access in cities throughout the US that had been in operation since the 1970s. This network was eventually interconnected with the others in the 1980s as the TCP/IP protocol became increasingly popular. The ability of TCP/IP to work over virtually any pre-existing communication networks allowed for a great ease of growth, although the rapid growth of the Internet was due primarily to the availability of commercial routers from companies such as Cisco Systems, Proteon and Juniper, the availability of commercial Ethernet equipment for local-area networking and the widespread implementation of TCP/IP on the UNIX operating system.

Growth

Although the basic applications and guidelines that make the Internet possible had existed for almost a decade, the network did not gain a public face until the

1990s. On August 6, 1991, CERN, which straddles the border between France and Switzerland, publicised the new World Wide Web project. The Web was invented by English scientist Tim Berners-Lee in 1989.

An early popular web browser was ViolaWWW, patterned after HyperCard and built using the X Window System. It was eventually replaced in popularity by the Mosaic web browser. In 1993, the National Centre for Supercomputing Applications at the University of Illinois released version 1.0 of Mosaic, and by late 1994 there was growing public interest in the previously academic, technical Internet. By 1996, usage of the word Internet had become commonplace, and consequently, so had its use as a synecdoche in reference to the World Wide Web.

Meanwhile, over the course of the decade, the Internet successfully accommodated the majority of previously existing public computer networks (although some networks, such as FidoNet, have remained separate). During the 1990s, it was estimated that the Internet grew by 100% per year, with a brief period of explosive growth in 1996 and 1997. This growth is often attributed to the lack of central administration, which allows organic growth of the network, as well as the non-proprietary open nature of the Internet protocols, which encourages vendor interoperability and prevents any one company from exerting too much control over the network.

Today's Internet

Aside from the complex physical connections that make up its infrastructure, the Internet is facilitated by bi- or multi-lateral commercial contracts (e.g., peering agreements), and by technical specifications or protocols that describe how to exchange data over the network. Indeed, the Internet is defined by its interconnections and routing policies.

As of March 31, 2008 1.407 billion people use the Internet according to Internet World Statistics.

Common Uses

The World Wide Web[54]

Many people use the terms Internet and World Wide Web (or just the Web) interchangeably, yet the two terms are not synonymous.

54. Besides most common and obvious uses such as email, chatting, file transfer, voice over Internet protocol etc etc.

The World Wide Web is a huge set of interlinked documents, images and other resources, linked by hyperlinks and URL s[55]. These hyperlinks and URLs allow the web servers and other machines that store originals, and cached copies of these resources to deliver them as required using HTTP (Hypertext Transfer Protocol). HTTP is only one of the communication protocols used on the Internet.

Web services also use HTTP to allow software systems to communicate in order to share and exchange business logic and data.

Software products that can access the resources of the Web are correctly termed user agents. In normal use, web browsers, such as Internet Explorer and Firefox, access web pages and allow users to navigate from one to another via hyperlinks. Web documents may contain almost any combination of computer data including graphics, sounds, text, video, multimedia and interactive content including games, office applications and scientific demonstrations.

Through keyword-driven Internet research using search engines like Yahoo! and Google, millions of people worldwide have easy, instant access to a vast and diverse amount of online information. Compared to encyclopaedias and traditional libraries, the World Wide Web has enabled a sudden and extreme decentralisation of information and data.

Using the Web, it is also easier than ever before for individuals and organisations to publish ideas and information to an extremely large audience. Anyone can find ways to publish a web page, a blog or build a website for very little initial cost. Publishing and maintaining large, professional websites full of attractive, diverse and up-to-date information is still a difficult and expensive proposition, however.

Many individuals and some companies and groups use 'web logs' or blogs, which are largely used as easily updatable online diaries. Some commercial organisations encourage staff to fill them with advice on their areas of specialisation in the hope that visitors will be impressed by the expert knowledge and free information, and be attracted to the corporation as a result. One example of this practice is Microsoft, whose product developers publish their personal blogs in order to attract the public interest in their work.

Collections of personal web pages published by large service providers remain popular, and have become increasingly sophisticated. Whereas operations such as Angelfire and GeoCities have existed since the early days of the Web, newer

55. Uniform Resource Locators

offerings from, for example, Wordpress, Facebook and MySpace currently have large followings. These operations often brand themselves as social network services rather than simply as web page hosts.

Advertising on popular web pages can be lucrative, and e-commerce or the sale of products and services directly via the Web continues to grow.

In the early days, web pages were usually created as sets of complete and isolated HTML text files stored on a web server. More recently, websites are more often created using Content Management System (CMS) or Wiki software with, initially, very little content. Contributors to these systems, who may be paid staff, members of a club or other organisation or members of the public, fill underlying databases with content using editing pages designed for that purpose, while casual visitors view and read this content in its final HTML form. There may or may not be editorial, approval and security systems built into the process of taking newly entered content and making it available to the target visitors.

Internet Access

Common methods of home access include dial-up, landline broadband (over coaxial cable, fibber optic or copper wires), Wi-Fi, satellite and 3G technology cell phones.

Public places to use the Internet include libraries and Internet cafes, where computers with Internet connections are available. There are also Internet access points in many public places, such as airport halls and coffee shops, in some cases just for brief use while standing. Various terms are used, such as 'public Internet kiosk', 'public access terminal', and 'Web payphone'. Many hotels now also have public terminals, though these are usually fee-based. These terminals are widely accessed for various usage like ticket booking, bank deposit, online payment etc. Wi-Fi provides wireless access to computer networks, and therefore can do so to the Internet itself. Hotspots providing such access include Wi-Fi cafés, where potential users need to bring their own wireless-enabled devices such as a laptop or PDA. These services may be free to all, free to customers only, or fee-based. A hotspot need not be limited to a confined location. A whole campus or park, or even an entire city can be enabled. Grassroots efforts have led to wireless community networks. Commercial Wi-Fi services covering large city areas are in place in London, Vienna, Toronto, San Francisco, Philadelphia, Chicago and Pittsburgh. The Internet can then be accessed from such places as a park bench.

Apart from Wi-Fi, there have been experiments with proprietary mobile wireless networks like Ricochet, various high-speed data services over cellular phone networks, and fixed wireless services.

High-end mobile phones such as smartphones generally come with Internet access through the phone network. Web browsers such as Opera are available on these advanced handsets, which can also run a wide variety of other Internet software. More mobile phones have Internet access than PCs, though this is not as widely used. An Internet access provider and protocol matrix differentiates the methods used to get online.

A Vodafone Internet WiFi Connection

Social Impact

The Internet has made possible entirely new forms of social interaction, activities and organising, thanks to its basic features such as widespread usability and access.

Social networking websites such as Facebook and MySpace have created a new form of socialisation and interaction. Users of these sites are able to add a wide variety of items to their personal pages, to indicate common interests, and to connect with others. It is also possible to find a large circle of existing acquaintances, especially if a site allows users to utilise their real names, and to allow communication among large existing groups of people.

Sites like meetup.com[56] exist to allow wider announcement of groups which may exist mainly for face-to-face meetings, but which may have a variety of minor interactions over their group's site at meetup.com, or other similar sites.

Political Organisation and Censorship

In democratic societies, the Internet has achieved new relevance as a political tool. The presidential campaign of Howard Dean in 2004 in the United States became famous for its ability to generate donations via the Internet. Many political groups use the Internet to achieve a whole new method of organising, in order to carry out Internet activism.

---

56. www.meetup.com

Some governments, such as those of Cuba, Iran, North Korea, Myanmar, the People's Republic of China, and Saudi Arabia, restrict what people in their countries can access on the Internet, especially political and religious content. This is accomplished through software that filters domains and content so that they may not be easily accessed or obtained without elaborate circumvention.

In Norway, Denmark, Finland and Sweden, major Internet service providers have voluntarily (possibly to avoid such an arrangement being turned into law) agreed to restrict access to sites listed by the police. While this list of forbidden URLs is only supposed to contain addresses of known child pornography sites, the content of the list is secret.

Many countries, including the United States, have enacted laws making the possession or distribution of certain material, such as child pornography, illegal, but do not use filtering software.

There are many free and commercially available software programmes with which a user can choose to block offensive websites on individual computers or networks, such as to limit a child's access to pornography or violence.

Internet as an Instrument of Mass Communication

If one is to even try to comprehend how Internet would change the very concept of Mass Communication as a whole in the mere five years to come, one would simply have to check his or her email. In 2005, Google, the most famous of the search engines ever to bless the Internet, offered free email accounts with unlimited storage capacity. While the concept of unlimited space was reason enough for people to sign up for their free email accounts, Google offered an ingenious concept of Google Talk, Google Chat, Email Search and above all Email News. This meant that you could no longer just check your mails and ever need to delete it, you could chat with your friends, search for a small note in the heap of a million letters, all the while reading the headlines and if needed the entire news. Google detected automatically the names of places typed and provided news and advertisements about that place. And if more information on anything else was required, one could simply search for it on the Internet using Google Search. Google is after all the world's best search engine. Today, almost 72 per cent of the world uses Gmail and about 98 per cent use Google as the preferred search engine.

If what Google was able to achieve with Gmail is contemplated in the real world, it would essentially mean – (1) the Post Office offering you a post box of unlimited storage capacity free of cost for your entire life and no postage ever needed for any number of correspondence, (2) an official dedicated towards maintaining the records of your mails and who at the time of being asked about a letter received ten years earlier from an aunt present it to you, in almost a second in its pristine condition, (3) and the same official also being a general tracker of sorts who when asked of anything in the world comes up with every information on it that possibly exists, (4) and lastly, an entire office or group of people working tirelessly to offer you information, including news, entertainment and gossips. And if all of these were indeed possible, it would have to be for free!

Certainly, such a thing had not even been thought of in 2000. Today, with high-speed Internet connectivity, movies, documentary and music videos in their highest resolution can only be watched on the Internet. The highest precision sound can only be accessed in the Internet. Internet makes it possible for a local village gossip to be heard side by side with the United States Presidential Address to the Congress. This is the true freedom of choice. Further, Internet cannot be brought down by any Government. Nor can it be censored! It cannot be banned nor brought to bear. This does have a critical bearing on everything; the opportunities and the responsibilities nonetheless are seemingly limitless.

THE WORLD OF MASS COMMUNICATION

- → Communication – What Does It Involve?
- → Models of Communication
- → Communication and Mass Communication
- → Mass Media
- → Roles the Readers and Audiences Play

"It's only the possibility of mass communication that makes man a social animal. . . without mass communication, man is just an animal."

The World of Mass Communication

Once upon a time, this planet was a planet without words. No words were written, nor even spoken! People lived a lonely life and died a stranger even to their neighbour. Only the idea to survive existed; beyond that there were no other ideas. Man was a silent being and led a miserable existence.

But then a glorious breakthrough occurred in the course of evolution. Man realised that he could not exist alone and that his existence could only be guaranteed if he could communicate in order to muster help and support of his neighbours. Hence, the art of communication was invented. In course of time, communication was also applied in influencing public opinion. Kings and Emperors proclaimed of their new laws through drum beaters, messengers, minstrels, writers and poets. Philosophers, thinkers and inventors wrote books. Poets wrote poems and songs. Eventually a system of communication involving the entire mass was evolved and a name was given to it – Mass Communication!

Communication – What Does It Involve?

Communication, whether it is meant for a large audience (such as a speech) or a single individual (for example, a simple conversation), whether written or oral or even without words involves a 'communicator' and a 'receiver'. In simple words, if you are giving a speech in the auditorium of your college, a communication is said to exist, where you are acting as a communicator and the audience—the receiver. Of course, the non-existence of any of you—either the communicator or the receiver—will lead to no communication. Similarly, in a simple conversation with your friend or friends, you will act as a communicator and a receiver intermittently.

In terms of communication involving written words, you are already very much accustomed to the different notices put by the principal on your college notice board. And of course, a communication can also exist without words, both verbal and written. A photograph of an aged woman being helped by a young lad to cross the street does communicate with you, doesn't it?

Models of Communication

A model is defined as something which is ideal, to be imitated, followed or to be propagated. While in theory, words are used to explain a phenomenon, a model explains the process by means of tables, charts and drawings.

The concern for communication has produced many models of the process of communication, listing the various elements, the interaction and relationships among the elements, and their relationships with the environment.

We shall discuss here some of the famous models of communication developed so far.

Shannon and Weaver Model

This model was developed by an acclaimed mathematician Shannon in 1947, and later perfected by Warren Weaver. Thus, it came to be known as Shannon-Weaver Model.

According to this model, there are five ingredients in a communication:

a) Source, who is a speaker,

b) Transmitter, the medium used to send the message,

c) Signal, which is speech or a message,

d) Receiver, and

e) Destination, which is the receiver.

The model can be illustrated as follows:

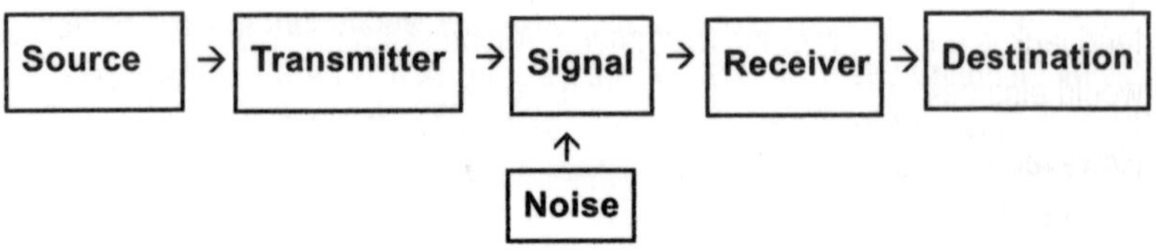

Berlo's S-M-C-R Model

This model is also known as Source – Message – Channel – Receiver model of communication. This model emphasises the importance of "thorough understanding of human behaviour as a pre-requisite to communication analysis", and assumes that the source and the receiver are matched in their standing to make the communication fruitful, failing which there will be gaps.

The model can be represented as:

Source   Message   Channel   Receiver

M

Schramm's Interactive Model

Wilbur Schramm analysed and presented communication in a new light and explained communication in various ways. He used Shannon-Weaver's model to further elaborate and clarify his concepts of communication. He conceived of decoding and encoding as activities maintained simultaneously by sender and receiver, and also made provisions for a two-way interchange of messages.

The model can be illustrated as follows:

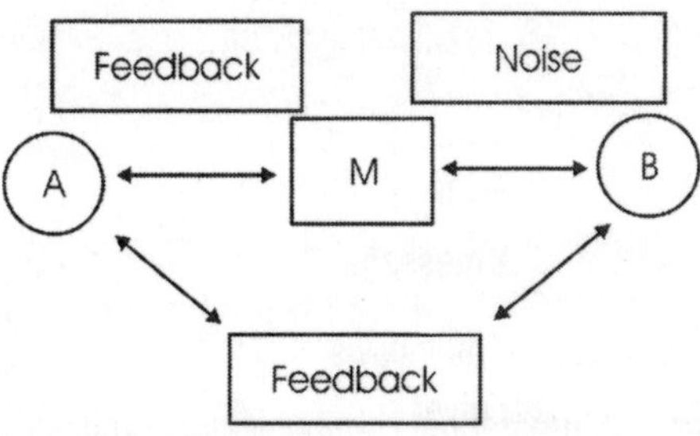

The model signifies that when A and B are exchanging the message (M), feedback is constantly being exchanged. Anyone who is receiving the message would also be reacting, thus providing a feedback.

However, there can be problems in comprehending the message correctly. This is caused by 'noise' which can make the message 'ineffective'. It means that the content of the message is determined by the receiver in a particular manner depending on his personal background, social status, economic position, etc.

It has been represented as follows:

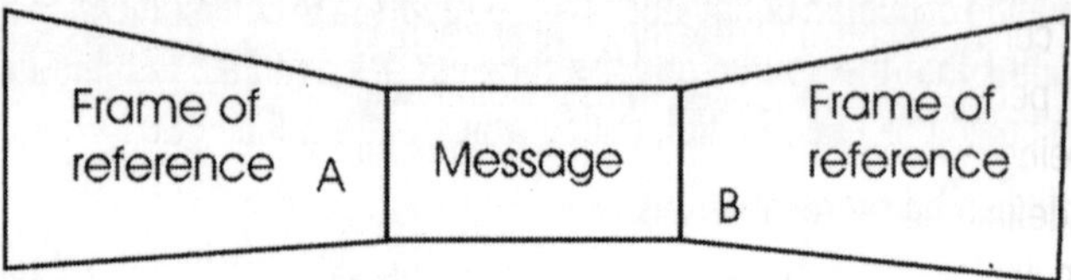

The above model shows that A is the source, while B is the receiver, and the receiver picks up from the message what he thinks is relevant to him, and discards the rest.

Dance's Helical Spiral

According to EX Dance, communication is stimulated in a circular model, and once the process of communication starts, it comes back full circle to exactly the same point from where it started.

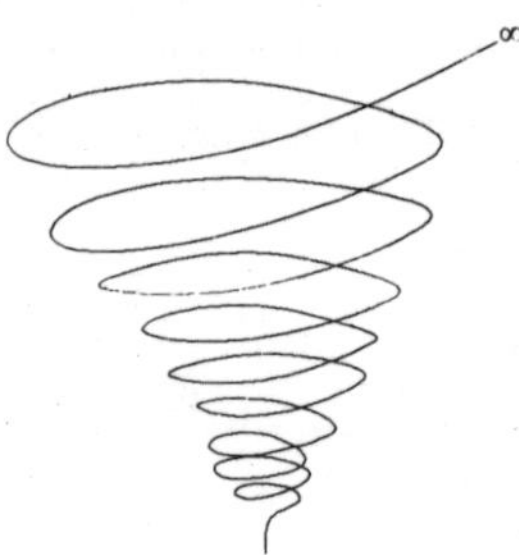

This model can be represented as follows:

This model is closer to interpersonal communication process, but fails to reflect or explain all areas of communication effectively.

Communication and Mass Communication

Now that we know what communication is, how it evolved and what it involves, let us try to understand what Mass Communication is and what does it involve.

In simple words, Mass Communication implies communication at a mass scale[57] . This further means that a simple conversation does not imply mass communication. For a communication to be called mass communication, it must involve a group of audience much greater in number than what is possible in simple conversation. For example, a speech in an auditorium filled with a thousand people can be called Mass Communication. Similarly, your same speech being re-broadcast from a local radio station to all the receivers in the region is definitely a Mass Communication between you and all the receivers in the region, which of course at times may make up at least a hundred thousand.

But your speech made to five of your best friends does not imply mass communication.

Mass Media

Mass Media as a terminology is derived from Mass Communication and is used to describe the different instruments of Mass Communication. The classic example of mass media are newspapers, newsmagazines, television broadcasts, radio broadcasts, journals, e-books, the Internet whereupon the different websites of varied interests and subjects are the 'online' version of newspapers, newsmagazines and journals. Apart from these, the illegal 'spam'[58] , SMS (Short Message Service[59]) and mass mailers[60] are also examples of mass communication. These are all, however, the inventions of the 21st century.

Characteristics of Mass Communication

Five characteristics of Mass Communication as identified by Cambridge University's John B. Thompson[61] are:

---

57. This is also how the terminology Mass Communication came into being.

58. Unsolicited emails sent to millions of Internet users all over the world featuring different advertisements, appeals, and the so-called newsletters, all of which you never seem to have ever subscribed. Though spam has been made illegal in the United States, in India it has become the instrument of choice of some political parties bombarding the Indian Internet users with political advertisements and propagandas.

59. SMS is being used in much the same manner as spam is being used today, at least in India.

60. Different political parties, industries and marketing houses send mass mails to prospective individuals with the hope of trying to influence their opinions in whatever subject this might be in. For example, the BJP led NDA Government decided to send mass mails to the individual head of all the families in the nation. The letter signed by the Prime Minister himself was intended to seek the support of the voters.

61. John B. Thompson is a Sociology professor at the University of Cambridge and a fellow of Jesus College. He has studied the influence of the media in the formation of modern societies, a subject on which he is one of the few social theorists to focus. One of the key themes of his work is the role of the media in the transformation

Firstly, it 'comprises both technical and institutional methods of production and distribution'. This is evident throughout the history of the media, from print to the Internet, each suitable for commercial utility.

Secondly, it involves the 'commodification of symbolic forms', as the production of materials relies on its ability to manufacture and sell large quantities of the work. Just as radio stations rely on its time sold to advertisements, newspapers rely for the same reasons on its space.

Mass Communication's **third** characteristic is the 'separate contexts between the production and reception of information', while the **fourth** is in its "reach to those 'far removed' in time and space, in comparison to the producers".

Finally, Thompson notes a **fifth** characteristic of Mass Communication, which involves 'information distribution'. This is a 'one to many' form of communication, whereby products are mass produced and disseminated to a great quantity of audiences.

Roles, the Readers and Audiences Play

As it has already been stated in the previous chapter, the readers are the true kings in the business of Mass Communication. And indeed all the troubles that newspapers, magazines, periodicals, television and radio broadcasts go through are just to serve them. This does imply that the people, in whatever capacity they might be attached with Mass Media, are the most important ingredient in Mass Communication. And this further implies that they greatly influence the policies of Mass Media, which has been discussed earlier.

But as all actions have equal and opposite reaction, the readers themselves are greatly influenced by the Mass Media. And indeed it is important that they be aware of their responsibilities as readers or audiences[62] .

---

of space and time in social life, and the creation of new forms of action and interaction beyond temporal and spatial frameworks. Influenced strongly by hermeneutics, he studies communication and its uses, and links it closely with social context. Other key concepts are the transformation of visibility, the media and tradition, and identity and the symbolic project. His book Ideology and Mass Culture is a study of what the theory of ideology entails in modern society. William Outhwaite of the University of Sussex dubs it a path breaking work which will undoubtedly become one of the fundamental texts in the theory of ideology. Thompson's essay 'The New Visibility' is employed as the basis for the study of media at Rhodes University, while his tome Political Scandal: Power and Visibility in the Media Age has been described by Amy Binder of Clemson University as 'excellent'. His work stands out for its recognition of the importance of the nature and development of mass communication.

62. Remember this includes you even if you are working for a paper

Responsibilities of the Readers and Audiences

Can you believe what you read? Is it the truth? And if yes, is it the whole truth or merely a part of the truth – a part that gives you a different impression from the one you would receive if you knew the whole story?

The Freedom of the Press implies that editors have the right to print almost all that they want to. Of course, the laws do try to stop them from being overwhelmed by the freedom guaranteed; it does not still give the readers and the people of our nation as a whole to rest easy. As the protector of the Constitution and stability and the integrity of the nation, the readers must remain vigilant and act like a watchdog. The readers must also learn to think as they read, listen or view. And above all they must be very careful and critical of news and views bombarded to their face.

Hence, they must

1. Cultivate the ability to recognise and understand opinions
2. Learn to distinguish between facts and opinions
3. Carefully consider each and every news source
4. Be careful of slanted news
5. Be careful of appeals to your emotions

Cultivate the ability to recognise and understand opinions

Learn to distinguish between facts and opinions

What are opinions, anyway?

Opinions simply put are points of views.

In fact, all knowledge is only but a point of view.

The above sentence is in itself a classical example of opinion. Now how would you deal with the above sentence? For one, you would read it and probably agree with it or perhaps not. This implies that you can either accept it or negate it.

Now take the following sentence for an example:

The aranyakas and upanisads are the jnankanda, of the Vedas, studied by the uttara mimansa, 'posterior interpretation', or Vedanta, 'End of the Vedas' school.

If you are a student of Theology, you will certainly agree with the above statement. And even go on to say that there is no room to disagree with it because it is a 'Fact', just like the fact that 'White is white' or 'Rose is a rose'.

In Mass Communication, a reporter, takes anything that really happens to be a fact. For example, if someone makes a speech concerning an event, the only known fact is that he made the speech, while the contents of the speech must be considered to be opinion. Here, however, it is not up to the reporter to determine what is fact and what is opinion. Instead it is the readers who must accept the responsibility to determine the truth.

The readers must also try to form their own opinion instead of taking the opinion expressed in the papers for granted.

Carefully Consider Each and Every News Source

The reader must learn how to question the legality of statements quoted in any news story. The source through which he or she derived his news is as important as the news itself. For example, if a reporter, while in a police beat is informed of a hit-and-run accident and reports the same as a hit-and-run accident based on the information derived from his beat thereof. The news might be completely misleading and false. Here however, still it is not up to the reporter to be careful. He will simple follow-up the story the day after by visiting the family, the mortuary, the site of accident and the police station.

Take another instance for example, during a party office beat, a reporter might be told something by a politician which could either be 'out of record' or an official statement. But even if it is official, it might not be public. Here, if the statement is published by the reporter, the politician may back up and say that he or she had never made such a statement. Of course, both the politician and the reporter are within their rights, the readers must then try to make sense out of these mêlée.

At times, a reporter might chance upon a scoop, or what could best be called privileged information, he might not be able to quote the person who provided him the information. However, it is understood that the news is true. Here, the reporter will implicate his story to have been based upon 'reliable sources' or 'mostly reliable source' or 'informed source' etc., etc.

The reporter while in doubt of publishing certain statements made might prefer to include such words as 'alleged...' and 'asserted...'

Here the readers are believed to be able to extract the real truth from the story.

Be Careful of Slanted News

The entire business of Mass Communication is run by humans not gods, and as such they are as individuals and as a group of individuals prone to all that weaknesses that vex mankind.

Reporters while investigating a story also unconsciously forms his own opinion about the news. Of course, he or she knows that his or her opinions or views about the news has importance and as an unwritten journalistic norm must not be implicated in the reporting of the news, it does at times, unwittingly though seem to reflect on his or her reporting.

I have myself been found to have unwittingly done so during the first days of my reporting. In one murder investigation back in Chennai, I found myself so involved with the story and the family of the murder victim that when my reports were published, they almost seemed to be emotional ramblings of detective instead of a news-report.

Here the danger of slanted news arises. When a reporter punctuates his news by opinions or personal views, he transforms the entire story. The story no longer becomes a fact but an opinion and most important 'not what happened but what the reporter thought happened'. Going through the ancient unwritten laws of journalism, this is the greatest of all blasphemy.

You might have been a bit surprised when I suggested the 'ancient unwritten laws of journalism'; this I have done so in great pain because the modern journalists all seem to be bent at breaking the holiest and the most 'foundationary' rules of journalism.

Take for instance, the approval of slanted news by the present day's editors of both print media and news broadcasts on television and radio. Since recent times, most Indian newspapers seem to be filled with slanted news. Sensationalism has given way to the 'reporting of news as it was'. These days, even the simplest of news seem to be based more upon the opinions of what the reporter thought to have happened and not what actually happened[63].

63. It would be rather a sin, if I pass this out without putting into words issues that mark modern trends in journalism. Like in the days of Yellow Journalism in the United States and even presently, when news have become much like a product you find in your general story, somehow, it needs to be gift-wrapped and made more attractive to the customer, here readers. Believe it or not, the publishers, owners of different media groups both in India and abroad want to make money and hence, as a result want to make their paper, channel or station more popular with the people, which in turn leads to unwarranted importance in sensationalism. This leads to more readership, more viewer/audience base and thence, more advertisement.

Here the responsibilities of the readers, viewers or audiences grow. You are bombarded with news, sensationalised and especially designed to influence your opinion in various ways. Now if you sit back and accept and agree to all that is being said or written you will certainly be in trouble.

You must at once learn to trace opinion of the reporter in the news. And that is not all. You must decide whether you want the truth or sensationalism, for if you just want sensationalism then it is you who is causing more harm to journalism then the reporters, editors or publishers.

Beware of Propaganda

In controlled Press (es) in countries like People's Republic of China, North Korea, US-occupied Iraq, Israel-occupied Palestine, Cuba, Angola, Nepal and so on. Even in our country in Kashmir, where the Press enjoys little freedom (being under implications of both the Indian Government and the Terrorist Organisation) , they might simply be forced to publish propaganda materials.

In our country, the Doordarshan being the National Channel directly under the Government, broadcasts certain programmes which are aimed at defaming Pakistan, similarly, the PTV, Doordarshan's counterpart on the other side of the border itself directly under the Pakistani Government broadcasts certain programmes of same type aimed at defaming the Indian Government and the Indian Defence Forces. Both simply are propagandas.

During the Second World War, Nazi Germany excelled in propaganda, that is false yet, made believable ideas. For example, Nazi Germany through its propaganda wanted the people in Austria to believe that Austria indeed was a part of Germany and the two long families had to be brought together. When Hitler rode to 'liberate' Austria, there was not a single shot fired. The entire government simply handed over the country believing the propaganda. Today,

---

In the recent years, the Mass Media business in India made the most profit during the Kargil War reporting the news of the war. It is an open window to the see through as to how, rather strangely both the Press in India and Pakistan sided with their respective Governments. Each reporting diligently different incidents featuring the exploits of their respective army, which while most of the time were entirely untrue. This is not prevalent only in the Indian Sub-continent though. Actually, we Indians and Pakistanis only seem to have learnt it from the Americans and the British. During the three Gulf Wars, both the US and British media openly sided with their Governments reporting 'what happened through the point of view of a British or US reporter' nor simply a reporter. But then in the modern days of Global Marketing, when the world has just become a big market reachable by and to all, such methods of grabbing the share of the market is usual and accepted. No revolution within the field itself, as yet would lead to change only perhaps the change in economic concepts and our way of Life, which strangely seems to reflect more like the American Way of Life, every day.

Austria is an independent country as it always was.

The Americans, on the other hand, have been extensively using propaganda. The George Bush government was able to convince the people through different propaganda machineries that the invasion of Iraq was a must for the very survival of United States.

However, all propagandas are not that harmful. For example, a simple notice in the newspaper may ask you to "Vote!" The other may say "Join the Green Peace". All these are intended to educate the people and are welcome.

These days all advertisements are propaganda. A certain product advertisement might ask you to "use it because Mr Sachin Tendulkar uses it". It is believed that because you and Sachin will be sharing something in common, the poor or rather middle-class individual will feel some sort of achievement, and this in turn will certainly influence him in buying that product. All advertisements employing known figures like actors, actresses, sportsperson, celebrities, so on and so forth are based on this fact.

Other advertisements are propaganda in the sense that they are simply misleading – "Certified by the American Specialists". The product might be certified by the American specialists, but what type of certification was provided and by what kind of specialists. Questions like these always remain unanswered. And the worst of all, what does 'American Specialists' imply? Does it mean that Indian Scientists are not trained or qualified enough to test and certify the products? Or has the 'American' just used it as a label – "Come on, the Americans certified it. The product must be good!" That's what the model seems to imply to us.

Now you as an end receiver, if not serious, might be forced to buy air packed in a cylinder just because the free, hugely available air is unfit to inhale.

All these devices are meant to catch you off-guard. People are easily fooled when they relax and take things for granted. If you don't bother to question the propaganda put before you, you will certainly be fooled. This is the greatest danger and indeed the greatest challenge of modern day mass communication.

THE PRESS

- Definition
  - Power and Responsibilities of the Press
  - What Regulates the Press? Libel Laws
- Civil and Criminal Libel
- The Author's Defences
- What Regulates the Press besides Libel?

"Freedom without restrictions can only lead to chaos. A Free Press is free as long as it is aware of its duties."

The Press

Definition

Press (1) *pres,* (all obs.) **preacher, prease, preasse, etc.**, prēs, vs.t. To exert a pushing force upon, to squeeze, to compress, to clasp, to thrust onwards or downwards, to squeeze out, to imprint, stamp or print.

Press (2) *pres, v.t.* To carry off **and** force into service, esp. in the navy: to requisition: to turn to use in an unsuitable or provisional way[64] .

Press (3) *noun, in modern journalism terminology (Always used with the capital P):* Printing, a printing organisation, newspapers, periodicals, radio broadcasting, television broadcasting, individuals associated with either print media, electronic media, online publication taken individually or collectively.

While it is not known as to how and when this interpretation of the terminology 'Press' came into existence, a popular and a safe surmise puts it to the very process of printing the early newspapers and journals.

Power and Responsibilities of the Press

The Press implied in journalistic terms literally has power to create revolutions, topple governments, create chaos, and at the same time bring an end to revolutions, save governments and bring peace. Truly, history is rampant with examples of such power wielded by the Press. The Boston Tea Party was planned at the house of a newspaper editor. The newspaper started by Dadabhai

64. Lanuua I Sidney, Ramson S W, Schwarz Catherine & others, Chambers English Dictionary, Allied Publishers Limited, India 1990.

Naoroji literally started the true freedom struggle in India. The Gulf War and the Iraqi invasion by the US and the allied forces were both termed as Media War, proving beyond doubt that half of the war could actually be won through the Press itself.

However, the same power of Press implies numerous things.

For one, the Press in a country like North Korea effectively has no power. Why? Because North Korea is a Totalitarian State with State imposed restrictions on the Press. In fact, in North Korea, newspapers always print the photos of President Kim as it is resolved that he is 'always in the news'. The extent of State monopoly is such that even textbooks of all subjects ranging from social sciences to engineering are available, though all authored rather strangely by President Kim himself.

This does seem rather odd to us. However, in North Korea, it is not. The Press cannot criticise the government or its officials. It cannot discuss the official policies nor try by itself to interpret them. It must print what it is told to, not what it wants to or should. Here effectively, the Press has no freedom and thus has no power. This further implies that without freedom the Press is nearly non-existent.

However, this is only one side of the story. In our country, the Press is guaranteed freedom and non-interference by the Constitution itself. This means that the Press wields a great deal of power than in other parts of the world.

The Press in India can openly criticise both the Prime Minister and the President [65]. The Press at the same time has the ability to change and influence the opinions of the people.

But here is the catch! With great power comes great responsibility.

---

65. Freedom of press in India - The Indian Constitution, while not mentioning the word 'press', provides for 'the right to freedom of speech and expression' (Article 19(1) a). However, this right is subject to restrictions under subclause (2), whereby this freedom can be restricted for reasons of 'sovereignty and integrity of India, the security of the State, friendly relations with foreign States, public order, preserving decency, preserving morality, in relation to contempt of court, defamation, or incitement to an offence'. Laws such as the Official Secrets Act and Prevention of Terrorism Act (PoTA) have been used to limit press freedom. Under PoTA, person could be detained for up to six months for being in contact with a terrorist or terrorist group. PoTA was repealed in 2006, but the Official Secrets Act 1923 continues. For the first half-century of independence, media control by the state was the major constraint on press freedom. Indira Gandhi famously stated in 1975 that All India Radio is 'a Government organ, it is going to remain a Government organ....' With the liberalisation starting in the 1990s, private control of media has burgeoned, leading to increasing independence and greater scrutiny of government. Organisations like Tehelka and NDTV have been particularly influential, e.g. in bringing about the resignation of powerful Haryana minister Venod Sharma.

If the Press in our country can criticise the heads of the Government both at national and regional levels, it cannot do so without keeping certain things in mind. For example, the Press can criticise the Prime Minister for a certain policy that he undertakes, it cannot however, criticise the Prime Minister individually for his personal activities outside the realm of 'public life'. Here journalistic ethics come in to play.

The founders of our Constitution while giving freedom to the Press also made sure that the same freedom did not overwhelm The Press; so they put in certain laws to regulate the Press. In due time, International laws were formed in order to regulate Press at the International level.

What Regulates the Press

Libel Laws

According to the Illinois Criminal code, **"(Libel is) A malicious defamation,** *expressed either by printing or by signs, pictures or the like tending to blacken the memory of one who is dead or to impeach the honesty, integrity, virtue or reputation or publish the natural defects of one who is alive, and thereby to expose him to public hatred, contempt, ridicule or financial injury."*

Now let us discuss the above given definition in following perspectives:

a. The **Defamation** Angle

The first noun we encounter is **'defamation'**. Defamation has been defined by an Iowa Court as *"taking from another's reputation"*. Now this does provide us with our first clue to an important point and that is—whether or not a person has been defamed, depends not so much on what has been said. But rather on what people think as a result of what has been said, or, more realistically, what a court judges to be the effect upon people's minds of what has been said.

Let's take for example the following sentence:

"Rajesh Sharma has been known to steal and thus it is not a surprise that the Maharaja's jewellery be lost in his custody."

The above sentence summarily convicts Rajesh Sharma. But that is not all. The readers who would read the sentence would also believe that Rajesh Sharma was indeed behind the heist. Here, essentially, the above surmise – what people think as a result of what has been said – becomes more realistic. True, Rajesh Sharma was an ex-convict, but that does not make him 'the man' behind the heist by default. The other side of the story also remains unexplored. The sentence, itself says that the Maharaja's jewellery was in his custody, which means that someone must have trusted him enough to have given him the custody of the jewellery. This does effectively pronounce that Rajesh Sharma is a rehabilitated man and that the above statement is totally unwarranted and out rightly defamatory[66].

Defamation in Action

Real Life Examples

Defamation case against DMK political speaker

By Our Staff Reporter

VELLORE, Dec 27: A defamation case has been filed on behalf of the Chief Minister, Jayalalithaa, in the court of the District and Sessions judge, Vellore, against the Dravida Munnetra Kazhagam (DMK) political speaker, Kritto Kasinathan of Chatram in Arni taluk of Tiruvannamalai district.

According to the petition filed by K. Balachandar, Public Prosecutor, Vellore district, Mr. Kritto Kasinathan in his speech made at a party public meeting at Keezhvallam in the district on June 29 made false imputations which tended to tarnish the image of Ms. Jayalalithaa and damage her reputation as Chief Minister in the estimation of the public.

The petition was filed on December 17 on the directions of the State Government under Section 199 (2) of the Criminal Procedure Code (Cr.P.C.) for an offence allegedly committed by the speaker and under Section 499 (defamation) of the Indian Penal Code (IPC), which was punishable under Section 500 of the IPC.

The judge, Mala, has ordered the accused to appear before the court on January 22. (*The Hindu*[67])

b. The **Malicious** Adjective

66. There are two kinds of defamation. Libel of course, being one, the other being slander. **Briefly put, slander is oral (spoken) defamation and libel is published or printed defamation.**

Since the spoken word preceded the printed word, slander is the parent of libel. There is today much in common between them. The differences, which are many, for the most part are based on the fact that slander, by its nature, reaches few persons whereas libel reaches many. Defamation by radio or television is, on the whole, treated more like libel than slander.

67. The Hindu 28th December 2003 issue

Now notice how *'defamation'* has been qualified with the adjective 'malicious' in the definition. Does this imply that defamation must be actuated by malice, for instance, that the publication of a defamatory statement must have been intended to do harm? Yes!

An interesting situation arises from this surmise – if a statement published in a newspaper is judged to be defamatory by a judge, it is granted that it was malicious. That's why it defamed a person, didn't it! If it was not malicious, then it would certainly be understood to be a 'wrong representation of the individual in question'.

Let us take the following examples:

1. Anirban Banerjee is an individual of dubious personality and savage and unclean habits. He is known to be medically dependent and an alcoholic.

2. Raju Biswas is a man of great intellect and ingenuity. He was the inventor of Boolean algebra and father of atomic science in India.

Now what if Anirban Banerjee is a professor at the local college and Raju Biswas, a young businessman?

The author of both the sentences has indulged himself in 'wrong representation of the (individual in question) Anirban Banerjee and Raju Biswas respectively'. However, there is a distinct difference in the treatment of both in his sentences. In the first sentence, malice is the most important theme. The author knowingly, seeks to maliciously defame Anirban Banerjee while he knowingly, seeks to misrepresent Raju Biswas who is of course, not the progenitor of atomic science in India.

Now do you think that both of the sentences constitute defamation?

The first sentence surely constitutes defamation, but the second sentence does not. Why? Because it is not malicious[68] . If some one was to write about my exploits in the Formula One Circuit, I would besides being amused and rather surprised not go ahead with the idea of suing the paper or the author. But if I were to be treated as Anirban Banerjee, I would surely go to the court.

c. The ***Tending...***

'Tending' is another word in the definition that begs to be discussed.

Now the very presence of 'tending' ensures presumption on the mind of the

68. "Actual malice", the intent to do harm, is a factor in various defences and mitigations to be discussed below. "Malice in Law" is presumed in civil cases and this accounts for the use of "malicious" in the definition.

judge, when he or she sits upon a defamation case. Surely, no one can judge or measure physically the damages caused by a defamatory statement. Of course, sentences like those discussed above can lead to much trouble for defamed individual; it cannot for sure be measured as to how many individual's mind or opinion was changed vis-à-vis the defamed individual. Here, the judge faced with a defamatory suit must assume such and such effect has been made by the defamatory statement on the defamed individual and the people who knows him personally or are mere acquaintances.

This also implies that it is not always necessary to take for granted that the publication in question has changed the attitudes of a multitude of people vis-à-vis the 'defamed' individual. You cannot parade witnesses and ask them whether their attitudes have changed and if so due to the publication of the 'defamatory statement'.

The court thus must decide not in quantitative level as to how many individuals have been influenced which of course amounts to absurdity but to qualitative level, as to who have been influenced.

Take for example the following statement:

1. *Anirban Banerjee is an individual of dubious personality and savage and unclean habits. He is known to be medically dependent and an alcoholic.*

Now Anirban Banerjee may not be much concerned by how many people were influenced by the above statement published by a newspaper. Because, for one, most of the people he deals with, know him well and would not ultimately believe in what has been written about him.

But then what about his nine-year-old son and twelve-year-old daughter? Both of them would, of course, have a hard time believing what has been written about their father, but above all, the published statement would still have an effect in their mind which would lead to the rise of suspicion with respect to their father.

This is what the qualitative level of individuals influenced is all about. For a father, like Anirban Banerjee, this gives him enough reason to fight for and the judge, enough reason to be dissatisfied with the publishers and the author of the defamation[69].

69. In fact, this factor leads to the rise of the present and now most quoted definition of libel – A publication is libellous of any person if its natural effect is to make those who read it think less of that person and "those who read it" can be taken to mean "a substantial number of influencing people in terms of the individual in question."

d. Or!

Now believe it or not, the final or in the series of or

...who is dead or to impeach the honesty, integrity, virtue or reputation or publish the natural defects of one who is alive, and thereby to expose him to public hatred, contempt, ridicule or financial injury is very important.

The final 'or' tries to make it clear that it is not necessary that the defamation be translatable into financial terms.

To explain it in simple words, financial injury not accompanied by loss of esteem usually is not libel; however, loss of esteem not accompanied by financial injury may be libel.

e. The **Public** Factor

The word 'Public' in the definition implies that ordinarily one may not be 'privately' libelled. This further means that the injury must arise out of the effect the words may be expected to have on others, not their effect upon the person libelled.

Civil and Criminal Libel

All the instances of libel discussed above come under the realm of 'Civil' libel. Further, defamation through printing, etc., can be said to have two major kinds of effect where the course of Law is supposed to intervene. One, where the injury is caused to an individual member of the society; the other, where the injury is caused to the society as a whole.

The first instance is covered under the civil libel. In such instances, the law allows the injured party to go to court and obtain redress for his injury. Like all civil actions, the matter is between the first party and the second, with the public only providing the means, through the courts, of 'refereeing' the contest. In a criminal action the public, having been wronged, acts directly through the courts to exact punishment.

It implies that defamation that might result in injury to the public on the one hand or injuries to individuals on the other might be quite different. Of course, without examining these differences in detail, it can be safely said that defamations

---

However, it is also reasonable to ask, "How much loss?" Such publications could range from the mildly disparaging to words which would cause almost everyone to shun the person for life. The best clue is in the definition above, which specifies 'hatred, contempt, ridicule'. While perhaps everyone could not agree in every case whether the effect of a publication would fit this terminology, at least it should be clear that mere disparagement is not defamation.

which have a tendency to cause a breach of the peace fall into the criminal category, while those which tend to cause injury or suffering to an individual constitute civil libel.

In the recent past, some newspapers in Nepal came under the hammer of criminal libel, when they resorted to asking youths to join the 'Maoist movement'. Their editorials in the opinion of the court far from defaming an individual, defamed the entire society as a whole leading to a breach of the peace amounting to criminal libel.

Criminal libel has a more interesting past and has been the feature of our regional newspapers during the independence movement. All editors and publishers who worked towards the awakening of the Indian soul during the independence movement were regularly charged with Criminal Libel. These days, criminal-libel actions are rare, at least, in our country. In countries like Israel, however, the Arabic newspapers published by Palestinians regularly face criminal libel. Similarly, in countries of former Soviet Union, South America, Angola, Zaire, Sierra Leone and the Eastern African countries still have regular criminal-libel actions.

However, most of these instances of criminal libel actions are not based on the fact that 'the society as a whole has been defamed'; most of these actions are based on the fact that a publication defamed a dead person. This is the other side of the Criminal Libel.

But then how can a dead person be defamed?

Actually, a dead person is a great candidate of defamation than a live one. This is because it is taken that an individual's reputation dies with him, suggesting that no civil action can be possible. Further, the defamation does not extend to his descendants, for instance, since it is his memory that has been blackened, not their reputation. Likewise, a member of an organisation cannot obtain redress when that organisation is ridiculed or falsely accused except in the rare case where he can show that he himself has somehow been identified[70].

Cyber Libel

Internet is one of the most recent instruments of Mass Communication and hence, whatever libel (civil or criminal laws) are applicable to the print or electronic

70 However, criminal action is possible in such a case, although such actions are rarely brought. Also the fact that malice is not assumed in criminal libel and must be shown.

media like Television and Radio broadcasts, they are applicable to the different websites individually based upon the country of their origin.

Cyber Libel in Action

Matt Drudge & AOL v. White House Communications

A pending case is all set to create a precedent for controlling information flow on the Internet. And the outcome will determine liability of Internet publishers and carriers for their writers' work.

Matt Drudge, the creator of the Drudge Report, manages a news service which includes a web page and e-mail distribution. 85,000 people subscribe to the service. The Drudge Report covers a broad range of topics from relatively insignificant events to world news and White House controversies.

Both Drudge and America Online, his Internet provider, were recently sued by White House Communications aide Sydney Blumenthal. The suit alleges 21 counts of libel, defamation, false light, invasion of privacy, intentional infliction of emotional distress, and slander. The August 11, 1997 Drudge Report said records confirmed Blumenthal had abused his wife. Blumenthal contends that he and his wife, Jacqueline Jordan Blumenthal, were defamed by the report. He and his wife sued after Drudge refused to reveal his sources.

AOL is being sued for displaying the report and for showing a reckless disregard for the truth. One defence for AOL is contained in the Telecommunications Act of 1996. One section of the act states: "No provider or user of an interactive computer service shall be treated as the publisher or speaker of any information provided by another content provider." Another defence is that Matt Drudge retracted the report. Timely retraction of false information can be used to show lack of actual malice.

Since the Internet is a relatively new medium, the outcome will likely set an important precedent[71].

Note: As a matter of deliberation, we will now confine ourselves to civil libel only. This is because almost all libel actions involving mass media are civil actions.

71. Cyber libel and the White House. David Corn. The Nation. January 12/19, 1998. Pgs 23-24.

Also remember, henceforth, libel in this book will be synonymous with civil libel unless otherwise specified.

Per Se and Per Quod

In the series of making distinction in various types of libel, we have already discussed in much detail civil and criminal libels, now in same instance; it is prudent we also discuss the two other types of libel – libel per se and libel per quod.

First let us take Per Se for discussion.

In some instances, certain words are taken to be libellous in and of themselves whenever applied to any person. These are libellous per se or in more simple words, libellous in itself.

Take for example:

Suman Rai is an animal.

... is an animal is libellous in itself.

Per Quod

Dangerous publications are not limited to such words only. Other words which may be innocent in themselves can prove to be dangerous in certain contexts. These are known as libels per quod.

Remember, the precise legal distinction between per se and per quod is not crystal clear as yet and it is for most instances based on an individual judge's interpretation. However, for our present level of deliberation it would indeed be enough to say that the mere evident meaning of the words used cannot help the author escape from a per quod allegation[72] . It is, thus, important for all concerned to look beyond the surface meaning of the words used.

This is not all. Even innocent-looking words at times may cause extreme harm just because of the way they were used.

For example, it is not libellous to say of a married woman that she gave birth to a healthy boy but to say so falsely in the second month after marriage is another matter.

72. The distinction under discussion has another important aspect when and if the case comes to Court. Because libel per se is obviously defamatory, it is not necessary for the plaintiff to show that in some specific way he has in fact suffered as a result of the publication. Libel per quod, on the other hand, requires proof that special damages were suffered.

In 1927, the *Darjeeling Advertiser* used to carry hotel guest lists. Of course, this was common feature in newspapers all over the 'civilised world', the publisher of the said newspaper however, found himself in the court when in one instance, it published 'Mr. and Mrs. Robin Smith' in its guest lists when it should only have published, 'Mr. Robin Smith.'

The honourable court at Darjeeling, much amused asked the publisher to pay Mr. Robin Smith a sum of Rs. 5 posthaste and apologise 'through letter and official stamp'. This was all done because Mr. Robin Smith became the target of a mockery at the Gymkhana Club where his friends sought to call him, "Mr. and Mrs. Robin Smith."

Identification

The identification of the 'person defamed[73]' is most important. In fact, without a defamed person being identified, no libel case can be made out of any publication. This, however, also implies that the said publication itself must clearly identify the defamed person and that there must not be any assumption whatsoever on the part of the court in terms of identification of the defamed individual[74] .

Take the following sentences for example:

1. (Darjeeling): Rajesh Sharma has been known to steal and thus it is not a surprise that the Maharaja's jewellery be lost in his custody."

2. (Darjeeling): Anirban Banerjee is an individual of dubious personality and savage and unclean habits. He is known to be medically dependent and an alcoholic.

3. (Darjeeling): Suman Rai is an animal.

It does not really matter whether the above instances were featured in local, regional or national newspapers. The fact remains that the publication itself puts the occurrence of the said issue to be at Darjeeling. This means that all the

73. This section will refer to the injured person as 'person', 'individual', etc., but it must be pointed out that - big Corporations and Partnerships are treated as persons under the Law and thus may be injured by libellous publications. However, it is up to the plaintiff to show that he (or the corporation or partnership) was the one injured by the publication. It is not enough that he show that a group of persons was injured and that he is a member of that group. The courts have ruled, as long ago as 1815 especially in the United States that criticism of a group does not in itself constitute a criticism of an individual member of that group. The only danger of libel in an attack upon a group is the possibility that a Court will determine that the injurious language clearly pertained to every member of the group and hence to the individual. In general, the smaller the group the greater likelihood of such a finding.

74. This simply means that the person libelled must have been identified in the publication as the person defamed.

individuals implied to in the above sentences live and work in Darjeeling. This in turn makes the identification of these individual easy given that Darjeeling is a small town.

However, if all the above instances were to be published in a national newspaper without precisely stating the occurrence of the said issue, a reader and most importantly a judge would find it really hard to identify the 'individual in question' as to where exactly they belong, and whom exactly was the publication discussing about. Here, identification is virtually impossible. And if this is the case, no libel is said to have been occurred.

Remember also that words alone cannot be used by the court for identification. The important thing here from the stand-point of the copy desk is that there are more ways of identifying a person than using his name, age and street address. Devices for concealing the name while telling the story can 'boomerang'. It is not necessary to show that all readers would be able to identify the person nor that a majority would or that a lot of people would. The disapprobation of the few who could identify the person might be as damaging as if the name itself were used.

Also the fact that identification need not be only words, for that matter. It has been established that a picture can identify a person as positively as the name. This underscores the importance of precision in carrying out the routines of newsroom and composing room. Many libel cases arise simply out of misidentification, cases in which X's picture are used where Y's was intended. The possibilities are obvious. We might be on perfectly safe ground in describing Y's crimes and running Y's picture, but we defame X if his picture – no matter how inadvertently – appears instead.

Publication

The publication of the libellous story, article, photo, so on and so forth is important. Without the publication, no libel is said to have been risen. I cannot, for instance, go to the court and say that a certain newspaper defamed me if I do have the published copy of the same in my hands.

In many instances, where simple mistakes and lapses have the potential to incite major libel suits against the publication, the same is averted by the editor or the sub-editor at the copy-desk itself. There are times when printing is halted mid-way, in order to correct the libellous mistakes.

What is not Libel?

Now that you are all scared and literally tied up by the strings of libel laws, you may yet not want to throw away this book and search for some other career.

Yes, a lawyer may make you believe that everything you write may account to libel but that is not the case. Given to you is a great power and with that great power you must show some restrain; but that does not mean you should be scared by your own power either.

Here is a list of what is not Libel:

- ☞ A publication which causes an individual much anguish but does not affect his reputation is not a libel.
- ☞ A publication is not libellous merely because it is false.
- ☞ A publication is not libellous merely because it causes financial injury.

And that's not all! Read ahead, we are just warming up.

The Author's Defences

Once, libel is assumed, it is given that its perpetrators – namely the author of the said article, story or news, the editor of the paper and its publishers, are liable to pay for the damages caused. However, in a civilised society, one is not guilty unless proven[75] and that all essentially has the right to prove their innocence. This leads to the concept of what is known in Law as Defence[76] .

A comprehensive list of all the complete defences in libel could include as many as nine. Let us discuss each, one by one.

1. Statute of limitations

Libel has a statute of limitations, which means that if a case is not filed in an appropriate court within a stated time after the commission of the libel, there is no recourse to law. It is like a demand draft you make at bank for someone. Unless and until the individual specified on the draft withdraws the money within six months, the money is said to have lapsed in the bank's account[77] . Of course, the length of time varies based on many factors.

---

75. Actually in our country one is assumed guilty on arrest and that he or she is not innocent until proven in a Court of Law. This is exactly opposite to what it is in the United States, where an individual is assumed innocent even on arrest and hence, read his or her right. It is only when proven in a Court of Law, that the said individual is to be guilty.

76. In US Defence

77. the issuing bank

2. Absolute Privilege

Absolute privilege protects judges, witnesses, legislators, etc., as participants in public and official proceedings, but has no bearing on reports of these proceedings.

3. One time only!

This actually means that no case can be filed in a court for a second time after having been settled once.

4. Out-of-Court Settlement[78]

Once an out-of-court settlement has been reached upon, no case can be pleaded in the said Court of Law .

Remember all these are based upon specific Laws of the Land which may change from state to state and also based upon certain norms of the individuals courts. Also the fact that all these do not specify language which means that libel in all languages is treated as libel, not as libel in Nepali, libel in Bengali or libel in English.

Complete Defences

Now before we go any further with our discussion on defences, it is important to make some observations.

All the earlier mentioned defences, namely: *1. Statute of limitations 2. Absolute Privilege 3. One time only! 4. Out-of-Court Settlement* are not what one might call complete defences. All these essentially are understood to be taken care of by the 'plaintiff's lawyers'. Take for example, Statute of Limitation. If the said statute specifies that the case be filed within three months of the publication, the plaintiff's lawyer would of course wait for the last day to file the case. Similarly, all the other defences can be easily taken care of.

Which leads to the question – *Where are my real and true defences?*

The complete[79] defences are just the one you are looking for.

78. The 'Out-of-Court' is a new thing in India, while a common feature in the United States where a majority of Court cases are settled 'out-of-the-Court'.

79. 'Complete' is used here to describe a defence which, if established, means that no damages of any sort may be recovered. The defendant need not establish any other defence. This is equally true of truth, fair comment and privilege.

Complete defences are very much important because they are the true protections against the libel hazard, which in turn makes it possible for newspapers to publish the great volume of defamatory material that they must.

Complete defences are made of *truth, statutory privilege and fair comment or criticism.* And all three are well established as complete, through qualified, defences[80] .

Truth

Truth is a defence in civil libel well established in Anglo-Saxon law as well as our own[81] . Believe it a not, there was once a time when it was held that the greater the truth the greater the libel. This was especially true during the evolution of modern newspapers in England. Due to limitations in technology, rumours were the mainstay of newspapers. However, at times based upon certain witness reports, truth came out blazing like the sun in the dark, rainy London sky. Most of these, of course, would have to do with either the Royal Family or the elite. And this certainly meant the greater the truth the great the libel.

But what is the rationale behind the truth as a defence?

Let us take the following sentences for example:

1. Rajesh Sharma has been known to steal and thus it is not a surprise that the Maharaja's jewellery be lost in his custody.

2. Anirban Banerjee is an individual of dubious personality and savage and unclean habits. He is known to be medically dependent and an alcoholic.

3. Suman Rai is an animal.

We previously assumed all these sentences to be defamatory and hence libellous because they were false. But what if Rajesh Sharma indeed is the man behind the jewellery heist? And if Anirban Banerjee is truly, a man of dubious personality and savage and unclean habits! And also the fact that Suman Rai is indeed the name of a goat!

This will imply that there has been no defamation. Truth thence, as the saying goes frees all.

---

80. Remember these are all qualified defences in some states only while some are qualified in other states. For instance, some states, as we shall see, qualify truth as a defence with the stipulation that the truth must be for good motives and justifiable ends. This is what complete, through qualified, defence means.

81. It is, however, not necessarily and usually a defence in criminal libel

But then there is the catch!

How far can one go in terms of the publication of truth?

Before we discuss that, let us first define truth, of course in journalistic terms. Now, some scholars might not subscribe to what I intend to divulge, the following surmise can then best be said to invite 'an open discussion'.

Truth in journalism is not merely 'what it is'.

A dictionary would define truth as –

Trōōth, n faithfulness: constancy: veracity: agreement with reality: fact of being true: actuality: accuracy of adjustment or conformity: in the fine arts, a faithful adherence to nature: that which is true or according to the facts of the case: the true state of things, or facts: a true statement: an established fact: true belief: known facts, knowledge[82] .

A journalist, however, would not be much happy with the above definition. To him truth is much more. In fact to him there are many different definitions of truth. This also leads to what can best be called different shades or perhaps flavours of truth.

Let us find out the different definitions of truth.

Note: All these surmises are based on the fact that they occur in practical terms vis-à-vis mass communication.

Half Truth

Let us examine the following sentence:

1. *Reshma is a dancer at a local bar.*

True, Reshma does earn her livelihood by dancing at a local bar.

Do you think this implies defamation? And if your answer is –

"No, because it is the truth."

...Then think again.

Reshma is uneducated, a widow and single parent of three young kids. She cannot surely earn a livelihood by begging. And her young children must be fed, clothed and sheltered. As single uneducated mother, she is forced to dance at a local bar.

---

82. Landua I Sidney, Ramson S W, Schwarz Catherine & others, Chambers English Dictionary, Allied Publishers Limited, India 1990.

So where does the above statement – *Reshma is a dancer at a local bar* – stand now! At best it is truth but only half. It is half-truth.

This is defamation. You cannot pass on half-truth to the readers. Why? Because, it is as damaging as a lie. And a judge might even take it to be malicious, knowingly intended.

The Naked Truth

Anamika gave birth to a healthy baby boy yesterday. Her husband, Suraj, however, was furious for she had done so in the second month of her marriage.

Now again, this is all true. Actuality at its best! However, again, is this defamatory? Yes. Even if both Anamika and her husband Suraj are celebrities, there is a line that separates a private fact and a public fact. While it is true that the people have a right to know about celebrities' life, what they do and what they don't, the above truth is too private in nature to be published.

Here, the naked truth cannot be a defence. Instead, a Judge might even, again, treat it to be malicious and knowingly intended.

The Yellow Truth

The Yellow Truth also known as 'fabricated truth' was the invention of the American Press back in 1890-1917. In fact, the era is also known as the era of Yellow Journalism.

Now what is a fabricated truth?

Fabricated truth defined in simple words, is truth well garnished with lies. What this means, is that while lies predominate, they somehow seem to be overwhelmed by the one single truth, which further implies that 'truth is maintained'.

Let us take the following example:

Einstein, a great scientist, was the father of all sciences.

Now how much of that is the truth. Einstein was a great scientist but surely he was not the father of all sciences. However, some scholars might want to contest that surmise. They might in fact try to even prove that Einstein was indeed the father of all sciences.

This is where the trouble lies. This statement obviously defames the entire society of scientists all over the world leading to criminal libel. But the publishers of the same could also contest the same surmise taking the help of the fact that indeed Einstein can be said to be the father of all sciences.

The judge can either based upon the arguments put by both the sides, lay down that a malicious defamation has been intended towards the entire scientific community and that the same was done intentionally. However, given enough proof, the judge might even declare that the statement published was correct and that Einstein was indeed the father of all sciences.

Here effectively, the Yellow Truth can become a defence for the perpetrators based on argument. And that it would not be wrong either to say that in most cases it does.

However, the fact still remains that Yellow Truth or fabricated truth is not truth in entirety and that the most enthralling part of it is actually a lie.

Yellow Truth began its life when the American newspapers openly started to rally themselves with either the Republican or the Democratic Party. Each side essentially publishing news, glorifying their leaders. The same is prominent today, in countries like North Korea, Angola, Nepal, Cuba, Libya and other totalitarian states.

But isn't the publication of truth, the fundamental duty of the Press?

Yes, but this depends from country to country and indeed even from state to state.

The rationale of truth as a defence might be studied in this light. If the Press is to perform its function in a democratic society, it must be free to publish the truth even though that truth may sometimes hurt. If some truth tends to incite riot, then the fact that it is a truth is no justification, hence the criminal libel complications. If the truth tends to cause injury, then it is justifiable to publish the truth only where there is good reason to believe the public will thereby be served, hence the common qualification that truth is a defence only when published for good motives and justifiable ends.

What is the effect of the defence of truth on what can safely be published and what may not?

It is given that words which are true may be published without fear of retribution even though they may be defamatory, however, several very important limitations must be observed.

And thse limitations are as follows:

1. *The burden of proof is on the defendant.* This means that we must not only ask ourselves whether the words are true, but also if we can we prove it. For it is

not up to the plaintiff to prove that the story is untrue; it is up to the perpetrator (publisher or the author) to show that it is true. This immediately involves us in the rules of evidence and the whole question of what the courts regard as proof of the fact.

While it is not possible to cover such a broad subject in this summary handling of the libel hazard, all that can be done to fulfil the level of our present deliberation is to remember this important fact. **No matter how sure the reporter is that his facts are correct, both in kind of proof that court will accept. The reporter's good faith in the matter, his belief that the facts are right, has no bearing on truth as a defence.**

2. *Facts, as journalism defines facts, do not qualify as truth as the law defines truth.* To justify a publication on the grounds that it is true, it is necessary to show that the facts that are reported are true. It is not sufficient that a paper [83]reported accurately what happened. For instance, if an informant tells a reporter that another person has committed a crime, the paper satisfies the journalistic definition of fact if it reports that he (informer) said it (or that it was said). In defending a libel suit, however, the paper must be able to prove that the accused person did in fact commit such a crime.

3. *The justification must be as broad as and specific to the charge.* If a person is labelled a 'notorious criminal', it is not sufficient to show that he has a criminal record or that he was once convicted of some petty crime. If a story accuses a person of embezzlement, it is not sufficient either to show that he merely 'diverted funds', which maybe a lesser crime nor is it sufficient to show that he has in fact been guilty of other crimes than embezzlement, even though they may be equally serious crimes. The paper must be prepared to prove embezzlement.

Summary: Remember truth is perhaps the most powerful defence in libel. It would be even more powerful if it were easier to prove to a court's satisfaction.

Statutory Privilege

A second complete, though again qualified, defence is statutory privilege. This is sometimes called qualified privilege to distinguish it from the absolute privilege attaching to judges, etc., described above. It is called statutory privilege because in most countries it has been established by written law.

---

83. Unless otherwise specified – paper in this book will imply a newspaper

The rationale of privilege returns us once more to the Fundamental Rights guaranteed by the Constitution and considerations of the public interest. The courts have protected the right to publish facts that may be damaging to the reputation of an individual. It would be contrary to the public interest if sources of information and ideas were so hedged around by fear of reprisal as to keep large parts of the public business out of the public prints.

As a consequence, newspapers and other purveyors of information are protected in spreading public affairs on the record to the extent, at least, that public and official proceedings may be fairly and truly reported without fear of libel.

It is clearly defamatory of a person to report that he has been charged with a heinous crime. It becomes possible to report such a fact because it is part of the procedure of a democratic society to try him for the crime publicly and officially. The right to such publication is, therefore, protected by giving immunity to such information.

We are safeguarded in reporting the charge, then, as long as it is official and part of a public record or proceeding – whether or not the charge subsequently proves to be true. This does not, however, give us the right to say a person is guilty of the crime before a court has so determined, and it does not give us the right to speculate on his guilt or innocence or to publish information lacking in similar authority which would tend to imply his guilt or innocence.

Since it is in many instances part of the written law, it is possible to examine a typical definition of statutory privilege. The New York Law defines it in the following terms - *"An action, civil or criminal, cannot be maintained against a reporter, editor, publisher or proprietor of a newspaper for publication therein of a fair and true report of any judicial, legislative or other public and official proceeding; or for any heading of the report which is a fair and true head note of the article published. This section does not apply to a libel contained in any other matter added by any person concerned in the publication, or in the report of anything said or done at the time and place of the judicial, legislative or other public and official proceeding which was not a part thereof."*

In one important respect this definition is not typical. This is a definition of privilege unqualified by use of such language as 'for good motives and justifiable end.' Only a handful of countries fail to include such a qualification. Thus in most countries, proof of actual malice is sufficient to nullify the defence of privilege.

All of the important things to remember about privilege (except those pertaining to the qualification mentioned above) are contained in the definition:

1. *A fair and true report* – This language makes it clear that newsmen must be vigilant even when reporting proceedings which are privileged. It is one of our most dangerous sources of libel that reporters and editors sometimes go beyond the factual reporting which is essential if the immunities of privilege are to be enjoyed, especially in reporting court trails that 'catch on' and command widespread interest.

2. *Any judicial, legislative or other public and official proceeding* – This phrase is extremely important because it establishes quite clearly the limits of the defence of privilege. For instance, the 'and' is especially significant, indicating that it is not enough that a proceeding be official nor is it enough that it be public. Legislative committee hearings, for instance, are official and ordinarily public. However, executive sessions of such committees are official but not public and hence do not carry immunity. A public meeting, even if it is sponsored by some public or semi-public agency is only public and not also official, hence not privileged.

A few countries have extended privilege to meetings which are public, though not official. This is far from being a generally accepted principle, however.

Some documents fall into the shadowy area between public and not public, official and non-official. The police 'blotter' is one of these. The blotter is the running record of the department's activities, usually kept by a desk sergeant. It is often his source of specific information in supplying news to reporters. Some countries have, by law, declared the blotter to be public:

(a) Most *juvenile* courts are always secret. Publication of such proceedings is not privileged and may also cause citation for contempt.

(b) *Grand jury proceedings* in countries like United States are secret and may not be reported. The indictment or failure to indict which results from these proceedings is privileged and may be reported. A report of a grand jury proceeding subjects the offending publisher not only to loss of privilege, should libel be involved, but also to citation for contempt.

(c) When, due to the nature of the testimony, a judge 'clears the court' – *orders the public from the courtroom* – the Press is similarly excluded and may not report the proceedings. The judge may permit the court or some court officer to be quoted as to the essence of the testimony and such may safely be given a fair and true account. Both contempt and loss of privilege are again at stake.

(d) Certain *pleadings* are not privileged until they become part of the record of a trial. In general, these are pleadings which are entered before trail commences.

The most dangerous example here is divorce pleadings. When suit is filed for divorce, attorneys for both parties file pleadings containing the grounds for divorce and answers thereto. Such material tempts the reporter because it often contains sensational disclosures. However, when a divorce is filed, who is filing against whom, charging what, is all part of the public record and may safely be reported.

In due course, pleadings become a part of the record of the court and public, provided that the case actually reaches open court. Only then are these documents privileged. In the frequent instances where the action is dropped or is settled 'in chambers', the pleadings are sealed and never do become a public record, hence are not privileged at any time.

3. *Does not apply to a libel contained in any other matter* – It is the proceeding itself that is privileged. Events which occur at the same time and place as the proceeding are not made immune. The great source of danger here is often the reporter's anxiety to improve his story with touches of colour. He is safe in supplying details not part of the proceedings as long as such details cannot be construed as commenting on the defendant's guilt or innocence. "The defendant visibly paled at the mention of the knife", "the witness wrung his hands fearfully", such comments are obviously not a part of the record (the court reporter does not record changes in skin tint or motor activity) and are not privileged.

Matter which has been stricken from the record is treated by the court as though it hadn't happened. Consequently, there is no protection in reporting the stricken testimony, however accurately, even when the fact that it was stricken is also duly reported.

Comments by officials about public and official proceedings are not part of such proceedings and are not privileged. Another major source of trouble is information obtained from policemen, prosecuting attorneys, court officials, and others. In order to get a better picture of the background of an arrest or civil or criminal court case, the reporter frequently seeks such information from persons who are able to supply it. He writes such matter into his story at the risk of libel. For instance, an arrest is always libellous, since it can invariably be said to reflect discredit. However, privilege attaches to any legal arrest, whether or not there is a warrant. Statements about the facts leading to the arrest made by the arresting officer or the desk sergeant or the district attorney are not privileged. Should the arrested person later be freed, he may appeal for libel; if he does and such non-privileged matter is made the basis for the case, the newspaper must resort to some other defence than privilege.

However, statements not a part of the proceedings which are not libellous do not destroy the privilege that attaches to the proceeding.

Fair Comment or Criticism

The third complete defence in libel is fair comment or criticism. Like truth and privilege it is a qualified defence, and again it is the absence of malice that largely defines the qualification.

This defence rounds out a triumvirate of rights which collectively is as important to the freedom of the Press as the provisions made by the Fundamental Rights itself. Along with truth and privilege, fair comment protects the publisher in the exercise of his editorial vigilance over public affairs against the crippling prospect of libel appeals.

It is not, however, a right reserved to publishers of the written word, nor to broadcasters of the spoken word but to all citizens, who are within their rights in criticising public officials and others who seek public approval, so long as the criticism are fair and reasonable and not malicious.

There is an interesting contrast between fair comment and privilege. Privilege is a defence. Even though there has clearly been defamation, as we have seen, such defamation may be defended on grounds of privilege. The establishment of fair comment, on the other hand, means that there has been no libel. In effect it says – these unkind words have been directed against the individual's work, not against his person; hence, the individual has not been defamed at all.

It follows from this conception that to avail itself of the defence of fair comment, the newspaper must have seen to it that the criticism has been of the individual in his capacity as a public official, etc., and that the publication is not defamatory of the person. For instance, it is reasonably safe to condemn the acts of a public official in vigorous terms but it is unsafe to imply that his imperfections as a public official carry over into his private life, or that the acts arise out of a general want of integrity or morality.

This distinction is important in the rationale of fair comment, which makes it possible for the public, and its agents in the Press, to be critical of the public personage's performance as such but not to defame his character.

But then what makes a person a public personage?

In general, it can be said that those who invite public approbation for their acts are the very ones who must accept disapprobation of the same acts. This further implies, as to what my late grandfather, Raghubir Rawat, always used to say, "If you want to be famous, you must be ready to bear the brunt of your fame."

Among the persons and institutions falling into the category of public personage are as follows:

- ➤ Officials of government, whether elected or appointed, and candidates for public office.
- ➤ Administrators of justice, including the judiciary and court officials.
- ➤ Institutions, both public and private, if their function is a matter of public concern, and the officers and employees of such institutions (universities, hospitals, churches, etc.).
- ➤ Authors, artists, actors, singers, sportspersons etc., including anyone who in cultural or entertainment pursuits appeals to public acceptance.

It is for the judge, however, to decide whether a person falls into this category.

In appraising privilege and fair comment a difficult distinction arises namely:

What is fact and what is opinion?

For it can be seen that statements of fact in many circumstances are defensible on the grounds of privilege; whereas statements of opinion, even arising out of the same facts, are defensible on the grounds of fair comment. But it is often up to the court to decide this ticklish problem.

In general, we can say that the acts of a judge or legislator during an official proceeding may be described factually (without actual malice) under the protection of privilege and his acts may be appraised (without actual malice) with the protection of fair comment, provided the criticism is fair and it is stated as an opinion.

Here is a list of elements in the defence of fair comment, which may be valuable at the copy desk in assessing the libel hazard in, say, a theatre or literary column:

1. Fair comment applies only where the subject of criticism is a matter of public interest or concern; it deals only with matters that invite public attention and tend to seek public approval.

2. The comment must be an intellectual appraisal or evaluation (not, for instance, the pretext for a personal attack).

3. It must be stated as opinion.

4. It must be the result of an honest opinion.
5. It must have a basis in fact.
6. It must be free from the imputation of corrupt or sordid motives.
7. It must be free of actual malice.

Where, then does the 'fair' come in?

The limitations upon the comment in terms of fairness are already present in the check list. To be fair it must not be malicious, it must be an opinion stated as such, and it must have a basis of fact.

It is worth noting that there is nothing here limiting the notion of fairness to temperate wording, or giving 'both sides', or freedom from bias, or providing a means of rebuttal. The wording may be vigorous, the ideas opinionated, the bias obvious and the defence of fair comment still appropriate.

Gross deviation from the facts can be the basis for wrecking the defence of fair comment. But minor deviations from the facts do not provide this basis. The judge must examine the criticism in its entirety and determine whether the facts are susceptible of the opinions expressed.

Perhaps the most important single thing to watch for in testing the prospects of defending a story, editorial, or column as fair comment is its imputations. If the motives of the performer or public servant are questioned, this can overthrow the defence.

A second key check is found in the relationship of the opinion to the facts (accuracy, once again, rises to our defence). It is important to remember that whereas in privilege it is the occasion that gives us protection, provided we confine our story to the official parts of the occasion and are free of malice, in fair comment there is no such simple test. A public official may appeal successfully despite the fact of his position. If a story falsely accuses him of complicity in some illegal act, we have no defence in the fact he happens to be a public official. But it is equally true that opinions relating to a public official's public capacity lose the protection of fair comment when they are grossly at variance with because he filed a public report late when in fact the report was filed on time. In this connection, the fact that the publisher, reporter, or editor believed the facts to be true does not free him from this requirement. And again, it is the defendant who must prove the truth of the facts forming the basis of the opinion if he is to avail himself of the defence of fair comment.

Other Complete Defences

The two complete defences that remain to be discussed are less securely anchored in law. The first of these is ***consent*** or ***authorisation***. In its simplest aspects, this is a rather obvious defence. If a person reads a story and approves it before publication and then, after publication, brings case for libel, the newspaper has but to prove that consent to publication was obtained. A libel has been committed but the defence is complete. No damages may be assessed. *"Consent does not include an assent obtained by fraud or duress or from... (an) incompetent person... (it) may be express or implied. If express, it may be written or oral."*

In its pure form, consent is rarely granted; or perhaps those foolish enough to grant consent to a damaging story are rarely foolish enough to appeal. But there are times when consent may be said to be implied. This is what is not clearly established in law.

For instance, when a person has availed himself of an opportunity to reply before publication to a defamatory charge, courts has held that he has given his consent to the publication implicitly. Such a defence holds, of course, only when the individual does not demand or indicate his wish that the story be withheld.

The complete defence of ***self-defence*** is also in a formative stage. Courts have held that a newspaper has a right to strike back against one who has begun a controversy against it. The newspaper 'may not only block or parry the blow-that is, deny the charges – but may also use reasonable affirmative force as, for example, by publishing statements exposing what it believes to be infirmities or misconduct of the plaintiff, though such statement be libellous and turn out to be false, provided they were made in good faith, on reasonable grounds, and without actual malice."

Thus even when libellous statements cannot be defended on the grounds that they are true, or that they are privileged, or that they constitute fair comment, it may be possible to defend them on the grounds of self-defence.

What Regulates the Press besides Libel?

1. Official Secrets Act, 1923

This is an act which consolidates the law relating to official secrets and deals with offences like spying and wrongful communication of secret information.

Section 3 of the Act makes it an offence if any person for the purpose prejudicial to the public safety and the interests of the state

(a) approaches, inspects, passes over or is in the vicinity of, or enters, any prohibited place; or

(b) makes any sketch, plan, model, or note which is calculated to be or might be or is intended to be, directly or indirectly, useful to an enemy; or

(c) obtains, collects, records or publishes or communicates to other person any secret official code or pass word, or any sketch, plan, model, article or note or other document or information which is calculated to be or might be or is intended to be, directly or indirectly, useful to an enemy or which relates to a matter the disclosure of which is likely to affect the sovereignty and integrity of India, the security of the State or friendly relations with foreign States.

In a prosecution for an offence punishable under section 3 (i) of the Act, with imprisonment for a term which may extend to 14 years.

2. Contempt of Court

Contempt of court and legislature is also one of the reasonable restrictions under Article 19 (2) of the Indian Constitution. Contempt of court was enacted for the first time in the year 1952. But under this act, there was no definite definition of contempt of court. Later on, contempt of court was again enacted in 1971, which was further amended in 1976.

According to this Act, a person is said to be an offender of contempt of court under the following circumstances:

- Charging the judge with inability and unreasonableness.
- Expressing doubts on the prestige, status, rights or fairness of the judiciary.
- Publication of any comment on the matters which are under the proceedings of the court and which may mislead the general public and which lead them to be prejudiced.
- To cast aspersion or to attempt in influence or the judge, jury, advocates or witness of any matters which are under the proceeding of the court.
- To interfere in the judicial administration.
- To threat the witnesses.
- To attempt to obstruct the police inquiry.
- Against the order of the judge, publication of the proceedings of the court or the publication of the picture of the accused.

- ➛ Publication of the report of the proceedings of the court and distorting the facts.
- ➛ Wrongful publication of the proceedings of the court and distorting the facts.

3. Copyright Act, 1957

According to the Handbook of Copyright Law[84] of the Ministry of Human Resource Development, Department of Secondary Education and Higher Education Government of India, *"Copyright is a right given by the law to creators of literary, dramatic, musical and artistic works and producers of cinematograph films and sound recordings. In fact, it is a bundle of rights including, inter alia, rights of reproduction, communication to the public, adaptation and translation of the work...."*

Under Section 14 of the Copyright Act 1957, the work of copyright has been comprehensively explained.

(1) For the purpose of this "Copyright" means the exclusive right by virtue of and subject to the provisions of this act.

(a) In the case of literary, dramatic or musical work, to do and authorise the doing of any of the following acts, namely

(i) To reproduce the work in any material form

(ii) To publish the work

(iii) To perform the work in public

(iv) To produce, reproduce, perform or publish any translation of the work

(v) To make any cinematograph film or a record in respect of the work

(vi) To communicate the work by radio diffusion or to communicate to the public by loudspeaker or any other similar instrument the radio-diffusion of the work

(vii) To make any adaptation of the work

(viii) To do in relation to a translation or an adaptation of the work any of the acts specified in relation to the work in clauses (i) to (vi)

Infringement of Copyright

Under Section 51 of the Copyright Act 1957, infringement of copyright has been discussed.

---

84. Controller of Publications, Government of India, Civil Lines, Delhi- 110 054

Copyright in a work shall be deemed to be infringed:

(a) when any person, without a licence granted by the owner of the Copyright or the Registrar of Copyrights under this Act or in contravention of the conditions of a licence so granted or of any condition imposed by a competent authority under this Act ---

(i) does anything, the exclusive right to do which is by this Act conferred upon the owner of the copyright, or

(ii) permits for profit any place to be used for the performance of the work in public where such performance constitutes an infringement of the copyright in the work unless he was not aware and had no reasonable ground for believing that such performance would be an infringement of copyright, or

(b) when any person ---

(i) makes for sale or hire, or sells or lets for hire, or by way of trade displays or offers for sale or hire, or

(ii) distributes either for the purpose of trade or to such an extent as to affect prejudicially the owner of the copyright, or

(iii) by way of trade exhibits in public, or

(iv) imports (except for the private and domestic use of the importer) into India,

any infringing copies of the work.

No Infringement

Section 52 of the Copyright Act lays down that the following acts shall not constitute an infringement of copyright, namely

(a) a fair dealing with a literary, dramatic, musical or artistic work for the purposes of ---

(i) research or private study ;

(ii) criticism or review, whether of that work or of any other work;

(b) a fair dealing with a literary, dramatic, musical or artistic work for the purpose of reporting current events ---

(i) in a newspaper, magazine or similar periodical, or

(ii) by radio-diffusion or in a cinematograph film or by means of photographs;

(c) the reproduction of a literary, dramatic, musical or artistic work for the purpose of a judicial proceeding or for the purpose of a report of a judicial proceeding;

(d) the reproduction or publication of a literary, dramatic, musical or artistic work in any work prepared by the Secretariat of a Legislature or, where the Legislature consists of two Houses, by the Secretariat of either House of the Legislature, exclusively for the use of the members of that Legislature;

(e) the reproduction of any literary, dramatic or musical work in a certified copy made or supplied in accordance with any law for the time being in force;

(f) the reading or recitation in public of any reasonable extract from a published literary or dramatic work;

(g) the publication in a collection, mainly composed of non-copyright matter, bona fide intended for the use of educational institutions, and so described in the title and in any advertisement issued by or on behalf of the publisher, of short passages from published literary or dramatic works, not themselves published for the use of educational institutions, in which copyright subsists:

Provided that not more than two such passages from works by the same author are published by the same publisher during any period of five years.

Explanation.-In the case of a work of joint authorship, references in this clause to passages from works shall include references to passages from works by any one or more of the authors of those passages or by any one or more of those authors in collaboration with any other person;

(h) the reproduction of a literary, dramatic, musical or artistic work-

(i) by a teacher or a pupil in the course of instruction; or

(ii) as part of the questions to be answered in an examination; or

(iii) in answers to such questions;

(i) the performance in the course of the activities of an educational institution, of a literary, dramatic or musical work by the staff and students of the institution, or of a cinematograph film or a record, if the audience is limited to such staff and students, the parents and guardians of the students and persons directly connected with the activities of the institution;

(j) the making of records in respect of any literary dramatic or musical work, if ---

(i) records recording that work have previously been made by, or with the licence or consent of, the owner of the copyright in the work; and

(ii) the person making the records has given the prescribed notice of his intention to make the records, and has paid in the prescribed manner to the owner of the copyright in the work royalties in respect of all such records to be made by him, at the rate fixed by the Copyright Board in this behalf :

Provided that in making the records such prison shall not make any alternations in, or omission from, the work, unless records recording the work subject to similar alterations and omissions have been previously made by, or with the licence or consent of, the owner of the copyright or unless such alterations and omissions are reasonably necessary for the adaptation of the work to the records in question;

(k) the causing of a recording embodied in a record to be heard in public by utilising the record, ---

(i) at any premises where persons reside, as part of the amenities provided exclusively or mainly for residents therein, or

(ii) as part of the activities of a club, society or other organisation which is not established or conducted for profit;

(l) the performance of a literary, dramatic or musical work by an amateur club or society, if the performance is given to a non-paying audience, or for the benefit of a religious institution;

(m) the reproduction in a newspaper, magazine or other periodical of an article on current economic, political, social or religious topics, unless the author of such article has expressly reserved to himself the right of such reproduction;

(n) the publication in a newspaper, magazine or other periodical of a report of a lecture delivered in public;

(o) the making of not more than three copies of a book (including a pamphlet, sheet of music, map, chart or plan) by or under the direction of the person in charge of a public library for the use of the library if such books is not available for sale in India;

(p) the reproduction, for the purpose of research or private study or with a view to publication, of an unpublished literary, dramatic or musical work kept in a library, museum or other institution to which the public has access :

Provided that where the identity of the author of any such work or, in the case of a work of joint authorship, of any of the authors is known to the library, museum or other institution, as the case may be, the provisions of this clause shall apply only if such reproduction is made at a time more than fifty years from the date of the death of the author or, in the case of a work of joint authorship, from the death of the author whose identity is known or, if the identity of more authors than one is known from the death of such of those authors who dies last;

(q) the production or publication of a translation in any Indian language of an Act of a Legislature and of any rules or orders made thereunder ---

(i) if no translation of such Act or rules or orders in that language has previously been produced or published by the Government; or

(ii) where a translation of such Act or rules or orders in that language has been produced or published by the Government, if the translation is not available for sale to the public :

Provided that such translation contains a statement at a prominent place to the effect that the translation has not been authorised or accepted an authentic by the Government.

Punishment of Crime

Under Section 63 of this Act, there is a mention of punishment of infringement of copyright. For infringement of copyright, there is a punishment of one year imprisonment or monetary fine or both.

4. Advertisers' influence

While editors might not accept the fact that they do get influenced by their clients, who buy spaces in their paper to market their products, it is a fact that papers draw most of their revenue through the selling of advertisement spaces. And at times, the advertisers might try to influence the editor into publishing fabricated stories of their products as well as in various other ways.

5. Readers'/Audience's influence

The readers, with respect to published works and audience with respect to television and radio are in fact the real boss in Mass Media. And believe it or it is they who influence the policies of the media. If you think that the readers are dumb and would read and accept everything forced upon them, you are certainly wrong. In a civilised and a politically active nation like ours, neglecting or ignoring the readers would lead to doom.

The more the paper publishes what the readers want the more the people accept it. This, in turn, blows up the circulation influencing in turn greater business houses to use the paper to advertise their products. The papers influence over its readers also improves.

However, this might also lead the paper into being trapped in the vicious circle of giving what the people want. There might not be a consensus as to what the people want. Teenagers might want more sensational news, while the intelligentsia of the society might not be very interested in cheap sensationalism. And hence they might move over to the other paper.

The publishers and the editors hence, like to go for the more intelligent balance of all kinds of news.

Right to Information Act

Every citizen has a right to know how the Government is functioning. Right to Information empowers every citizen to seek any information from the Government, inspect any Government documents and seek certified photocopies thereof. Some laws on Right to Information also empower citizens to inspect any Government work or to take sample of material used in any work.

Right to Information includes the right to:

➢ Inspect works, documents, records.

➢ Take notes, extracts or certified copies of documents or records.

➢ Take certified samples of material.

➢ Obtain information in form of printouts, diskettes, floppies, tapes, video , cassettes or in any other electronic mode or through printouts.

Information means any material in any form, including records, documents, memos, e-mails, opinions, advices, press releases, circulars, orders, logbooks, contracts, reports, papers, samples, models, data material held in any electronic form and information relating to any private body which can be accessed by a public authority under any other law for the time being in force.

Record includes:

➢ Any document, manuscript and file

➢ Any microfilm, microfiche, and facsimile copy of a document

➢ Any reproduction of image or images embodied in such microfilm (whether enlarged or not); and

➢ Any other material produced by a computer or any other device;

- An applicant cannot ask for opinions/advice/views under the RTI Act, unless the
- opinion/advice/view is already on record.

However, under Section 4(1)(d), an applicant can ask for 'reasons' behind an administrative or quasi-judicial decision of a public authority, especially if he is the 'affected person'.

Right to Information Act v/s Official Secrets Act

Official Secrets Act was formulated in 1923 during the British rule, and continued to be in exercise in the independent India as well. Right to Information is a fundamental right and an integral component of a democratic country like India. It grants the citizens right to obtain data from the government or government-owned organisations by paying a certain amount of fee. However, many deals and contracts are often hidden from the public knowledge under the shelter of Official Secrets Act. Debates are, thus, going on whether or not Official Secrets Act be repealed, though the conclusion on the same still remains pending.

THE NEWS

- → The Saloon Incident
- → What does News Imply?
- → How to Judge News
- → Who Decides?
- → What is News?
- → What do Readers Read?
- → Today's Heterogeneous Audience
- → Serving Dual Masters
- → The Basic Appeals
- → Identification
- → Unknown
- → Identification to Work
- → How New must News be?
- → Wavering Interest
- → Differences
- → The Sum Aggregate of Interest
- → Creating Interest
- → Effects of Declining Competition
- → The Rewards of News

"If Mass Media were to be a commercial enterprise. . ..their main product would be News"

News

The Saloon Incident

It is six o' clock, Sunday morning, when Jagarnath Mishra in a hurry, slams the door behind him. The wooden door of the old and shabby saloon rattles and clinks as its bolts are almost plucked from the decayed wood. A minute later, Om Narayan Gupta follows, slamming the door behind him.

Rahul Rawat, a young journalist meanwhile, watches the activities forgetting ominously to queue at the milk booth. Curious to see the two gentlemen at such a neighbourhood, Rahul walks towards the dirty sideway leading to the saloon. He then looks around and being satisfied that there was no one puts his ears on the door. He hears words that are obscure and through crack on the door sees only silhouettes. Rahul then decides to look around for a better vantage point. There is no fear of getting caught. He simply must listen to what the men are talking about.

After a short search, Rahul finds a hole on a window and peeps through it. Now, clearly visible, he sticks his ears further into the hole to hear their conversation.

"Jagarnath Babu, you must understand that if the Congress were to align with your party, you will still be in the opposition. The Congress simply does not have the numbers to put you into power in the legislature. However, you can by influencing your party members not to align with Congress, make it possible for us to counter the Congress effectively."

"But I would certainly be playing a traitor to my party, if I were to do whatever you ask me."

"Come on, Jagarnath Babu, it is not the first time that you changed loyalties. You already betrayed our party when you joined the PDF."

"I did not betray the party; it was all because of Somesh babu and his chamchas, who kept picking on me."

"The past is past, Jagarnath Babu. Anyway we are ready to offer you 10 crore up front if you influence your party in not aligning with the Congress."

"10 crore...!"

"Yes, 10 crore and up front. We have all the faith in you."

Rahul walks straight to his editor and sits down smiling. He takes out a cigarette from his pocket and lights it. The editor knows Rahul is on to something. He asks his secretary to leave the office for a while and sits down.

"Good News," Rahul says smiling.

"Tell me about it."

"What I have is the scoop of a life time..."

"Good."

"Jagarnath Mishra has been brought. The PDF will not be aligning with the Congress. And the no-confidence motion that Congress and the PDF is to bring tomorrow morning in the legislature will not be brought because the PDF will abstain," Rahul says smoking rapidly.

"You mean that the PDF will just remain absent in the Legislature tomorrow and destroy all of Congress' hope.

"Absolutely!"

"How much has Jagarnath Mishra been offered?"

"Just 10 crore."

"10 crore!" The editor takes the cigarette from Rahul's hand, takes long whiffs and exclaims after a twinkle on his eyes. "You were able to record this conversation on tape, weren't you?"

Rahul smiles and says, "Yes." [85]

---

85. Reproduced with permission from PRESS TIMES INDIA, a novel by BARUN ROY: Roy, Barun, Press Times India, Mandalay Books Pvt. Ltd (India), 2004

What does News Imply?

We have now been accustomed with the denomination 'News'. The newspapers deal with the news and hence, the name 'newspapers' was the simplest of surmises we came upon. But what does news imply?

News implies three things:

1. Action

2. People

3. Interest

In simple words, Action, People and Interest are the three ingredients that make up news. The absence of any, thence, leads to what your editor would say, "It is not news!"

Let us examine each in detail.

1. Action

Someone must be doing something in order to be in the news. Action thence implies, 'something that influences people directly'.

For example take the following:

> **Kosovska Mitrovica, April 18 (Reuters):** Two Americans and a Jordanian were shot dead in Kosovo yesterday when emotions over Iraq apparently boiled over into a gun battle between members of the UN law enforcement mission.

As you can find out from the above paragraph that an action has occurred and this action is that of the **Killing of two Americans and a Jordanian.** Now this will have implications all over the world and most importantly in the United States and Jordan.

Here the ingredient **Action** is very much evident.

2. People

It must also involve **People** both in terms of its implications and appeal.

The above paragraph which tells us about the murder of the two Americans and a Jordanian involves not just a whole lot of people but also nations. While the Americans will be hurt and feel the need for revenge, the Jordanians will also feel the same. However, Iraqi people on their part would like to stress that the ongoing occupation of their motherland by the American compelled them to act in such a manner.

Here again the ingredient people is very much evident.

3. Interest

Do you think that the above paragraph has the element of **Interest** in it? Definitely, as already stated a lot of people, involving nations and indeed the world itself will be interested in the event. As such the event will have implications all over the world.

Thus the above paragraph fulfils all the criteria to be called news.

How to Judge News

The selection and play of the news is perhaps the heaviest responsibility of the copy desk[86] . In almost everything else he does the editor acts primarily as a technician. As such, he is mainly responsible to a set of technical standards. As a 'gate keeper' of the flow of ideas and information to his readers, he has a higher responsibility, a responsibility not only to the specific aims of his own newspaper, not only to the standards of the editor's craft, but also to the public his newspaper serves.

A mere technical competence in the selection and play of the news is sufficient in some newsrooms; a slavish devotion to the attitudes of the ownership is a chief ingredient of success in others. But fortunately in many other newsrooms the editor has a higher and more severe taskmaster: the information requirements of the reading public. To serve it well with the ideas and information that are the ingredients of the democratic process is the real vocation of the news editor.

Not all copy editors are concerned with this problem all the time, and some are little concerned with it any of the time. The man on the rim usually has little to say about how the news is to be judged and displayed. But every editor, at least every promising one, is potentially a news editor. In that sense he can be said to be serving his news editor's apprenticeship while working on the rim. It behooves him, then to pay heed to the decision-making process.

Who Decides?

Newspapers differ extensively in the point at which major news decisions are made. On many smaller ones, all decisions except possibly a few 'close ones' are

86. Table at which copy-readers work, often semicircular in shape; the city editor may sit in the slot at the centre

made right on the desk by the man in the slot. In others, the news editor functions apart from the desk as the chief news decision maker. Often the managing editor leaves routine matters to the news editor but decides the top play each day. Some metropolitan newspapers arrive at major news judgements during a Page One conference of a number of top editors. In still other newsrooms, at least some of the decisions are made for all the resident editors by wire from highest echelons of the chain ownership.

However, it is perhaps the typical situation that someone along the news-stream, usually at the desk itself, is responsible for making the decisions about what news gets into the paper, in what detail, and with what prominence and position. He will here be referred to as the news editor.

We have already studied extensively the news editor's role as a manager of the flow of news. Our present problem is to take a close look at the decisions he must make about what goes into the paper and how prominently.

What is News?

Of course, you have already been exposed to the question of "What News implies?" If you are still not sure what it is, that's fine. Neither does a lot of people and most eminent editors these days!

Although the effort has at least been made, little is known about what readers prefer in their newspapers and there is little agreement on what part reader preference should play in the editor's judgements about what goes and what doesn't go. Until a lot more research has produced a clearer understanding about reader's preferences, editors will have to fall back on their experience and 'news sense'.

'News sense' has been too often regarded as something instinctive or innate. It is important to understand that it is learned and that it differs substantially from one practitioner to another. It should then follow that the apprentice news editor can learn to be an astute judge of news and that such a learning process can benefit from a sound theory of what makes news.

Perhaps the most widely quoted definition of news is that devised by the late Willard G. Bleyer, who said: *"News is anything timely that is interesting and significant to readers in respect to their personal affairs or their relation to society, and the best news is that which possesses the greatest degree of this interest and significance for the greatest number."*

Such a limited definition is helpful in that it brings into the picture some notion of the elements that are the ingredients of news decisions. It points up the rather obvious fact that news must be new – or relatively so. It brings both 'interest' and 'significance' into the picture – but not into focus.

It also puts some stress on the fact that what is news is dependent in large measure on what newspaper reader regard as news. It perhaps has the fault that it implies that news is 'something' that can be grasped by the study of news. It is probably closest to the truth that news values can be grasped only by the study of people and their reaction and interactions. Furthermore, there are no 'right' and 'wrong' answers. There are no objective criteria. What one editor sees as news for his readers may get only the scantiest attention from another.

If there are no objective criteria, what can the fledging editor do to prepare himself to make decisions about the selection and play of news?

My ambition here will not be to pretend to answer that question in 'easy lessons'. It is rather to propose that the editor can become a better judge of news by giving a lot of attention to what interest people. He can carry that forward into a study of how people differ in their interests and reading preferences and finally he can become a student of the dynamics of reading preferences: how changing times are reflected in changing reading patterns.

What do Readers Read?

First, let us review what is known about what newspaper readers prefer. On the basis of a highly tentative and limited study of reader interest in 10 national and 20 regional newspapers, I have drawn up the following conclusions among others[87] :

1. The reason a reader brought one newspaper rather than the other could usually be traced to features, rather than news[88] .

87. Only newspapers in English were taken into consideration.

88. A rather interesting incident occurred in the Darjeeling Hills almost three years ago. The Statesman started its NB Plus Page being published from Siliguri. This was effectively done to concentrate on the Hills and give to the Hills its first 'truly daily newspaper'. Earlier people had to read a day old newspaper. However, the NB Plus Page, more than being news oriented was a feature paper, publishing stories, essays and articles on the various facets of the Hill life. The Statesman became easily the best selling newspaper in the Hills. The Telegraph followed it later shifting its base similarly to Siliguri and starting its own North Bengal & Sikkim. However, it could not muster much support from the readers because its North Bengal & Sikkim was too news oriented. There were no features, which meant readers still preferred The Statesman and its NB Plus Page.

2. When readers were asked to tell what they disliked most in their paper, the majority of them said, 'sensationalism'. Yet practically everyone who made the charge seemed to have read as much crime and scandal as the average person.

3. Most readers wanted a paper which could be read in a hurry.

4. More adults read the best comic strip in a newspaper, on the average day then they did the front-page banner story.

5. The average reader of a metropolitan daily spent more time on the features than on the news.

6. A picture page in a newspaper was 'read' by a third more adults than anything on the front page.

7. Kolkata correspondents, even during a political campaign, were read by fewer than 10 per cent of all adult readers.

8. A surprisingly large number of women seem to turn first to the classified column on deaths, marriages and births, in spite of the fact that they rarely recognise the names of any persons mentioned.

9. Fewer than 10 per cent of all male readers and 3 per cent of all women readers were interested in business and financial news during normal times.

10. The average person read a very small part of his paper; a great many men read nothing but sports news and the comics and a great many women read no news at all.

Now remember, this is neither a very encouraging picture nor the final word on the subject.

Some of these findings have been supported by subsequent study; others are still 'areas open discussion' at best. However, it is not that they are of no value to us. They do show that the average adult Indian newspaper reader is interested in other things in his newspaper besides the solid news of the day that is the chief concern of the copy desk.

It is a mistake, however, to assume from these data that what the public wants in its newspaper is infotainment[89] only. The readers want news in a right balance with the infotainment feature.

89. A mix match of Information and Entertainment

Today's Heterogeneous Audience

Editors in British Raj were not faced with this problem. Their reading public was relatively homogeneous. The man who could afford a newspaper and read it was for the most part an opinion leader in the community. He sought the solid news of what was happening in his country and indeed in the entire of the British Empire which would help him maintain this leadership. The problem was to obtain the news, not to leaven it with entertainment material to attract a diverse audience.

Every major change in Indian newspaper since that time reflects the effect of an increasingly heterogeneous audience on publishing policies. When James Augustus Hicky founded the first of the 'papers' *The Bengal Gazette*, he sought a mass audience not only by making the paper cheaply affordable to all but by including material, factual and otherwise, which would tap an audience not therefore attracted to daily newspapers. A change in the news values of the time was effected by including regular police reporting for the first time. The process was repeated late in the last century when the 'Independence Movement' came on the scene, again by lowering the appeal and the price and rewriting the definition of news. Then in the early 1910s it happened again with the emergence of the some of the most important regional newspapers openly supporting *Swaraj*.

This should be sufficient evidence that news values have a dynamic quality and that they, above all, are subject to what newspaper readers want their paper to contain. Newspapers have not so much changed their values since the British Raj as they have added values and changed their relationships. The news of commerce that was such a large part of earlier newspaper readers were relatively wealthy men engaged in commerce, it was appropriate that news of commerce should predominate. The addition of the housewife and factory worker to the newspaper reading public then necessitated the addition of material of particular interest to them but it has not supplanted material not of interest to them. News has not declined in volume through the years so much as it has declined in the *proportion* of non-advertising space devoted to it. The broader appeal has produced larger circulations, which have increased advertising patronage, which in turn has made larger papers possible.

So the increasing heterogeneity of the newspaper audience – the increasing breadth of the newspaper's – has forced changes in its composition in the direction of more 'popular' appeals. But it has not altered the newspaper's duty to present as much as possible of the most significant news. The special legal position accorded the newspaper forces upon it certain responsibilities to the public which 'other entertainment media' do not enjoy.

Serving Dual Masters

The question of what goes into the paper is a larger one than simply finding out what readers want and then giving it to them. To exist, the newspaper must serve two masters, the public taste and the public wealth. To fail to broaden its appeal sufficiently can mean extinction, as the owners and editors of the *Beacon* learned too late. *Beacon* was a fine old paper that had a powerful appeal – for a limited audience especially among the youths in the Darjeeling Hills and others on the fringe of that stratum. The stratum declined under the impact of a changing society and the *Beacon's* circulation declined with it – to below the break-even point. On the other hand, to fail to serve its other master, the public wealth, is to neglect its primary and legally sanctioned place in the common wealth.

The reading public must be its own best judge of the popular interest, but to a certain extent the editor must be a discriminating judge of the public interest.

This should help make it clear that entertainment material has its place in the newspaper but that it cannot be given such a prominent place as to push the solid news out of the picture. Much of the entertainment material does not come through the news stream, anyway. The comics, for example, are chosen by higher headquarters and are not ordinarily handled by the desk. Nevertheless, the news material itself provides the editor with a never-ending choice in how to use his space. Essentially, it is the choice between material that is primarily of entertainment value and material which is primarily of news value. Since this is the part of the paper that concerns the copy desk, it is here that we come to grips with the editor's role as the selector and displayer of news.

Once we have seen that what the newspaper offers its readers is only partly news, we must still look at how news differs if we are to devise a set of principles as a guide to news judgement. Perhaps the most useful way of looking at the matter is to analyse the news in terms of its appeals to the newspaper reader. Such an approach is valid, however, only if we recognise that there is no such thing as an 'average' reader. Readers differ widely in what appeals to them. But the reader is capable of making his own selection from what we offer him. He acts, to a certain extent at least, on the basis of the appeals the material has for him at a given moment. Thus one reader's path through the paper may coincide at only a few points with the path of another.

The Basic Appeals

The question now is: what are the basic appeals if any to this readership, considering its very diversity? The traditional formulation has at least these eight parts:

(1) Timeliness

The more recent the news is to the time of its publication, the timelier and more interesting it becomes.

(2) Nearness or Proximity

The closer the event takes place to the reader, the more interesting it becomes.

(3) Importance or Prominence

The greater the implication of the event, the better.

(4) Names

More names quoted in the news, interests more readers to read it.

(5) Conflict

Conflict offer drama on the otherwise stale practical life. It also whets the readers' interest and makes them read more.

(6) Variety

Events that are strange and unseen and unheard of add to the interest of the readers.

(7) Human Interest

Events and things that appeal to the emotion of the readers.

(8) Humour

Everybody loves a good laugh.

This list is perhaps valuable as a starting point but it is limited in a number of respects. In the first place, it concentrates on the event, rather than on the impact of its telling on the reader. It also seems to confuse what interest readers and what ought to interest them. It leaves us far short of a theory of news that will provide a solid underpinning for the editor learning to make day-by-day judgements of news.

Remembering that we are not only concerned with what interests our reader, we must nevertheless examine his motives in choosing what he will take time to read, rejecting the rest. It is the proximity of the story to him, the prominence of the news personality in his mind, for instance, that contributes to this decision. We must examine him as an individual and as a member of various groups – family, close circle of friends, business associates, clubs – to get a clearer picture.

Identification

An extensive study of personality and motivation is neither possible nor necessary at this point. The author would like to suggest that the study of one psychological mechanism will bring us closer to the individual and the decisions he will or will not make than any of the customary lists of news 'elements'. This is the mechanism of Identification. The suggestion is that the degree to which the individual reader identifies himself with places, persons and events in a news story is the best measure of the 'worth' of that story for him. We need add only the matter of timeliness (among others) to get a fairly predictive picture of what his news interests are, and thus what he will probably choose to read or choose to reject.

This should give us a clearer conception of such 'elements' of news as those listed above.

Do we really mean proximity, for instance, or are we actually concerned with the degree to which the individual identifies himself with persons and places that are nearer him in space? Perhaps sheer spatial distance, then, is not so important. Perhaps the reader is impelled to read about what is near him in every respect, not just physically near. The reader can be expected to be more interested in an accident at a familiar place, not because it is nearer than other but because he can visualise it. He may have an even stronger identification with a street farther away that was the scene of a near-accident of his own. His personal identifications may be strong at great distance – the town where he grew up, a small hilly town in the Darjeeling where he first fell in love. The point is that sheer 'proximity' is not sufficient to explain his interest in places and events.

Some editors have learned the fallacy of pure geographical proximity by discovering for themselves the intense interest of their readers in solutions to local problems of other communities. They have ranged far to find comparable communities with similar problems and have carried detailed accounts of their solutions. Readers in Nagaland learned in detail how others had solved the drug addiction problem. Readers in Darjeeling Hills learned how others dealt with public transportation problems. The intense interest these stories aroused adds to the conviction that it is not so much proximity but identifications that affects reader's interest.

A similar analysis may give us a clearer picture of persons in the news. Is it their prominence that affects the interest of newspaper readers in certain personages? Or is it the degree to which readers identifies themselves with them? Compare reader interest in two events, the progress of diplomatic negotiations over constructing an oil pipe originating in Iran and crossing through the countries of Afghanistan and Pakistan before reaching India, and the culmination in a flamboyant Bollywood wedding of a widely heralded romance of two movie stars. Clearly the prominence of the diplomat representing Indian interest in a conference featuring Iran, Afghanistan and Pakistan that may even affect war and peace far exceeds that of the movie personalities. Yet that isn't what readers respond to in choosing the inconsequential story dominated by radiant personalities over the consequential story relatively lacking in personalities. Perhaps the identification concept comes closer to something basic in this choice. It could be that readers identify more readily with the movie personality whose every mannerism they know through the peculiar intimacy of the movies than with a vague name, soon forgotten.

So do names make news? Well let's say that personalities produce responses.

Unknown

It is typical of a student that he looks upon news as the unknown, rather than in terms of reader experience and identification. According to his way of thinking, a story is worth printing in proportion to its being outside the knowledge of its reader. That which is already a part of his experience is, by this definition, not news. This notion is illustrated in the author's news editing lectures year after year. In the typical situation, the student news editor scrambles to his job on the desk in a blazing heat, switches on the fan, removes his sweater as he looks over the file, rubs the perspiration of his face with his handkerchief as he sets to work – and fails to give any sort of play to the weather when it comes to making his decisions about the news. When he is scolded for this oversight, he has a ready answer: "But everybody knows it's hot!"

This is superb reasoning under the notion of 'the unknown', he has developed about news but it breaks down under examination through the identification principle. That weather stories attract consistently high readership is shown through various surveys. Weather, by its very nature, is a story that almost everyone knows all about. Its high readership cannot be attributed to its supplying information in the realm of the unknown but rather in the realm of the partly known. These and other data lead us to the conclusion that interest can in large measure be attributed to the reader's participation in the event. The reader who saw the fire reads the story a little more closely than the reader who wasn't there. The concept of identification is perhaps the best explanation for this apparent fact.

The notion of conflict is another frequently noted 'element' in news values. Perhaps other mechanisms are operative here, but it is possible that this, too is largely a matter of psychologically 'choosing up sides': that readers respond more readily to a story involving a conflict angle because they identify with one or more of the participants and get a vicarious thrill out of the clash.

As to human interest, this would appear to be a catch all for those stories that are obviously worth little or nothing as news in any strict sense but nevertheless worth telling because readers will 'get a kick'. It is the sort of thing that conscientious readers abhor at 'trivia' but rarely fail to read. Here the identification notion has its application. Human interest pieces are pure identification. They are the little things that have happened, or could easily happen to self or neighbour.

Identification to Work

All this might make it appear that identification is a factor in the motivation of news-paper readers that gives all the breaks to inconsequential material. This need not be the case. Actually, it can be harnessed to make significant news more immediately interesting. This is, in fact, the device of the person who seeks to popularise science. He does what he can to shift the scientific story from the impersonal facts of the laboratory to an emphasis on what a new development means or could mean for the average citizen or his descendants. Or he tells it in terms of a battle against ignorance or disease with a 'hero' and a 'villain'. In any case, by shifting the focus and simplifying the language, he is making it possible for the reader to identify himself with the outcomes or possible outcomes of a scientific effort.

Thus, consequence enters the picture. Consequence may attach to a story intrinsically. The Kargil Invasion by the Pakistani Forces had consequences which was apparent immediately to even the most unsophisticated reader. But it may be less apparent in such cases as the Balance of Property Policy or Point

Four Programme of the Indian Government. In these instances consequence may have to be attached to the story if it is to get the readership it deserves.

How New must News be?

Timelessness deserves special attention. In a sense it is the simplest of the dimensions of news to understand: 'If it isn't new, it isn't news.' But actually, in day-to-day decisions that must be made on the desk, 'the time element' is perhaps a more difficult aspect of news than that simplification would imply.

For a news-story is rarely new. It is either part of a story that has been developing over weeks or months or years (or even civilisation) – a new development in an old story – or it is less than new in its resemblance to countless stories very much like in that newspapers have been printing for generations. So it is seldom possible to say 'this is new, that is old'. Decisions are based on considerations more like this: "this is a relatively new, relatively unexpected development which relatively few of our readers have already been exposed to, at least in relatively little detail".

There are clues here to two facts of present-day news and newspapers:

(1) That most of what is news today is a new development in unfolding story: rioting in Patna or Samastipur in Bihar is not a new story but a new development in the on going racial tension prevalent through generation; an oil discovery in Bombay High is less new than it is a phase of the battle for resources for defence and industry, for example during the Kargil War.

(2) That the newspaper rarely has a chance to 'break' a story given today's television's virtual instantaneousness. This has further changed the newspaper's role from the supplier of first intelligence of an event to a supplier of fuller detail.

Study of almost any newspaper front page will illustrate the latter point. Take a typical one chosen at random. Of the seven stories getting published above the fold, three are in the Political arena, one originates in the Parliament or that involving the National Government, two are of either sports or natural disasters and a third of a man-made disaster including crimes, riots and political conflicts. All three stories involving the Parliament and the National Government tell of new developments of varying magnitude in policy formulations that have been going forward for months; the Parliament story could be about final passage of a Bill which has been before the Parliament for weeks; of the two sports or natural disasters, one could be of a major Indian victory in cricket the rivals like

Pakistan or Australia, in natural disasters, a flood or a landslide which has been in the news for days but is threatening anew; the second is more than half-a-day old and has been told repeatedly in earlier newspapers and television and radio newscast: the accident has had no earlier newspaper play but is hours old on the television and the radio. Since these seven stories received top play in the newspaper in question, it must be clear that its editors do not make their decisions on the basis of newness alone.

Wavering Interest

There is an additional factor complicating the time element. It is almost certain fact that some stories, by their very nature, gain in interest, relatively speaking, with the passage of time while others decline in interest rapidly and drop out of the news almost at once. The sheer magnitude of the original story may keep it on the front pages for some days. The cyclone that hit Orissa or the disastrous earthquake that left thousands homeless in Latur for example, remained at the top of front pages for several days after the event because of its overwhelming impact, plus the fact that early stories left many unanswered and partly answered questions. Then there is the fact that big stories tend to produce little ones of a similar nature in their wake. There was a rash of infant deaths in a Government Hospital in Kolkata first reported by *Aaj Tak* Television news-channel captivating the nation's attention. (There undoubtedly were no more infants dying than ever before. But the similarity to that highly dramatised news-story lifted such death out of the routine and brought them to the attention of the audiences.)

But something more basic than sheer magnitude seems to operate to keep some stories alive where others of equal original impact die out almost immediately. Perhaps the answer lies in something like 'suspense' – the residue a story leaves due to the fact that some of its elements are unresolved and await further developments.

Take two Mig 21 Jet Fighter crash stories involving the Indian Air Force and the death of the pilots. One which told of a technical snag aboard the aged fighter jet just before the crash raised the question whether the Mig 21 was too old to be operated as the prime fighter jet by the Indian Air Force. A spark of suspense is retained until this question is officially answered. Another plane crash due to a bird hit is also followed by an investigation and the story is dutifully covered but with little element of suspense. The common reader here finds his interest in the story waning.

It would appear, then that some stories raise as many questions as they can initially answer and create varying degrees of suspense that keep interest in them alive, while others answer most of these questions at once and require little in the way of follow-up. This is one of the facts complicating the simple notion that news has to be new. However, this discussion should not be construed as a brief for 'stale' news. No newspaper can survive which does not give an effective answer day in and day out to the question: What is new? In news judgement as it might at first appear – Newness is relative and has validity only in relation to other factors in news worth.

Differences

So far we have concentrated on the content choices made by the individual reader of the newspaper. My surmise is that such an examination is first necessary in order to attempt to get at the basic mechanisms concerned: why readers choose one story over another. It must be clear; however, that the variation among readers is extensive and we are not very close to realistic applications of the theory until we examine reading preferences in terms of aggregates.

The Darjeeling newspaper reader who happens to come from, says, Mumbai, may respond emphatically to news of his former state (Maharashtra), but this fact is of importance to news editors of Darjeeling papers only if there happens to be a concentration of Mumbaikars in the paper's actual or potential reading public. They know, however, that there is such a concentration of ex-Bhutanese and ex-Bangladeshi and this fact is relevant to the aggregate worth of stories originating in those countries.

Age differences in reading preferences are of interest in the same way: elderly people have special interests, such as old-age pensions and financial security and health. Where there is a normal distribution of ages, this is relatively not pertinent to the editor who makes decisions for an aggregate of the population; but it has or should have important consequences in the news judgements of editors, perhaps in a city like Tokyo, where the proportion of elderly persons is unusually high.

The Sum Aggregate of Interest

It should go without saying that such a thing as community interest exists and that it must be assessed carefully by the news editor. A reader's interest in certain stories can be profoundly affected by their relevance to the community's interest and activities. Darjeeling is interested in tea, oranges, tourism, mountaineer, etc., whether or not these stories originate in Darjeeling itself; Mumbai is interested in stock market, Bollywood; N. Delhi, in Parliament, Call Centre Prospects; International Diplomats, Kolkata., in the arts, dramas, writers, debates, small-scale industries; Srinagar in Tourism, Terrorists and rebuilding; Bastar in Naxalites, water, wheat; Hyderabad, in Information Technology, Hotel Industries etc., etc. Each community has its special cluster of interests and the news editor must go systematically about discovering what they are, what their basis is, and their intensity.

Thus, the editor is not only concerned with what makes the individual make the choices he does but how many individuals make similar choices and in what directions. For this reason, the editor must be a student not only of the psychology of reading habits but also of the aggregations of his own community. What are its ethnic origins, what are its industries, what are its community interests, what is its history, what is its age distribution? These are only a few of the special qualities of the community that provide clues to what its members, in the aggregate, are interested in.

Creating Interest

So far we have proceeded on the assumption that the editor needs only to recognise the intrinsic interest value of a story and to act upon it. It is very likely, however, that the news editor has it in his power to create and develop interest as well. Sometimes newspaper are accused of arousing interest in matters which have no intrinsic news worth – relaying day by day the details of an obscure murder trail, for instance. This may be true enough of some newspapers some of the time. For our purposes, it merely illustrates the fact that the choices the editor makes of what to run and what to ignore plus the decisions he makes about the size and position of headlines, the nature of accompanying art, etc., do have an effect upon reader response, and that this can be (and is) implemented constructively to arouse interest in a consequential news development that does not necessarily contain intrinsic interest.

What interest the members of his reading community (and what, thereby, they are likely to read) is not, however, the sole and final consideration in an editor's judgements about what goes into the paper and with what emphasis. It has been suggested earlier that the final decision-making process is a dual one. The editor, in selecting and recommending certain segments of the glut of occurrences, must ask not only "What do people want?" but also "What is it in the public interest that they should have?"

Making judgements about what the reader should have is tough. It occasionally prompts beginning news editors to withhold stories on the grounds that the public would be better off if they did not know about them. A former associate of the author's brought in a pat example of this sort of judgement during the first week of his news editorship in *Beacon*. A particularly ugly regional controversy had been raging, though ultimately having already passed its peak, was still very much in the news. Our young friend was fed up the whole thing and his personal leanings were such that he deplored its effect on the public morale. So he left the story out. He was fortunate in having a superbly reasonable and understanding editor to give him another chance.

However, this does imply one of the most asked questions – "Is it in my power to suppress this story?"

This question is not just asked by a news editor but all journalists, reporters and photographers alike.

In an article **Bringing Death Closer** by **James F. Vesely[90]** , Vesely dwells over the realm of the above mentioned question in an interesting manner when he writes:

Suddenly, all the theories about taste and responsibility were washed away by the power and intensity of a single photograph.

Late in an early summer afternoon, four editors were standing in the newsroom of The Sacramento Union, staring at a black and white print showing the limp body of 7-year-old Lamphone Keovoravoth.

Should we run the photo? Will we offend our readers by depicting death so closely? Is it really news? If we didn't have the photo would the story even make page one? What are we selling with this paper, information or emotion?

He further writes:

These are no longer easy questions in today's competitive marketplace. Editors know that a dramatic local story can bring a barrage of telephone calls the next day, readers angry at the impersonal and exploitative press.

Newspapers seem to take the brunt of reader anger in these situations. The very nature of print seems indelible, with its power to plant a message in the mind.

The impact of a single, black and white photo prominently displayed can last in a community's conscience long after the news has moved on to other events.

---

90. FineLine: The Newsletter On Journalism Ethics, vol. 1, no. 2 (May 1989), p. 7.

Still, the boy is limp in the policeman's arms. His hair is wet from the river.

The story is full of the small details that serve us as compilers of human tragedy: the boy was swimming in a dangerous part of the Sacramento River, despite many public warnings about the strong current; he disappeared beneath the surface of the river and then was dramatically rescued by a member of the Drowning Accident Rescue Team (DART); the family, poignantly Cambodian refugees, grieves by the banks of the river.

The conversation in the middle of the city room goes like this –

Photo Editor: "Best shot we've had in weeks. The photographer did a phenomenal job just getting there. Run it."

News Editor: "It's either this or the swearing-in of the president of Brazil. Let's run it."

City Editor: "It will be all over television. We have the photo. Even if we focus on the rescue attempt, it's still our best local story. I'd run it."

(Newsroom debates most often distil toward internal considerations.)

The photographer got the shot, how could you throw his work away? What do we have that's better? Another story from 5,000 miles away! We have the photo. We can't put it in the drawer and not use it, can we?

Of course we can...

Seeing death in the eye of a man about to blow his brains out was not a legitimate news function, the debate suggested, it was only the basest reason for starting the presses at all.

And yet, the photo before us this summer afternoon overcomes these deliberations with its own overwhelming logic. The rescuer holds in his open arms the life of a young boy. The boy still breathes, but barely. Doctors place the boy on their critical list and then, within a few hours, and despite their urgent work, the boy dies.

In the end, we are left with the only decision we can make. The photo will run because not to run it is the greater error. Even if the community and, sadly, the family are offended by the photo, we reason the greater offence is to withhold news.

Our detractors will say we could run the story, inside the paper, but skip the photo since it does nothing but exploit grief.

But the truth of the matter to the editors gathered in the newsroom is that the photo is the story. It is not just facts which become news.

If only facts were needed, stenographers would find work in city rooms. News and emotion are one. This photo brings an event to an emotional pitch.

If we cannot bring emotion to the news pages, then we can rarely tell a story because in the end, facts are not enough to tell the sorrow and joy.

(James F. Vesely is editor of The Sacramento Union, Sacramento, CA. He is also vice-chairman of the APME Ethics Committee.)

In a similar article titled *'As life passes by A Journalist's role: watch and wait' by Deni Elliott*[91] , another interesting view is observed.

Given the choice of shooting a picture or saving a life, what do you do? Photojournalist Ross Baughman says that if you're on the job, there's no quandary. You shoot the picture, of course.

Although I'm queasy about how the theory plays out in extreme circumstances, I think Baughman is right. Society needs one profession charged with documenting reality. If we're going to do a good job of governing ourselves, we need representations that are neither hidden in shadows nor painted by hype. Journalists can't provide that without the special privilege of watching life's drama from the sidelines. They can't provide that without the special obligation to stay out of life's way.

Sometimes journalists should come to the aid of an individual, but in general, they should put their duty to document first, even if someone is hurt or killed. And, not only should journalists be free from prosecution when they witness crimes, they should also be praised for their willingness to put their own physical and psychic safety aside to provide a look at the underbelly of life.

More than a decade ago, Baughman, then a photographer for AP, persuaded a Rhodesian[92] *cavalry unit to let him accompany them on a mission into the interior. It was rumoured that the white army was torturing and killing black civilians. The army denied the charges and the civilians weren't talking.*

Dressed like the soldiers so that he could be inconspicuous, Baughman photographed the 25-man unit while they burned down homes and tortured men,

91. FineLine: The Newsletter On Journalism Ethics, vol. 2, no. 7 (October 1990), p. 2.

92. Zimbabwean when it was known as Rhodesia

women and children. His photos won a Pulitzer Prize. His choice not to intervene won him international disfavour.

Baughman says that he could have stopped some of the atrocities, if he had been so inclined. "I would have been able to make the soldiers feel inhibited. I could have said, 'Gee, fellows, do you think this is necessary?'"

Or he could have protected the victims. "It would have been possible for me to poke my head into the next hut and shoo the people out the back, giving them a few extra seconds," Baughman said.

But he knew that style of reporting would have offered no more than what people already knew. It's no surprise that military units use threats to achieve their ends. "If you're going to find out if they're really going to pull the trigger, you have to wait," Baughman said.

With photos and stories, voters need to be brought face-to-face with parts of reality that they would like to deny. The disenfranchised, those living outside of the law, need their stories presented and their faces shown.

What entices people to attend dog fights? What's going on in the minds of young gang members who make city streets unsafe? We won't get answers waiting for these people to come forward and explain themselves. The explanations provided by arresting officers are obviously suspect. Yet we don't fully understand our society unless we get these stories from the perpetrators' point of view.

Journalists should watch and wait when the reality they are collecting is information that citizens need and when they alone can be trusted to get that information out.

No one questioned the judgment of the photojournalists who, in 1963, shot pictures of Buddhist monks who self-immolated in protest of the Vietnam War. The world needed that statement.

However, 20 years later, when two Jacksonville, Alabama videographers shot tape while a man attempted suicide by dousing himself with lighter fluid and lighting a match, the community was appalled that no one interceded.

In the second instance, the journalists should have put the man's life first. The drunken, out-of-work roofer's story of individual despair did not carry the same weight — the same need to be told at all costs — as the story of a religious group giving lives in protest of war.

But the line that separates one from the other is not that distinct. How about if six people had attempted suicide in the park? What if the roofer said that he was protesting some social ill? What if photojournalists happened upon the monk alone in a field rather than before a crowd of hundreds on a street in Saigon?

When journalists stumble upon life-threatening scenes with no context within which to judge what's going on, they should help if they're needed. But when they set out to do a story that they think may involve crime or pain, they should be prepared to watch rather than to react.

Society needs journalists who put professional duty before their desire to help. It's the same kind of need that society has for attorneys who are willing t o defend those guilty of heinous crimes, despite their own horror at the crimes committed.

At times, playing the role of observer and documenter of events can be a dirty job, but it's the journalist's job to do it.

(Elliott is director of the Ethics Institute, Dartmouth College)

The point of all this is that when we discuss 'what the public should have', we are not talking about spoon-feeding the news in motherly fashion, removing anything that might upset the collective tummy. What we are talking about is striking a balance between what the reader demonstrably tends to respond to, whether it is significant or not, and what is significant and therefore worthy of inclusion, whether or not it contains elements of emotional response.

Effects of Declining Competition

What most readers want is, apparently, a reasonable balance between what informs and what entertains. Perhaps no two of them agree on just what balance is; and so it should not be surprising that newspapers disagree on that score, too. But something has been added to the situation which requires that most editors give closer attention to balance than ever before. The steady decline in the number of competing newspapers has placed a new responsibility on those who make news decisions.

When a modest-sized city supported half a dozen daily newspapers that means that some could strike their balance sharply in favour of solid news and have sufficient patronage to let others pick off the semi-reader who prefers a paper balanced heavily on the side of entertainment and general fluff. Now most news editors make their decisions for newspapers that must be all things to all people. They must strike a balance that will guarantee against insolvency while at the same time discharging their public duty to see to it that plenty of 'hard' news is offered, even though only a small proportion of all readers choose to read it.

The Rewards of News

Dr Wilbur Schramm[93] , in an interesting study of psychological processes involved in reader choices of available communications material, proposes that the significant difference lies in the reward the item offers. Essentially, the suggestion is this: that the appeal a story has for its reader can be dichotomised into immediate and delayed rewards. Although any news item has in its elements of both appeals, one unusually predominates over the other. The story which carries its own built-in 'bang', or, in more scholarly terms, tends to provide an immediate reduction of tension, can be said to have an immediate reward for the reader. The story which offers its reward in the form of information which can later be used in one way or another to solve problems is of the delayed reward type. Dr Schramm offers proof that the distinction is valid by showing that significant difference in the reading of these two types of material can be noted between children and adults, less educated and more educated readers, etc.

This concept is discussed here because it provides a useful picture of what he is balancing when the editor balances between that which is significant and that which is merely interesting. The problem of making the significant item also interesting or at least readable is a very different job. Like the concept of identification, it has the advantage of describing the story and its impact on the reader.

93. Psychological Processes in Mass Communication, Schramm, Wilbur, Dr. Sacromento, Pg 23 – 45, 2005/7/6

Reporter

- Who is a Reporter?
- How do Reporters work?
  - Establish a News Beat
  - Give a Special Assignment
  - Follow a Tip
  - Create a News Story
- Interview
  - Definition
- Prepare Yourself for the Interview
  - Structured Interview
  - Semi-structured
  - Unstructured

"A Reporter like a foot soldier gets his hands dirty gathering news; most of the time to the extent of risking his life. Without him Mass Media cannot exist."

The Reporter

There is no bigger word in Media than 'Reporter'. The Reporter is indeed the backbone of all mass communication. In many ways reporters are like the frontline soldiers who are the ones to get their hands dirty. They are the ones who in the open, risk every thing for the local thug's displeasure to being shot covering a riot by the police. The importance of the reporters is also such that in a newspaper or a television news channel, a reporter through his courage and intelligence can single-handedly increase the readership or the viewership of a newspaper or television channel by his reporting.

A CNN TV Reporter

But in reality, the reporter needs to be a bit demystified. True, he is no less than an investigative detective, a lone soldier fighting a lonely war, or a scholar, his aura of practicality must be understood.

A reporter essentially is a person who collects such information part or whole of which could be used in the newspaper publication. I was recently asked by a professor at a particular institute, whether a 'reporter was essentially a person who collected news'. I certainly replied in the negative. Why? Because a reporter is not the collector of news. Remember news is just a concept, an idea at best. A reporter only collects information from different sources that go on to make news in its subsequent publication in the newspaper.

Thus, for our present surmise, it must be understood that a reporter collects information part or whole of which could be used for publication by the newspaper.

Who is a Reporter?

Well, this might be tough question to answer; however, here are some of the simplest of surmises:

1. A reporter is essentially an enthusiast. He or she is interested in everything that surrounds him or her.

2. He or she is an initiator. While in a conversation, he or she likes to ask questions. He or she is not afraid of talking or approaching people in order to know about them or what they do.

3. He or she is force to reckon with, strong in character, he or she is aggressive when it comes to extracting answers to their questions.

4. He or she is curious about everything.

5. He or she is a genuine person and above all fair.

6. He or she likes to write. Writing comes natural to him/her.

Besides these a reporter desires for facts, accuracy, and has a good education to fall back to.

Reportage

Reportage sometimes refers to the total body of media coverage of a particular topic or event, including news reporting and analysis: 'the extensive reportage of recent events in x'. This is typically used in discussions of the media's general tone or angle or other collective characteristics.

Reportage is also a term for an eye-witness genre of journalism: an individual journalist's report of news, especially when witnessed firsthand, distributed through the media. This style of reporting is often characterised by travel and careful observation.

Literary reportage is the art of blending documentary, reportage-style observations, with personal experience, perception, and anecdotal evidence, in a non-fiction form of literature. This is perhaps more commonly called creative non-fiction and is closely related to New Journalism. The prose of such reporting tends to be more polished and longer than in newspaper articles.

Investigative Reporting

Investigative Reporting is a type of reporting in which reporters deeply investigates a topic of interest, often involving crime, political corruption, or some other scandal.

De Burgh (2000) states that: 'An investigative journalist is a man or woman whose profession it is to discover the truth and to identify lapses from it in whatever media may be available. The act of doing this generally is called investigative journalism and is distinct from apparently similar work done by the police, lawyers, auditors and regulatory bodies in that it is not limited as to target, not legally founded and closely connected to publicity'.

An investigative journalist may spend a considerable period researching and preparing a report, sometimes months or years, whereas a typical daily or weekly news reporter writes items concerning immediately available news. Most investigative journalism is done by newspapers, wire services and freelance journalists. An investigative journalist's final report may take the form of an exposé.

There is no more important contribution that we can make to society than strong, publicly-spirited investigative journalism.

– Tony Burman, editor-in-chief of CBC News

The Investigation

The investigation will often require an extensive number of interviews and travel; other instances might call for the reporter to make use of activities such as surveillance techniques, analysis of documents, investigations of the performance of any kind of equipment involved in an accident, patent medicine, scientific analysis, social and legal issues, and the like.

Investigative journalism requires the scrutiny of details, fact-finding, and physical effort. An investigative journalist must have an analytical and incisive mind with strong self-motivation to carry on when all doors are closed, when facts are being covered up or falsified and so on.

Some of the means reporters can use for their fact-finding:

1. Studying neglected sources, such as archives, phone records, address books, tax records and license records

2. Talking to neighbours

3. Using subscription research sources such as LexisNexis

4. Anonymous sources (for example whistleblowers)

5. Going undercover

Investigative journalism can be contrasted with analytical reporting. According to De Burgh (2000), analytical journalism takes the data available and reconfigures it, helping us to ask questions about the situation or statement or see it in a different way, whereas investigative journalists go further and also want to know whether the situation presented to us is the reality.

Consequences

Some of the potential consequences for the subjects of successful investigative journalism include:

1. Indictment and conviction

2. Loss of job

3. Loss of professional accreditation

4. Payment of fines

5. Loss of personal and professional reputation

6. Domino consequences for family members/associates involved in unrelated criminal acts discovered through the process of investigation

Consequences for society as a whole include:

1. Revision of institutional policies

2. Changes in the law

Professional References

In *The Reporter's Handbook: An Investigator's Guide to Documents and Techniques*, Steve Weinberg defined investigative journalism as:

Reporting, through one's own initiative and work product, matters of importance to readers, viewers or listeners. In many cases, the subjects of the reporting wish the matters under scrutiny to remain undisclosed. There are currently university departments for teaching investigative journalism. Conferences are conducted presenting peer reviewed research into investigative journalism.

News Presenter

A news presenter is, broadly speaking, a person that presents a news show on television, radio or the Internet. The term is not commonly used by people in the industry as they tend to use more descriptive, and sometimes country-specific, terms. Examples include 'news reader', 'newscaster', and 'news anchor'.

Newscaster

A newscaster is a presenter of a news bulletin who is himself or herself a working journalist, and a participant in compiling the script to be delivered in a news bulletin.

Prior to the television era, radio news broadcasts often mixed news with opinion and each presenter strove for a distinctive style. These presenters were referred to as commentators. The last remaining news presenter of this type is Paul Harvey[94] . The term newscaster came into common use to distinguish presenters of straight news broadcasts from commentators.

However in the UK, ITN's presenters are referred to as newscasters (and have been since the 1950s), whilst those working at the BBC are called news readers.

News Anchor

In the United States and Canada, presenters of news broadcasts are referred to as news anchors (sometimes anchorperson, anchorman, or anchorwoman) instead of 'newscasters'. An anchor traditionally is a television personality who presents material prepared for a news programme and at times must improvise commentary for live presentation. Many news anchors are also involved in writing and/or editing the news for their programmes.

---

94. Paul Harvey Aurandt (born September 4, 1918), better known as Paul Harvey, is an American radio broadcaster for the ABC Radio Networks. He broadcasts News and Comment on weekday mornings and mid-days, and at noon on Saturdays, as well as his famous The Rest of the Story segments. His listening audience is estimated at 22 million people a week. Harvey likes to say he was raised in radio newsroom

The term 'anchor' was coined by producer Don Hewitt. PBS cites its first usage as being on July 7, 1952 to describe Walter Cronkite's role at the Democratic and Republican National Conventions. According to Hewitt, the term was in reference to the 'anchor leg' of a relay race.

How Do Reporters Work?

How does newspaper staff go about securing news? There are four main ways of locating news:

1. Establish a News Beat

Many reporters for city newspapers have definite beats or 'runs'. These are people to whom they go regularly in search of news. A beat may include, for example, the local police station, offices of the political parties, organisations and so on. A reporter 'covers' his beat as the first step in finding news stories. He is expected to contact each source of news at least once for every issue of the newspaper. When he finds news, he is expected to write it in proper form, regardless of how unimportant it may seem to him, or report it to the editor, who will assign the story to another reporter.

2. Give a Special Assignment

The editor or another staff member makes assignments to reporters for every important news event. An assignment usually includes the catch line or title of the story, the name of the person to see, the time when the story is due, the number of words to be written, and in general what the story should contain.

Assignment ideas come from many sources, but the main fountain of story information is the newspaper's '*Future Book*'. This is a loose-leaf folder with a page for each issue of the paper. As soon as anything is known about a future activity, an entry is made in the *Future Book* for each issue in which a story about this event might conceivably appear. For example, a classical dance might be entered on the pages representing the two or three issues preceding the date of the dance, and for the issue following. As plans and preparations for the dance go forward, new information will be available for each of the advance stories. Then there will probably be enough new facts available for one follow-up story in the issue following the dance.

3. Follow a Tip

A reporter learns that something is going to happen, or hears about something that has just happened. Using this tip as a starting point, he tries to find more information about the event. A tip differs from a beat in that it represents news which probably is not related to any of the newspaper's regular beats; it differs from an assignment in that it leads to a news event previously unknown to the editorial staff. (It may, of course, then become the subject of an assignment.) A reporter who is alert and keeps his eyes and ears open will hear about many news events that would not ordinarily reach the paper through beats or assignments.

4. Create a News Story

Invent a story! Of course, you can't make up a news story about an event that didn't happen, much as you might wish to! But there are certain kinds of stories waiting for an imaginative reporter to think of them. For instance: who is the shortest man in the town? The tallest? Occasionally you might like to investigate a question such as this: Are there some facts in the history of the town that are not commonly known? Perhaps a look into the files of your paper or a talk with an elderly man who has been witnessing everything happening in the town for many years will help you find them.

Interview

Definition

First let us find out the correct definition of Interview:

Journalism Schools[95] and scholars all over the world have defined interview differently. Here is how they see it:

The questioning of a person (or a conversation in which information is elicited), often conducted by journalists; 'my interviews with teenagers revealed a weakening of religious bonds'.

Also,

A conference (usually with someone important); 'he had a consultation with the judge'; 'he requested an audience with the king'.

95. I have consistently used the word 'School' in this book which denotes Institutions and colleges. Some of the most renowned colleges imparting journalism in the United States are known as Schools. I

Princeton University[96]

A series of orally-delivered questions designed to elicit responses concerning attitudes, information, interests, knowledge, and opinions. Interviews may be conducted in person or by telephone, and with one teacher or a group of teachers. The three major types of interviews are: (1) structured, where all questions to be asked by the interviewer are specified in advance; (2) semi-structured, where the interviewer can ask other questions in addition to the specified questions; and (3) unstructured, where the interviewer has a list of topics, but no or few specified questions.

West Michigan University

A record of a conversation between an interviewer and a subject. The intent of the interviewer is to provide for readers an overview and understanding of the subject being interviewed.

A social experience, depending on one person, the interviewer, asking a series of questions of another person or group of people.

Contact with an informant, or group of informants, in order to obtain information for a research project.

Sociology Essentials

The questioning of an individual for the purpose of obtaining information related to the investigation.

Fire Notes

A face-to-face or telephone questioning of a respondent to obtain desired information.

Social Science – S.chaef

In order to get information, a reporter must meet the person 'in the know' and converse with him or her. Here upon meeting the person also known as the source of the information, the reporter asks him a set of questions aimed at demystifying the subject in which he is working. This is how the scenario might go:

Rahul Rawat walks straight up to the door and knocks at it. A young house maid opens the door and upon seeing Rahul asks him to wait at the living room, while she calls Mr Ramendra Nayaran Roy, an eminent politician from the town.

96. See Bibliography for All

Meanwhile, Mr Ramendra walks down the stairs from his study room and meets Rahul, who upon seeing him stand up to shake his hand.

"When I received your call, I was a bit busy so could not fix a meeting right away. I hope I have not caused you much trouble." Mr Ramendra says.

"Of course not, Mr Roy." Rahul replies. "Now should we start?"

"Yes, by all means."

Rahul carries on with his questions, "You have in the recent time been trying to align with the regional parties predominant in the hills today, like the Communist Party of Revolutionary Marxist and People's Democratic Front. Why is it then that just before the elections you have decided to fight the election alone?"

"I have been contesting elections as an independent candidate for last 30 years. Yes, it is true that since past six months, I had been trying to reach an agreement with these regional parties – where we could field one consensus candidate who represents all of the Darjeeling Hills. But our ideologies and strategies have once again clashed and we have not been able to reach any sort of agreement. Thus, I was compelled to once contest the election as an independent candidate," Mr Roy replies.

"There has also been allegation in some quarters that you are an opportunist, who upon winning aligns with whichever party offers you the most?"

Mr Roy smiles. "In the 30 years of contesting election as an independent candidate, I have won 5 times, without any party's support. I have fought in the Parliament for the rights of our people, but you must understand that I have to be an opportunist so that I can extract from the Government more of all that is due to our people and our region. But beyond that I do not think I am an opportunist. My negotiations for the good of our people cannot be taken to be my indulgence in opportunism."

This is the heart of reporting – the most fascinating and interesting part of newspaper work. A reporter asks questions to be sure he understands. When he is finished, he has the pleasure of being on the 'inside' of knowing what's going to happen, often before many of the people who are directly affected know about it.

Prepare Yourself for the Interview

In one of the interesting definitions of interview put together by the West Michigan University, we were introduced to something more than the mere definition. Let us go through the same again.

A series of orally-delivered questions designed to elicit responses concerning attitudes, information, interests, knowledge, and opinions. Interviews may be conducted in person or by telephone, and with one teacher or a group of teachers. The three major types of interviews are: **(1) structured,** where all questions to be asked by the interviewer are specified in advance, **(2) semi-structured,** where the interviewer can ask other questions in addition to the specified ones, and **(3) unstructured,** where the interviewer has a list of topics, but no or few specified questions.

As you can see that there are three types of interviews:

1. **Structured**: Where all the questions you ask have already been jotted down. In this case, the interviewer merely acts like a questioning machine. He asks his questions and jots down the answer and then moves on to the other. Here the main stress is laid on the prior preparation by the interviewer or the reporter, who must study not just the subject he would be dealing with, but also the person he intends to interview. This means, he would have to know what the intended respondent is like. Is he/she well loved, renowned etc., how much knowledge does he have with respect to the issue in hand, so on and so forth.

However, this type of Structured Interview has certain drawbacks, which a reporter can find out easily. A reporter needs to be a conscious person when he interviews any one. It is true that he has to prepare before hand, which means study the subject, but while interviewing if he asks only the specified questions, there might be a chance that he might miss the most important of things. The entire concept of **Structured** Interview implies that the interviewer knows somehow or at least has an idea as to what the replies to his questions would be. This is how he will construct his questions before hand. But there might be such situations when the respondent might surprise the reporter and he might be left dumbfounded when his follow up questions would not stand a chance to be asked. Here the reporter must formulate his own questions based upon the respondent's replies.

2. **Semi-structured**: This type of interview is such that the reporter formulates a set of questions as a back up and a starter of sorts. However, he or she does not entirely rely upon them. Once the interview gains momentum, he consciously asks question impromptu based on the person's reply and his own interpretation of those replies. This is how all reporters prefer to interview.

3. **Unstructured**: An unstructured interview is one where a reporter walks straight into the office of the respondent and starts asking questions. Here an

experienced reporter can be able to carry and complete the interview getting all the information that he wanted, an amateur reporter on the other hand might make a nuisance of himself.

Covering News

What happened? You worked hard on this issue of the newspaper. It is attractive. The leads are interesting and the stories are well written. You used names wherever you could. But it just didn't 'click' with your readers. All the comments you heard were:

"It's all stale news. We heard it last week."

"They only print their own and their friend's names; we want to read about other people."

So what do you do now?

Emphasise the future and explain the past by doing the following things:

1. Keep news stories of past events short

Make your report of a past event brief. And state only essential facts. If the event was properly covered by advance stories, your only reason for a past story is to introduce new facts. However, you must remember if you have nothing new, you have no story.

2. Emphasise the why angle

Your story of a past event – even when the facts are well known to your readers – can be meaningful if you interpret these facts. Tell WHY the decision was made, what led up to it. Explain WHY the team was able to win, what this means to the next game. Interview news sources who can give you reasons for news events or suggest solutions to problems. Readers may know WHAT happened, but they rarely know WHY.

3. Feature the future while reporting the past

Does this sound impossible? It is one of the most important skills a reporter learns.

Serving Your Entire Community

Every newspaper serves a particular group of people whose interests are similar because they live and work in the same area, or do the same type of thing. The newspaper's job is to cover the news of this group, or 'community', completely and impartially. Readers must be confident that every bit of worthwhile news about community happenings, past, present, and future, will be reported.

The community served by a local newspaper is a broad one. It covers more area and more people than most reporters or their readers realise. And to obtain this news, you must reach upward, downward and outward from your primary topics. In doing so, you will improve your paper's coverage of your community, vitalise your news pages, and increase reader's interest.

And in order to achieve this, you must:

1. Realise that every person is a news possibility!

2. Try to involve as many people as you can in a story. This also means that you use as many different names as you can

3. Cover all the annual activities

4. Try to reach beyond the neighbourhood walls

5. Balance your news

6. Try to reach all your news sources

Eyewitness Reporting

All stories on future events, and many on current or past ones, are obtained by interviewing news sources. Major stories of past events may, however, be written by reporters who actually participated in the events or were present when they occurred.

This kind of reporting is common in daily newspapers, which deal with news of the recent past. In stories of fires, court trails, or meetings, for example, most of the action is seen by the reporter, and his interviews with news sources merely add to his own impressions.

However, you will face a major problem in covering any of these events. How will you sort and condense the vast array of facts, details, figures, and just plain words? Stories you obtained from a news source will already be condensed and key thoughts emphasised; your story will be relatively easy to organise. But not so with eyewitness stories! You will have to start with everything that happened, including much trivial detail that wouldn't deserve to be printed. Then you would have to do two things: first, place the key thought and other important facts, discarding ideas containing little news value; and second, condense the story into a brief, direct statement whose length reflects the overall news value of the story.

Making a Meeting Report Interesting

A story that tests your skill in deciding what is important and what is not is the report of a meeting such as those involving many different parties. Many things may be discussed and voted upon. You must decide which of these have news value and which are mere details.

The mechanics of writing an interesting meeting story are simple. First, attend the meeting personally and make your own notes. Second, select the event or decision that affects the largest number of people or that seems most interesting and important. This is your key thought; feature it in your lead. Third, give all the facts concerning your featured event. Finally, discuss other happenings in the remaining paragraphs of the story in the order of their importance, leaving the least important to the last.

Covering a Speech

There will be times when you will be assigned to write a story about an assembly featuring a political speaker. Reporting a speech accurately is difficult. You must shift among the many words spoken, find the essential facts, and then present these facts in an interesting way. A speech story is in a way similar to an interview story, for you must show the personality of the speaker and indicate how he is received by his audience.

Here is how you should do it:

1. Obtain background information about the speaker

2. Listen for the main idea in the speech

While listening to the speech, try to grasp the subject of the talk and the principal arguments or information presented. Make notes of them. Try to see what the speaker's aim or purpose is – what he wants you to understand.

3. Copy two or three interesting quotations

Copy, in the exact words used any of the speaker's statements that seem to express his purpose. You can even record the speech.

4. Interview the speaker if possible

You can learn more about the speaker's personality if an opportunity arises to interview him briefly, before or after the meeting. Ask a few questions about his experiences or his principal ideas in the speech. Any understanding you gain will help you write a clearer story.

5. Begin the lead with a direct quotation

The speech story closely follows the written pattern of the standard news story. The lead should start with direct quotation of an outstanding statement made by the speaker. If the statement is long, place it by itself in the first paragraph, and then present the other essential facts in the second paragraph.

The following are examples of good speech story leads:

"Opportunities in industry..."

6. Briefly identify the speaker and occasion

A phrase or sentence in the lead or second paragraph is adequate for this purpose. Tell who he is, when he spoke, and to whom. Then go on with your report of what he said. Other biographical information can be reflected in your summary of his talk or left for the final paragraphs.

7. Vary your manner of presentation

In writing the rest of the story, mix paragraphs of direct quotation, indirect quotation, and summary. One problem is to avoid repetition of "he said." This can be accomplished by using synonyms or suggesting this meaning in other ways.

Colourful News Features

"Features are the wide screen, 3-D, technicolour side of the newspaper business. They provide scope, extra dimension, and, above all, colour to the daily news diet", says Don Duncan of the Tacoma news-Tribune, writing in Student and Publisher.

A feature is anything in a newspaper that is not straight news or advertising. Features are the 'frosting on the cake'. If well chosen and well written, they add variety to any newspaper. Most features are based in some way on news events. In fact, newspapermen use the word 'feature' to identify a news feature, which tells of human interest items, presents entertaining news, or explains and interprets facts. Other types of features are related to news. They include editorials, most columns, personality interviews, fashions, editorial cartoons, and movie and television reviews. Successful newspapers include non-news features but limit them. Some of these features are book reviews, crossword puzzles, comics, and humorous cartoons. Almost any topic that would interest or entertain readers is an appropriate feature subject.

Finding and Writing News Features

News features may be identified in three ways. First, they report news events, although the news content is not as important as the way the stories are written. Second, they are written informally, with extensive use of descriptive verbs and entertaining phrases. Their leads are designed to attract readers rather than to recite essential facts. They may have surprise endings. And third, they may be printed on news pages or on the editorial page.

Features Develop from Observation

The reporter who finds and writes news features must be a keen observer. Details that go unnoticed by the average individual are yours to see and write about. Watch and listen for insignificant happenings that might develop into features.

Extend your powers of observation as you collect facts for your story. Train yourself to notice details. What was your news source wearing? What mannerisms did he have? What did he do with his hands and feet while you talked? What was going on around you during the interview? Teach yourself to absorb them and to recognise their news value, even if you may not use them in your present story.

Entertaining or Human Interest News Features

News features may be divided generally into those that entertain and those that inform. The examples presented so far in this chapter have been of the entertaining or human interest variety. This type of news feature appeals to the emotions of your readers. Since the news value is slight, the way these stories are written becomes vital to their success.

Subjects for entertaining news features are everywhere around school. You often uncover them on your beat or while following out a routine news assignment. What would be dull facts, if you recited them in straight news form, come to life when you develop them imaginatively into a news feature

Alertness, observation, and luck may help you find the best of your human interest features. Watch for unusual happenings, peculiar situations, sayings that make you laugh, or clever ways of doing things. Daily newspapers often publish features about sad or touching subjects, but your readers prefer the lively, humorous kind.

Writing Entertaining News Features

Step 1: Get all the facts

Clever writing will never hide a shortage of facts. Obtain them from news sources, personal observation, interviews, by asking questions, and by searching the morgue or libraries. Take thorough notes on main ideas, figures, names, and quotations.

Step 2: Determine your approach

Consider your material. How will you handle your facts? How will you portray the people involved? Will you build up to a climax or surprise ending? Will you improve your story if you tell it as seen through the eyes of a participant? Every feature story deserves individual treatment.

Step 3: Write your lead

The lead does not have to tell all essential facts, but it must include the most eye-catching information, attract readers, and tell your readers what kind of story to expect.

Step 4: Tell your story in the best possible way

No specific rules can be laid down for organising your story. The impression you wish to leave dictates your plan. In most cases a chronological or narrative arrangement is well suited to entertaining news features. Your reader does not expect to leave this kind of story at any point as he does a news story. He must stay with it to find out what happened. Sometimes a surprise ending, such as the one used in the news feature about the tip, may enliven your story.

Step 5: Use imagination and colour

Imaginative, original writing makes a news feature successful. Here is your opportunity to unleash action verbs and descriptive words that must be restrained in ordinary news writing.

Step 6: Stick to the facts!

Guard against the tendency to use your imagination to change or distort the facts. You are free to tell them in the most interesting way you can, but you must report what happened faithfully and accurately.

News features that Inform

Many outstanding news features are written to inform readers, rather than to entertain them. These are careful, thorough studies of particular situations, or activities.

Because news features that inform are not often related to a current event, it can be used whenever space permits. In addition, it is likely to be longer than a human-interest story. You are still responsible, however, for providing an attention-arresting lead and for using clear, colourful language and good news style. Since the informative news feature is 'educational', you must present facts in a special way designed to keep your reader's attention. The humour or the timely news 'peg' which makes him read entertaining features may be lacking here, and you must make up for it with especially good writing.

To write an informative news feature, you must follow the same steps as you do for an entertaining one. Here, again, your lead is important. Your lead sets the tone for the rest of your story. You may use an informal approach that may not be practical in a straight news story, but bear in mind that your story is based on facts. The impression you create must be that of truth, although you may write informally and imaginatively.

Describing a Personality

Interviewing to describe a personality

Interviewing someone for the purpose of writing about him as an individual differs considerably from interviewing someone to obtain news facts. You are now considering the news source as a person; up to this point, you have been interested only in the facts he has to tell you.

Writing a Personality Story

1. Make plans for your interview

Find out as much as you can about the individual you are to interview. Use directories, the newspaper morgue, or the library. Talk with people who know him. Decide on a topic or 'tie-in' for the interview. Prepare a brief set of questions. If the interview goes easily, you may not use them all; but by having questions ready, you will never be at a loss for something to say.

2. Prepare for the interview

Make an appointment with the person you are to interview.

Check your personal appearance. Neatness will help your create a good impression as you meet your subject. Carry two or three sharpened pencils and a small pad of paper. Make brief notes on facts and main ideas and put down the exact words of any statements you may wish to quote.

3. Enjoy your interview

Be pleasant and courteous. Begin the interview by getting acquainted. Relax and enjoy the conversation. Use a few questions to lead your subject into talking easily about himself. Concentrate on what he says. As you listen, decide what kind of story you want. After the interview, check facts, figures, and spelling with your subject. Be sure to express your thanks.

4. Picture your personality

Notice what he looks like. Study his face, his smile, his expression, his clothes, the way he moves his hands or eyes. While he talks, think what words you would use to describe him. Jot down quickly any words or phrases that seem especially vivid and appropriate.

Next, listen to the person behind the voice. How does he make statements? What is his attitude towards his subject? How would you describe his voice and his manner of speaking?

5. Write your story

Put the story on paper at once, while impressions are fresh in your mind. An interview story falls easily into the inverted pyramid pattern, although some of the less formal techniques suggested for news features may fit the kind of story you are preparing.

Your lead should identify the person, and feature an important fact or quotation relative to the 'tie-in' or main topic of your interview. How well do these leads make the identification, set the theme for the story, and begin to describe a colourful personality?

Informal writing, bits of personal description, and direct quotations help make your subject come alive. You aim is to describe this individual so well that he or she seems to step right out of the printed page and talk with your readers. For example, the use of bits of personal description in the story can help you emphasise particular points: 'the quiet-voiced writer....'

Arrange to have a photograph of your personality accompany the story, if at all possible.

The 'Inquiring Reporter'

A story related closely to the personality story is the symposium interview, or 'inquiring reporter', in which a number of people are asked the same question.

Here the topic is important, rather than the person. The symposium is popular because it enables your paper to use many names in the story and because it tells what people are doing and thinking.

In preparing a symposium, you ask many people a given question. It is usually desirable to ask a large number of people, and then select the most representative or informative answers. How well you choose your question affects the story's success. Any subject of interest to your readers is acceptable. A good question will furnish informative, entertaining, and often humorous replies.

☞ Relate your question to a current event: What do you think about the new district hospital coming up in place of the historic Eden Sanatorium....

Covering Sports

All types of news stories and features may be written on sports topics. Each item is prepared according to standards for its particular style.

1. Advance story: Unlike daily national newspapers, regional newspapers cannot publish fresh accounts of games or meets. Most stories of past events are one to two weeks old; fans already know the results. Therefore, the most important story on a sports page is the future or advance story. It tells about coming games, compares teams and players, discusses team records, gives line-ups, and tries to stir up enthusiasm.

Information for an advance story may be obtained from many sources.

2. Report of an event

Time is an essential consideration for the sports page.

Good accounts of games are written as a result of eyewitness reporting. In this sense, they are similar to reports of speeches or meetings. You observe carefully taking notes on spectacular action. If the scorekeeper's records are available to you, you may depend on these for basic facts; but you must add colourful highlights gained by personal observation. If these records are not available, you must keep the necessary records yourself, and at the same time watch for outstanding plays. Post-game interviews with players, coaches, and officials will add to your understanding of the event. From all these facts and impressions, you will select items to feature in your story.

3. Review or summary

Summary stories, giving results of several games or reviewing a complete season, may serve several purposes:

- To review and highlight the activities of an entire sports season.
- To summarise the events in a major or minor sport when space cannot be allocated for reports on individual games.
- To publicise and summarise the results of intramural competition, as well as other minor sports activities.

Sports summaries need not be routine recitations of scores and dull facts. Use the names of outstanding players. Briefly but vividly describe the highlights of the season. Even in intramural summaries, where many games must be mentioned in a limited space, emphasise a few outstanding games, getting colourful action words and players' names into your descriptions. Then combine the high points of other games into a few brief sentences, or list the scores. If you try to be 'fair' by writing one short sentence about each game, you will have a dull pattern ot sentences monotonously repeating the same idea, and no one will want to read your story.

4. General sports news

Valuable news stories on the sports page may relate to buildings, equipment, awards, rules, schedules, coaching staff, or other items of interest to sports readers.

5. Features

Do you want your sports page to look as though your purpose is to keep your readers informed and entertained? Use features! Almost any kind of feature is suitable.

Entertaining and informative news features will liven up the page. Seasoned or year's end summaries are best if treated as informative news features. Interpretive stories about new rules, sports history, styles of play, or game backgrounds add interest. Humorous incidents are always worth space for the attention they attract.

A sports personality or 'Player of the Week' story outlines a sports accomplishments, tells of his other interests, activities, and ambitions. Coaches and physios also make fine subjects for personality sketches.

To add life to your page, try:

- Quizzes on present or past sports events
- Summaries of little-known facts about athletics
- Readers poll on 'Athlete of the year'
- Statistics on team effort or individual players' records
- Quotes or predications for city sports writers and TV commentators
- Prediction contests, with subscriptions or published interviews as prizes

Editorials on athletic and games topics are usually of interest to readers. However, the informality of the sports page suggests that comment is more effective when given the personal touch possible only in columns or by-lined stories.

Write your Sports Story Informally but Correctly

Some sports reporters feel that the informal style of a sports page permits sloppy writing. Nothing could be further from the truth. Successful informal writing can be done only by those who have mastered the techniques of formal composition. When this has been accomplished, you have a basis for stretching these standards into an informal style. Without this training, your attempts at informality may end up as poor writing.

Good sports writing follows the standards for news writing that you have learned in previous chapters and have applied in writing news stories. The following points deserve special comment.

- **A good sports lead is complete and concise:** Write your sports lead as you would for a news story. It should start with the key thought and contain the essential 5 W and 1 H facts. You need not search for the 'wow' element. It is right there in the outcome of a game or in the close competition coming in the next game. Make your 'wow' stand out by beginning your lead with the subject of the first sentence, by keeping your lead short and by using simple sentences.

- **Use colourful but not trite expressions:** Informal words and phrases, sports slang, specific details, and imaginative language give a reader the 'feel' of being present at sports events. Good sports writing should be colourful, sparkling, and descriptive. But it is easy to go too far, using hackneyed expressions or inventing new terms which serve no purpose except to confuse readers.

⇨ **Use the proper form of address:** When referring to an athlete for the first time, use his full name ('Rahul Dravid' for example). For each other reference in the same story, use his last name only. Say 'Dravid' not 'Rahul' even though the latter form may be preferred on other news pages.

⇨ **Keep the time element in mind:** No news becomes stale more quickly than sports stories. Past games fade rapidly from people's minds because new ones are always coming. Your readers think, "If we won, we have to keep winning; if we lost, we can do better next time!"

⇨ **Use box scores properly:** Box scores list detailed statistics for a game, meet, or season, in small fonts. In most newspapers, there is no room for box scores of individual games. League standings and sometimes individual scoring records may be squeezed in.

⇨ **Interpret the facts if you are qualified to do so:** Because of their informal style and the kinds of topic covered in them, sports stories often contain some opinion. If the writer is familiar with the sport about which he is writing, and if he has learned to observe intelligently and to make competent judgements, such interpretation is acceptable to readers.

Answer two questions before inserting your opinion into a sports story.

- Are you thoroughly familiar with this sport?
- Are you stating the facts upon which your opinion is based?

If you cannot answer 'Yes' to both questions, you are running the risk of editorialising in an unacceptable way.

Plan an Interesting Sports Page

Sports space in your paper should be allotted in proportion to other news, features, and advertising, taking into consideration the amount of interest in sports and the athletic activities showed by your readers. Typically, sports news appears on the last page, sometimes the third, of a four-page paper. Advertisements usually fill part of the page, posing a problem to the sports editor. In four-page papers, advertising is divided between the sports page and the second news page. If the advertising is well planned and arranged by the advertising staff, a reasonable amount of space is left for sports news. Some papers keep approximately the same amount of advertising on the sports page week after week, varying the second news page according to the total volume of advertising. When the paper has six or more pages, the sports display can be improved by leaving the sports page, as well as the editorial and front pages, free of advertising. An alternate plan, more pleasing to your advertisers, is to allow two facing inside pages for sports, printing advertisements on both pages.

As you plan a sports page, keep in mind that athletics are vigorous and fast moving. A page that reflects this vigour and speed is possible if you consider several points.

- Plan stories and photographs well in advance. Make assignments to reporters according to your sports events schedule, bearing the time element in mind.
- Arrange for various kinds of material on the page: advance stories, reports, photographs, features, columns
- Cover all sports, major and minor.
- Feature advance stories rather than reports of past events.

The Editor and His News Desk

- Making the News Meaningful
  - The Inverted Pyramid style of Writing
  - The Block Paragraph
  - The Impersonal Tone of News Writing
- How to write a News Story
  - Step A: Obtain all the facts
  - Step B: Write your lead
  - Step C: Plan and write the body of your story
  - Step D: Use good newspaper paragraphs
  - Step E: Use direct quotes to brighten your story
  - Step F: Name your authority
  - Step G: When you have finished stating facts, stop writing!
- Other Important Things to be Kept in Mind
  - Keep your sentences simple
  - Use simple words
  - Don't use too many words
  - Use nouns as modifiers
  - Use colourful words
  - Use verbs for description
  - Personalise your news
  - Learn to distinguish between fact and opinion
  - Never editorialise in a news story
  - State the opinions of news sources
  - State your facts accurately
  - Tell the whole truth
  - Ask yourself – which is the right word?
  - Never use first or second person pronouns
  - Use pronouns properly
  - State time correctly
  - Names must be spelled correctly

"The Editor may be the Captain of the Ship, responsible singularly for all the collective mistakes of his team but the most important task that he and his legion of sub-editors, copy editors and proof readers are dedicated to is making the news meaningful".

The Editor and His News Desk

Making the News Meaningful

Possibly the largest single ingredient in meaningful writing is readable writing. The term 'readability' usually is used to describe the stylistic factors in writing which make it easier to read. Readable writing is presumed to be the meaningful writing.

Readability has been given a good deal of attention in the news services and newsrooms in recent years. It has almost become a cult. However, concern with readability in the newspaper profession is perhaps only a century old. Using simple sentence was the old times editor's injunction to the reporter, as they are writing for the people

An enthusiastic application of readability formulas has not solved all the problems of reading people with news of complex events. But it has helped to a great extent. Some of the conditions under which newsmen operate tend to militate strongly against readability.

For example:

1. The Inverted Pyramid style of writing

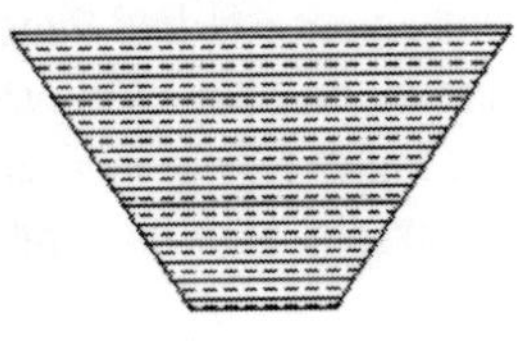

The diagram shows the most common and effective way of arranging a news story. The top-heavy look is intentional: the arrangement puts the 'big' facts first and the 'little' details last. Study the news story that follows. Note how each fact has more news value than the others following it.

Sourav targets history in victory .

Calcutta, March 9: History is on everyone's lips, particularly those of political leaders on each side of the border. India team leader, Sourav Ganguly, is also speaking of history, of a different kind.

"We will change it this time" – the words shot out in a sharp burst when the captain was reminded of India's poor record in Pakistan.

Forget goodwill and revival of friendship, when Ganguly and his boys take the field on Saturday in the opening one-day match of the 'historic' series, the only force driving them will be the desire to win.

"It's good to start an away series as favourites, our team knows how to handle this pressure," Sourav said at the end of the conditioning camp here.

India will tour Pakistan after 15 years to play a full-fledged series (five ODIs and three Tests) as an offshoot of the peace initiative launched by the leaders of the two countries.

The Telegraph, Siliguri, Wednesday, 10 March 2004

The reasons for writing a news story this way is the reader finds the information he wants more readily and understands it better; the reporter thinks more logically while preparing it; and the editor may adjust its length to the space requirements because it meets the cut-off test. The first paragraph after the lead contain essential details and the last paragraph of the story may be eliminated if there is no space for it.

Many news stories could be improved and the appearance of news pages enlivened if the last paragraph was cut off – or better yet, not written!

Each news story of any consequence is told three times in a newspaper: in the headline, in the lead, and in the body of the story. A long story in a daily newspaper may even have a fourth telling. In a story about a major disaster, for example, six or eight paragraphs after the lead may cover the main facts;

then the entire event may be told again in detail, from the beginning. Small local newspapers do not have the space or need for this kind of reporting.

Ninety-five percent of all news stories fit readily into the inverted pyramid arrangement. As you select facts for each paragraph, remember to apply the same standards as you did when arranging facts for your lead.

Explain your key thought first. Then, tell the other facts of the story in the order of their importance. Consider their news value, by the news elements contained, to determine their importance.

2. The Block Paragraph

Although it is no longer the dogma that it once was, the block paragraph habit persists. Its theory is that a paragraph must stand as a unit, so that if last-minute reassembling requires changes in paragraph order, a particular paragraph will not depend for its meaning on what went ahead of it.

It can be seen that this militates against the use of the transitions mentioned above. A paragraph that begins "Earlier..." may not work in another position in the story. Thus we are almost faced with a choice between the effective transitional phrase and the block paragraph traditional. Most newsmen today would unhesitatingly choose to junk the latter.

3. The Impersonal Tone of News Writing

The separation of news from opinion is largely responsible for this tradition of the newsroom. It is undoubtedly a sound one, but clearly comes in to conflict with readability, or at least with what the experts consider to be one of the most important ingredients of readability.

There have been sign, however, of a relaxation in the impersonal tone of news writing. At any rate, the impersonal tone is a precondition of news writing that tends to conflict with principles of readability.

How to Write a News Story

Step A: Obtain all the facts

⇴ Study your notes carefully to get the story clearly in mind. Be sure you understand the main idea of the entire story. Consider the news value of each fact and its potential interest to the readers of your newspaper. This will help you determine how to approach the assignment and what to emphasise.

⇾ Use the facilities of your newspaper morgue or the library to obtain additional information about your topic and to learn what has already been printed about this subject. If you now decide that you lack essential information, interview your original news source or others to fill in the gaps.

Step B: Write your lead

This is the most critical step you will take. The quality of your lead determines whether your story will be accepted by your editors and your readers.

Step C: Plan and write the body of your story

Consider whether the body of your story can be presented better in inverted pyramid arrangement or in a chronological order. Usually, you will have no alternative, since most news stories follow the inverted pyramid plan. However, the story you are preparing might be better presented wholly or partially in chronological order; therefore, this choice should be considered. Assuming that you will arrange your facts in an inverted pyramid, presenting them in the order of descending importance, you will:

⇾ **First, explain your key thought**: In the paragraphs following the lead, give details about your key thought. This is the most newsworthy idea in your story, so it should be explained first.

⇾ **Then, explain other facts in the order of their news value**: If your story is woven around a unified topic, all of the body will be devoted to amplifying and explaining your key thought. Within these paragraphs you should be careful to arrange the details in the order of descending importance. However, at least half the news stories you write will include facts not closely related to your key thought, and often not related to one another. Determine the news value of these facts and write the most important ones first.

Step D: Use good newspaper paragraphs

You have learned in English classes that a paragraph is a carefully organised group of sentences about the same general subject, and that a well-written paragraph includes a topic sentence which gives the main thought of the paragraph. You will need to keep this definition in mind as you write newspaper paragraphs, but you must also consider the special demands of a news page.

⇾ **A newspaper paragraph is about one topic or one aspect of a topic**: This holds true for any paragraphing you may do, whether for formal composition or news writing. Consider only one topic as you write a paragraph.

A newspaper paragraph must be short: Because of narrow newspaper column, paragraphs must be brief to improve page appearance. A very useful length is 30 to 40 words – about two sentences. Paragraphs should seldom exceed 75 words. Even long lists of names should be broken into short paragraphs. One of the rules of newspaper makeup is that white space around a story makes it more attractive to the reader.

A newspaper paragraph starts with significant words: As you write paragraphs, consider carefully the subject matter you plan to include. Just as in your lead, put the key thought of each paragraph at the beginning and describe it in live, interesting, hard-working words. Most of the steps that you follow in constructing good lead paragraphs will help you build successful paragraphs in the body of your story.

Step E: Use direct quotes to brighten your story

Quotations add variety, informality, and interest to your story. By using them, you can include in a natural way the names of your news sources and other important people, as well as additional names that you might overlook in preparing your story. Furthermore, quotes allow you to print opinions without editorialising, that is, without making them appear to be your own ideas. And finally, quotes draw the reader into your story because the person quoted seems to be speaking directly to him.

The customary way of including quotes in news stories is to use them in alternate paragraphs; for example, you might present a paragraph of straight facts followed by one of quotation, next a paragraph of straight facts followed by one of quotation, next a paragraph of straight facts, then one of quotation. Vary this plan to fit the paragraph of straight facts, then one of quotation. Vary this plan to fit the particular story you are writing.

Some caution is necessary in employing direct quotes. When you put someone's words in quotation marks, you become directly responsible to that individual for the accuracy of the remarks you print. You and your newspaper could get into serious trouble if you misquoted someone on a controversial issue, even by printing a single wrong word. The only safe way to use a quotation is to copy it exactly in the words of the person who says it. This requires extra attention while you are interviewing. Listen closely for short statements which may be worth quoting, and take careful notes. Develop your own system of 'shorthand': abbreviate words, leave out articles, conjunctions, and prepositions, invent symbols for words and names you use frequently. Your news source will usually be willing to wait while you copy short statements, if you do not take too long.

Step F: Name your authority

If you begin news leads like those above, one can almost hear your readers asking the question, "Who says so?" Statements of this kind need an authority to back them up – the names of the people who said them, and perhaps when and why the statements were made.

Generally, you must include an authority with three kinds of stories: announcements of special or unusual future events, announcements of changes from established custom, and statements of personal opinion. You should also name your authority for any news that you do not obtain from personal observation, for instance, that given to you by a news source. This protects you in case the information is incorrect. Then, too, by printing the name of your news source, you say "Thanks", and improve your chances of obtaining more news from him for the next issue.

The authority for a story based on an opinion or a controversial statement should be a part of your lead, but it is never the key thought. It belongs at the end of the last sentence in your lead. When you use the name of your authority in stories other than the three special kinds listed above, the name belongs in a later paragraph.

Step G: When you have finished stating facts, stop writing!

Check your story for the 5 W and 1 H facts. Whether or not these were included in your lead – and in most stories you will not use all six in the lead – usually all should appear somewhere in your story. Make sure you have answered all necessary and important questions.

When you have written the last fact of your story, write -30-, which means "The End," in the centre of the next line on your paper:

- 30 -

Resist the temptation to add a conclusion. A news story needs no summary at its end. Your story does not gain by having a moral pointed out – if it had one in the first place. It is childish to add an advertising 'plug', such as, "Let's everyone come out to see this fine show." This is one of the hardest, yet simplest, decisions for beginning reporters to make.

Other Important Things that Must be Kept in Mind while Writing for a Newspaper

1. Keep your sentences simple

Limit most sentences to one clause. (Each clause contains a subject and verb; an additional clause in a sentence starts with a word like and, but, who, which, or that.) Extra clauses can be made into new sentences. A few sentences containing more than one clause add variety, but many complicated sentences make your reader lose interest because they are too hard to understand.

2. Use simple words

Simple words help your reader understand the stories you write. Avoid using complicated or unfamiliar terms. Your vocabulary does not have to be large. Everyday words are best for news stories.

Also ensure that each word in your sentence should convey a definite idea and means what you intend.

The use of simple everyday words will ensure that your reader gets the idea you are trying to convey.

3. Don't use too many words

A common fault among beginning reporters is the use of too many words to express an idea. Learn to keep your paragraphs short and to the point. Readers don't like reading long paragraphs.

4. Use nouns as modifiers

To shorten sentences and state facts directly, news English often uses a noun as a modifying word. This process eliminates many prepositional phrases, which slow up reading.

5. Use colourful words

Certain topics lend themselves readily to the use of colourful words. Descriptive or action stories are especially adaptable, but all your stories will be improved if your sentences draw word pictures.

As you write your sentences, visualise your story. Give your reader a vivid impression by selecting bright, active, meaningful phrases. Your descriptive terms need not be unusual; choose common words, readily available in your vocabulary and easily understood by your readers.

6. Use verbs for description

Professional news writers find this trick effective to shorten sentences and turn out vivid copy. Verbs, which are active words in themselves, will furnish live and colourful description, replacing duller adjectives and adverbs. One way of doing this is to take the thought from a modifier and use it as the main verb of the sentence.

Another method is to use participles in place of adjectives, or infinitives in place of weaker phrases or clauses. These verb forms, like all verbs, carry a strong element of action.

7. Personalise your news

People make news. To report news effectively, you must tell about the people responsible for it. Use names in your stories whenever you can. Names sell newspapers. Names are what readers want in their news!

Your story must be more than a list of names, of course. It is "What happened?" that makes news in the first place. But "Who did it?" is the next question to answer. If a name is important enough, place it in the lead. If not, introduce it when it may be included in a natural way. A quotation is one successful method of adding names.

8. Learn to distinguish between fact and opinion

Every reporter must acquire the ability to distinguish between fact and opinion.

A fact represents an actual event or situation. It is a statement of what took place, or what plans were made, or what someone said. When you write a story about a future occurrence, you actually report what someone told you, or what has been planned. You cannot argue about a fact. If there is a discussion about what happened, it really concerns what people believe took place; in other words, they are discussing their opinions. The truth of the matter remains unchanged, even though no one may know exactly what that truth is.

An opinion is what someone thinks or wishes. That person may be your news source, or another individual, or you as the reporter. What someone said may include opinion and fact. It is a fact that he made the statement, but what he said may have been his personal opinion, or it may have been a true statement concerning what happened.

9. Never editorialise in a news story

Remember you are a reporter and your job is to report. It is the job of the newspaper editors to state their opinions in editorials. The newspaper reader does not want to be bothered with what the reporter thinks about a news event; he wants to know what happened. If he wishes an opinion, he will turn to the editorial page for thoughtful comment by an expert who is paid to analyse and criticise. The editor's opinion is far more valuable to the reader than that of the unknown reporter.

10. State the opinions of news sources

Opinions may be included in news stories, but they must be the opinions of news sources, and not of reporters. Opinions are identified as such by stating them as quotations, direct or indirect. Direct quotes may be used only when you copied exactly what your news sources said. All quotations should be checked with your source after your story is written, to verify the accuracy of your statements.

11. State your facts accurately!

Never try to twist and change the facts as according to your needs. The readers will never trust you if you do that and your integrity as journalist will always be on the line. State your facts accurately and as they are.

12. Tell the whole truth

Be sure to tell the whole truth about a story. Do not hide any thing. Remember the people has right to know about everything that goes around them.

13. Ask yourself – which is the right word?

News English has certain policies to help you select the right word and avoid the wrong one. Study the following sections to be sure you are following newspaper style.

13a. Never use first or second person pronouns

Except in direct quotations, news stories are impersonal. They are written in the third person; first and second person pronouns such as I, me, we, us, and you are not used. The presence of one of these pronouns suggests that the reporter may have drifted into editorialising. Their effort is to bring the writers or readers personally into the story.

Once in a long while, you may need to use first or second person to tell your story. In these cases, it is best to do so and not use a stilted expression like "this reporter" in place of 'I' or 'me'. This might happen in an interview story when the reporter asks a question, or in an eye-witness account. But these are not common news stories, and each would have a by-line showing the name of its writer.

In editorials, the first person plural (we or us) is used, even though you may be expressing the opinion of one person only. This custom does not apply to any other kind of newspaper articles.

13b. Use pronouns properly

All news stories should be written in the third person, except for direct quotations. But even third person pronouns may be used incorrectly. Particular troublemakers are they and them. Every pronoun must refer to an antecedent noun. If a pronoun refers to the wrong noun, the meaning becomes obscure.

Another problem with third person pronouns arises when you employ the plural form of a pronoun to refer to a singular antecedent.

Worse, yet a pronoun may be used without any apparent antecedent.

13c. State time correctly

Properly naming the day that an event happens is not difficult. However, a common error made by the beginning reporter is to think of the day he writes the story, rather than the day it will be read. Telling about an event that is to happen next Wednesday, for a paper published next Thursday, he mistakenly writes 'next Wednesday' instead of 'yesterday'. Or, for an event that will take place two weeks for now, but only five days after the paper is published, he writes 'Tuesday, April 19', instead of "next Thursday."

To state time correctly, use this guide

- Establish in your mind the day your story will be read. Figure forward or back from that day to the time of your news event.
- Write 'today', 'yesterday', or 'tomorrow' to name the day the paper is issued, the day before, or the day after.
- For events happening within a week before or after the publication date, state the day. Write 'last Tuesday' or 'next Tuesday', if there could be confusion as to which you mean.
- For any other time, use the date. Write 'March 12', not 'March 12th', nor 'the 12th of March'. Do not include the year unless your date is more than a year away.

13d. Names must be spelled correctly

It cannot be repeated too often that 'names make news'. A reader is delighted when his name is printed. But that delight turns to disappointment, and even to anger, if his name is misspelled. The following steps may help you get names right:

⇨ Learn the correct name when securing the story. Take time to copy it accurately. If it is given orally, ask for the spelling.

⇨ Look up the name if there is any doubt. Your news desk or morgue usually has a directory. The extra time is well worth the effort!

⇨ When the name is correct, type or print it carefully – don't write it – in your copy. Then there can be no excuse for typists' or printers' mistakes, and proofreaders can accurately check your copy against the proof.

BROADCASTING

"An organisation called Search for Extra Terrestrial Investigation (SETI) broadcasts every day without break messages to the outer space. These messages contain information about humanity, songs by groups such as Beatles etc. The message is broadcast in the hope that some day some where an Extra Terrestrial World would hear it and reply. . ."

Broadcasting

Broadcasting is the distribution of audio and/or video signals which transmit programmes to an audience. The audience may be the general public or a relatively large sub-audience, such as children or young adults. There is a wide variety of broadcasting systems, all of which have different capabilities. The smallest broadcasting systems are institutional public address systems, which transmit spoken messages and music within, for example, a school or hospital, and low-powered radio or television stations transmitting programmes to a small local area. National radio and television broadcasters have nationwide coverage, using re-transmitter towers, satellite systems, and cable distribution. Satellite radio and television broadcasting can cover areas as wide as entire continents, while Internet channels can distribute text or streamed music and speech worldwide. Individuals can also make use of Internet services to stream or podcast sound or video.

The sequencing of content in a broadcast is called a schedule. As with all technological endeavours, a number of technical terms and slang have developed. A list of these terms can be found at list of broadcasting terms[97] .

97. Incorporated in the Glossary

Television and radio programmes are distributed through radio broadcasting or cable, often both simultaneously. By coding signals and having decoding equipment in homes, the latter also enables subscription-based channels and pay-per-view services.

The term 'broadcast' originally referred to the sowing of seeds by scattering them over a wide field. It was adopted by early radio engineers from the mid-western United States to refer to the analogous dissemination of radio signals. Broadcasting forms a very large segment of the mass media. Broadcasting to a very narrow range of audience is called narrowcasting.

Economically there are a few ways in which stations are able to continually broadcast. Each differs in the method by which stations are funded:

1. In-kind donations of time and skills by volunteers (common with community broadcasters)

2. Direct government payments or operation of public broadcasters

3. Indirect government payments, such as radio and television licences

4. Grants from foundations or business entities

5. Selling advertising or sponsorships

6. Public subscription or membership

Broadcasters may rely on a combination of these business models. For example, National Public Radio, a non-commercial network within the United States, receives grants from the Corporation for Public Broadcasting (which in turn receives funding from the US government), by public membership, and by selling 'extended credits' to corporations.

Recorded broadcasts and live broadcasts

One can record and produce live broadcasts. The former allows correcting errors, and removing superfluous or undesired material, rearranging it, applying slow-motion and repetitions, and other

A TV Studio Control Room in Olympia, Washington

techniques to enhance the programme. However, some live events like sports telecasts can include some of the aspects including slow-motion clips of important goals/hits etc in between the live telecast.

American radio network broadcasters habitually forbade pre-recorded broadcasts in the 1930s and 1940s requiring radio programmes played for the Eastern and Central time zones to be repeated three hours later for the Pacific time zone. This restriction was dropped for special occasions, as in the case of the German dirigible airship Hindenburg at Lakehurst, New Jersey in 1937. During World War II, pre-recorded broadcasts from war correspondents were allowed on US radio. In addition, American radio programmes were recorded for playback by Armed Forces Radio stations around the world.

A disadvantage of recording first is that the public may know the outcome of an event from another source, which may be a spoiler. In addition, prerecording prevents live announcers from deviating from an officially-approved script, as occurred with propaganda broadcasts from Germany in the 1940s and with Radio Moscow in the 1980s.

Many events are advertised as being live, although they are often 'recorded live' (sometimes called 'live-to-tape'). This is particularly true of performances of musical artists on radio when they visit for an in-studio concert performance. This intentional blurring of the distinction between live and recorded media is viewed with chagrin among many music lovers. Similar situations have sometimes appeared in television ('The Cosby Show is recorded in front of a live studio audience').

A broadcast may be distributed through several physical means. If coming directly from the studio at a single radio or TV station, it is simply sent through the air chain to the transmitter and thence from the antenna on the tower out to the world. Programming may also come through a communications satellite, played either live or recorded for later transmission. Networks of stations may simulcast the same programming at the same time, originally via microwave link, now usually by satellite.

Distribution to stations or networks may also be through physical media, such as analog or digital videotape, CD, DVD, and sometimes other formats. Usually these are included in another broadcast, such as when electronic news gathering returns a story to the station for inclusion on a news programme.

The final leg of broadcast distribution is how the signal gets to the listener or viewer. It may come over the air as with a radio station or TV station to an antenna and receiver, or may come through cable TV or cable radio (or 'wireless cable') via the station or directly from a network. The Internet may also bring either radio or TV to the recipient, especially with multicasting allowing the signal and bandwidth to be shared.

The term 'broadcast network' is often used to distinguish networks that broadcast an over-the-air television signal that can be received using a television antenna from so-called networks that are broadcast only via cable or satellite television. The term 'broadcast television' can refer to the programming of such networks.

Legal Definitions

The Copyright, Designs and Patents Act 1988 defines a broadcast as a transmission by wireless telegraphy of visual images, sounds, or other information which is capable of lawful reception by the public or which is made for presentation to the public. It thus covers radio, television, teletext et al.

Broadcast-Safe

Broadcast-safe or broadcast legal or legal signal is a term used in the broadcast industry to define video and audio compliant with the technical or regulatory broadcast requirements of the target area or region the feed might be broadcasting. In the United States, the Federal Communications Commission (FCC) is the regulatory authority, in most of Europe, standards are set by the European Broadcasting Union (EBU).

Broadcast Safe Standard Definition video

Broadcast safe 625 video

Broadcast safe standards for 625 lines of Standard Definition (Inaccurately referred to as PAL, a colour encoding that is usually used with such systems) video are:

1. Commonly used No. of Vertical Lines = 625 (576 visible active video)
2. Commonly used Frame rate = 25 Hz (25 frame/s)
3. Commonly used TV Resolution = 720 x 576 (576i)
4. Black levels = 0 mV or 0 IRE
5. White levels (Chrominance amplitude):

a. 700 mV p-p or 100 IRE - 100% intensity setting which corresponds to 100.0.100.0 colour bars.

b. 75% intensity corresponding to 100.0.75.0 colour bars, also referred to as EBU Bars.

Broadcast safe 525 video

Broadcast safe standards for 525 lines of Standard Definition (NTSC) video are:

1. Commonly used Frame rate = 30 frame/s black and white, 29.97 frame/s colour

2. Black level = 7.5 IRE for NTSC in the US, 0 IRE in Japan.

3. Blanking level = 0 IRE

4. White levels = 100 IRE, 714 mV

5. Maximum signal level = 120 IRE

6. Minimum signal level = -20 IRE

Non-Standard Video

Video gear aimed at consumers sometimes produces video signals which are not broadcast safe. Usually this is to reduce the cost of the gear, and because a non-standard video signal in the home might not create the problems that one might find in a broadcast facility. Some potential flaws:

1. VHS and 8 mm: These formats are prone to time-base error, and in their non high-band versions transmit noticeably less detail and more noise than is normal for standard definition TV.

2. Older videogame systems: Before the sixth generation of videogame consoles, most videogames generated a video signal lacking the half scan line needed to make interlace happen. This subtle simplification caused NTSC sets to scan 240p instead of 480i, with similar results for PAL. While this actually improved picture quality for the kind of images that videogames of this era generated, such a signal would cause problems in a broadcast environment.

*VGA to NTSC converters: VGA runs at true 60 frame/s, not the slightly slower rate of NTSC. Some low cost VGA to NTSC converters could not correct for this, and would generate an NTSC signal with accelerated timing. Most TVs had no problem displaying this, but such a signal would rapidly deteriorate if recorded onto analog VCRs that are unable to compensate for the increased framerate.

Broadcast Safe High Definition Video

Digital broadcasting is very different from analog. The NTSC and PAL standards describe both transmission of the signal and how the electrical signal is converted into an image. In digital, there is a separation between the subject of how data is to be transmitted from tower to TV, and the subject of what content that data might contain. While data transmission is likely to be a fixed and consistent affair, the content could vary from High Definition video one hour, to SD multicasting the next, and even to non-video datacasting. In the US, 8VSB transmits the data, while MPEG-2 encodes pictures and sound.

Dead Air

Dead air is a phenomenon whereby a broadcast which normally carries audio or video unintentionally becomes silent or blank (also known as unmodulated carrier). The term is most often used in cases where programme material comes to an unexpected halt, either through operator error or for technical reasons, although it is also used in cases where a broadcaster has 'dried up'. It is the duty of all concerned to rectify the problem quickly. In many parts of the world dead air is among the worst things a broadcaster can do.

This is different from being off-the-air. When a station is off the air, the transmitter is not active and there is no signal at all. Dead air is where a carrier signal is being transmitted, but there is no modulation of that signal.

In the United Kingdom, any radio station which transmits dead air for more than ten minutes without rectifying the situation, broadcasting an announcement, or otherwise warning its listeners, can be penalised and may be fined up to £25,000 per minute by the independent regulator and competition authority for UK communications industries, Ofcom.

Dead air can also apply to television broadcasting, generally when a television channel has an interruption to its output, resulting in a blank screen or in the case of digital television, a frozen image, until output is restored or an apology message is broadcast.

Having dead air during commercials or sponsorship announcements can cost networks considerable advertising revenue.

Examples

An example of dead air was a Chris Evans radio transmission for the British Virgin Radio station. As a promotional stunt, Evans did not arrive for work, and his show went to air carrying nothing for about twenty five minutes.

Another case was BBC Radio 4's failure to broadcast Big Ben's midnight chimes on New Year's Day 2003; after announcing the chimes, a technical error caused the station to fall silent for a minute. This was caused by the correct feed not being fed up. Ironically, the chimes were supposed to be coming via a new link which the BBC had installed in Westminster to avoid dead air.

On September 11, 1987, Dan Rather walked off the set of the CBS *Evening News* when a late running US Open tennis match threatened to delay the start of his news broadcast. The match then ended sooner than expected but Rather was gone. The network broadcast six minutes of dead air before Rather was found and returned to the studio. There was considerable criticism of Rather for the incident.

Outside Broadcasting

Outside Broadcasting is the production of television or radio programmes (typically to cover news and sports events) from a mobile television studio. This mobile control room is known as an 'Outside Broadcasting Van', 'OB Van', 'Scanner' (a BBC term), 'mobile unit', 'remote truck', 'live truck', or ' production truck'. Signals from cameras and microphones come into the OB Van for processing and transmission. The term 'OB' is almost unheard of in the United States.

A typical OB Van is usually divided into 5 parts.

1. The first and largest part is the production area where the director, technical director, assistant director, character generator operator (sometimes called a chyron operator) and producers usually sit in front a wall of monitors. This area is very similar to a Production control room. The technical director sits in front of the video switcher. The monitors show all the video feeds from various sources, including computer graphics, cameras, video tapes, or slow motion replay machines. The wall of monitors also contains a preview monitor showing what could be the next source on air (does not have to be depending on how the video switcher is set up) and a program monitor that shows the feed currently going to air or being recorded. The dirty feed (feed with graphics) is what is actually transmitted back to the central studio that is controlling the outside broadcast. A clean feed (without the graphics) could be sent to other trucks for use in their production. The video switcher is usually operated by 1 person called the Technical Director or Vison Mixer in Europe. That person is responsible for putting all the video sources to air as directed to. Behind the directors there is usually a desk with monitors for the editors to operate. It is essential that the

directors and editor are in connection with each other during events, so that replays and slow-motion shots can be selected and aired.

2. The second part of a van is for the audio engineer; it has a sound mixer (being fed with all the various audio feeds, on-field microphones, etc. The audio engineer can control which channels are added to the output and will follow instructions from the director. The audio engineer normally also has a dirty feed monitor to help with the synchronisation of sound and video.

3. The third part of the van is video tape. The tape area has a collection of video tape machines (VTRs) and may also house additional power supplies or computer equipment.

4. The fourth part is the video control area where the professional video cameras are controlled by 1 or 2 people to make sure that the iris is at the correct exposure and that all the cameras look the same.

5. The fifth part is transmission where the signal is monitored by and engineered for quality control purposes and is transmitted or sent to other trucks.

A BBC Radio Outside Broadcasting Van at New College, Oxford. Photo by BBC

Television Studio

A television studio is an installation in which television or video productions take place, either for live television, for recording live to tape, or for the acquisition of raw footage for postproduction. The design of a studio is similar to, and derived from, movie studios, with a few amendments for the special requirements of television production. A professional television studio generally has several rooms, which are kept separate for noise and practicality reasons. These rooms are connected via intercom, and personnel will be divided among these workplaces.

Studio Floor

The studio floor is the actual stage on which the actions that will be recorded take place. A studio floor has the following characteristics and installations:

Al Jazeera News Room Studio Floor Under Construction

1. Decoration and/or sets
2. Cameras on pedestals
3. Microphones
4. Lighting rigs and the associated controlling equipment.
5. Several video monitors for visual feedback from the production control room
6. A small public address system for communication
7. A glass window between PCR and studio floor for direct visual contact is usually desired, but not always possible

While a production is in progress, the following people work in the studio floor:

1. The on-screen talent themselves, and any guests – the subjects of the show.
2. A floor director, who has overall charge of the studio area, and who relays timing and other information from the director.
3. One or more camera operators who operate the television cameras, though in some instances these can also be operated from PCR using remote heads.

4. Possibly a teleprompter operator, especially if this is a news broadcast.

Production Control Room

The production control room (also known as the 'gallery' or Studio Control Room (SCR) is the place in a television studio in which the composition of the outgoing programme takes place. Facilities in a PCR include:

1. A video monitor wall, with monitors for program, preview, videotape machines, cameras, graphics and other video sources

2. Switcher a device where all video sources are controlled and taken to air. Also known as a special-effects generator

3. Audio mixing console and other audio equipment such as effects devices

4. Character generator creates the majority of the names and full screen graphics that are inserted into the program

5. Digital video effects and/or still frame devices (if not integrated in the vision mixer)

6. Technical director's station, with waveform monitors, vectorscopes and the camera control units or remote control panels for the camera control units (CCUs)

7. VTRs may also be located in the PCR, but are also often found in the central machine room

Production Control Room for The News Hour with Jim Lehrer, taken November 7, 2005 during an interview with Gen. Peter Pace.

A Vinten Remote Camera Control Unit Station at the Al Jazeera SCR in London

Master Control Room

The master control room houses equipment that is too noisy or runs too hot for the production control room. It also makes sure that wire lengths and installation requirements keep within manageable lengths, since most high-quality wiring runs only between devices in this room. This can include:

1. The actual circuitry and connection boxes of the vision mixer, DVE and character generator devices.
2. Camera control units.
3. VTRs.
4. Patch panels for reconfiguration of the wiring between the various pieces of equipment.

In a broadcast station in the US, master control room or 'MCR' is the place where the on-air signal is controlled. It may include controls to play back programmes and commercials, switch local or network feeds, record satellite feeds and monitor the transmitter(s). The description of an MCR given above usually refers to an equipment rack room, which is usually separate from the MCR itself. The term 'studio' usually refers to a place where a particular local programme is originated. If the programme is broadcast live, the signal goes from the production control room to MCR and then out to the transmitter.

Other Facilities

A Make-up Room, at the Theatre Royal, Wexford, Ireland

A television studio usually has other rooms with no technical requirements beyond programme and audio monitors. Among them are:

1. one or more make-up and changing rooms

2. a reception area for crew, talent, and visitors, commonly called the green room.

Television Crew

- Pre-production
- Director
- Producer
- Casting Director
- Researcher
- Writer
- Make-up Artist
- Production Designer
- Costume Designer
- Production
- Floor Manager
- Assistant Floor Manager
- Camera Operator Cinematographer
- Production Manager
- Technical Director
- Boom Operator
- Gaffer
- Dolly Grip
- Key Grip
- Runner
- Stunt Coordinator
- Gallery/Control Room Team

Television Director - Director

Production Assistant

Vision Mixer or Switcher

Aston, Chyron, or Graphics Operator

VT Operator

Post-production

Editor

Sound Editor

Foley Artist

Publicist

Composer

Title Sequence Designer

Post-Production Runner

Specialist Editors

Special Effects Coordinator

ADR Editor

The Matte Artist or Bluescreen Director

Television Crew

Television crew positions are derived from those of film crew, but with several differences.

Pre-production

Everything before the shooting of the film is known as the pre-production stage. People involved in this stage include the director, the producer, the scriptwriter, the researcher, the set designer, the make-up artist, and the costume designer.

Director

A television director is usually responsible for directing the actors and other filmed aspects of a television production. His role differs from that of a film director because the major creative control will likely belong to the producer. In general, the actors and other regular artists on a show will be familiar enough with their roles that the director's input will be confined to technical issues. The director is responsible for all creative aspects of a movie. The director would most likely assist with hiring the cast (and possibly the crew). He helps decide on the locations, creates a plan of shooting, and sets a mental layout of shot by shot in his mind's eye. During shooting, the director supervises the overall project, manages shots, and keeps the assignment on budget, and schedule. Although the director holds much power, he is second in command after the producer, who ultimately hired him (unless he holds both positions). Some directors are also the producers of their programme, and, with the approval of the funding studio, have a much tighter grip on what makes the final cut than directors usually have.

Producer

In the entertainment industry, a television producer (compare to film producer) is generally in charge of, or helps to coordinate, the financial, legal, administrative, technological and artistic aspects of a production. In television, a television producer can be given one of the following titles:

Associate Producer

Performs limited producing functions under the authority of a producer; often in charge of the day-to-day running of a production. Usually the producer's head assistant, although the task can differ. They are frequently a connection between everyone making shooting possible (the production team) and the people involved after filming to finalise the production, and get it publicised (the post-production team). Occasionally credit for this role is given to the product's financial backer, or the person who originally brought the assignment to the producer.

Assistant Producer (AP)

In the UK, this is the closest role to that of a film director. An Assistant Producer often doubles as an experienced researcher, and takes direct charge of the creative content and action within a programme. The title of Director is usually reserved only for drama productions and those which bear most similarity to films, or for those who control a multi-camera shoot from the gallery.

Coordinating Producer

Coordinates the work of two or more producers working separately on one or more productions.

Co-producer

Typically performs producing functions in tandem with one or more co-producers (working as a team, rather than separately on different aspects of the production).

Executive Producer

Supervises one or more producers in all aspects of their work; sometimes the initiator of the production; usually the ultimate authority on the creative and business aspects of the production (except to the extent that a film director retains creative control). If the title is designated correctly, the executive producer would arrange for the project's financial backing and attempt to maintain a well-budgeted production. Far too often, the executive producer's role is given falsely to a power player in the equation, sometimes an actor, an actor's agent, or someone else who aided in the production of the project.

Line Producer

Supervises the physical aspects of the production (not the creative aspects), including personnel, technology, budget, and scheduling. The line producer oversees the project's budget. This involves operating costs such as salaries, production costs, and everyday equipment rental costs. The line producer works with the production manager on costs and expenditure.

Segment Producer

Produces one or more components of a multipart production.

Supervising Producer

Supervises one or more producers in some or all aspects of their work; usually works under the authority of an executive producer.

Casting Director

Casts the actors.... Usually one of the first crew members attached to the project. In fact, when a Television Pilot is initially cast the Executive Producer and Casting Director are often the only crew members.

Researcher

Researchers research the project ahead of shooting time to increase truth, factual content, creative content, original ideas, background information, and sometimes performs minor searches such as flight details, location conditions, accommodation details, etc. It is their task to inform the director, producer, and writer of all ideas, and knowledge related to what task is being undertaken, or what a scene/event/prop/backdrop needs to be included to make the show factual and ultimately more believable.

Writer

The writer creates and moulds an original story, or adapts other written, told, or acted stories for production of a television show. Their finished work is called a script. A script may also have been a contribution of many writers, so it is the Writers Guild of America's task to designate who gets the credit as being 'the Writer'[98] . 'Written By' in the credits, is a Writers Guild of America assigned terminology meaning 'Original Story and Screenplay By'. A screenplay or script is a blueprint for producing a motion picture, and a teleplay is the replica for a television show. Writers can also come under the category of screenwriters. Screenwriters, (or script writers), are authors who write the screenplays from which productions are made just as a writer does. Many of them also work as 'script doctors', attempting to change scripts to suit directors or studios. Script-doctoring can be quite lucrative, especially for the better known writers. Most professional screenwriters are unionised and are represented by organisations such as the Writers Guild of America.

Make-up Artist

A professional makeup artist is usually a beautician, who applies makeup to anyone appearing on screen. They concentrate on the area above the chest, the face, the top of the head, the fingers, hands, arms, and elbows. Their role is to manipulate an actor's on-screen appearance whether it makes them look more youthful, larger, older, or in some cases monstrous. There are also body makeup artist who concentrate their abilities on the body rather than the head. Makeup itself is material to enhance the beauty of the human body, but can also change the appearance, disguise, or costume someone. Along with the makeup artists, the hair stylists, costume designers, and dress technicians all combine their effort into transforming an actor into a character, or a person into a presenter.

Production Designer

The production designer is the person with the responsibility of the visual appearance of a production. They design, plan, organise, and arrange set design, equipment availability, as well as the on-screen appearance a production will have. A production designer is often referred to also as the set designer, or scenic designer. They are trained professionals, often with MFA degrees in scenic design.

The set designer is responsible for collaborating with the theatre director to create an environment for the production and then communicating the details of this environment to the technical director, scenic artist and props master. Scenic designers are responsible for creating scale models of the scenery as well as scale drawings. The set designer also takes instructions from the art director to create the appearance of the stage, and design its technical assembly. The

98. In the United States for example. In India we do not have any such organisation.

art director, who can also be the production designer, plans and oversees the formation of settings for a project. They are fully aware and conscious of art and design styles, including architecture and interior design. They also work with the cinematographer to accomplish the precise appearance for the project.

Costume Designer

The costume designer makes all the clothing and costumes worn by all the actors on screen, as well as designing, planning, and organising the construction of the garments down to the fabric, colours, and sizes. They greatly contribute to the appearance of the film, and set a particular mood, time, feeling, or genre. They alter the overall appearance of a project with their designs and constructions, including impact on the style of the project, and how the audience interprets the show's characters.

Production

Everything, while the shooting of the film is in progress, is part of the so-called 'production' stage. People involved in this stage of production include the cinematographer, production manager, the technical director, the boom operator, the gaffer, the dolly grip, the key grip and the stunt coordinator.

Floor Manager

The Floor Manager is the Director's representative on the studio floor, and is responsible for giving instruction and direction to crew, cast and guests. It is closest to the role of an Assistant Director, as the job frequently entails barking orders to keep a production moving to schedule. The Floor Manager is always in direct contact with the Director via talkback in the gallery.

Assistant Floor Manager

An Assistant Floor Manager (frequently abbreviated to AFM) is responsible for setting a stage and prompting contributors on the studio floor and ensuring that everyone knows their place in the script, freeing the Floor Manager for other duties. They often oversee a team of Runners. Increasingly, Assistant Floor Managers are being asked to assist with the design and preparation of props, as well as setting and resetting the action on the studio floor.

Camera Operator/Cinematographer

As the head member of the camera crew, the camera operator uses the camera as coached by the director. They are accountable for maintaining the required action is correctly filmed in the frame, and needs to react instinctively as the proceedings take place. If the camera operator is also a cinematographer, he also helps establish the theme and appearance of the show. The cinematographer or director of photography regulates the lighting for every scene, is responsible for framing some shots, chooses the lenses to be used, decides on film stock and guarantees that the visual appearance of the project follows to the director's initial foresight. However, the cinematographer would usually not manoeuvre the camera on the set, as this is usually the exclusive role of a camera operator.

Production Manager

The production manager performs deals concerned with business about the crew, and organises the technical needs of the production. This would involve many things ranging from gaining the correct equipment with the exact technical requirements, to arranging accommodation for the cast and crew. The production manager reports their expenses and needs to the line producer.

Technical Director

In a production control room (PCR), the technical director has overall responsibility for the operations. The technical director is responsible for the proper working of all the equipment in the PCR. They also match the quality and the output of all the cameras on the studio floor through the camera control units. It is their responsibility to supervise all the other crew members working in the PCR. The technical director also coordinates the working of the whole crew and looks into any technical problem which arises before, during or after the shooting of a project.

Boom Operator

The boom operator is an assistant of the sound engineer or 'sound mixer'. The main responsibility of the boom operator is microphone placement, sometimes using a 'fishpole' with a microphone attached to the end and sometimes, when the situation permits, using a 'boom' (most often a 'fisher boom') which is a special piece of equipment that the operator stands on and that allows precise control of the microphone at a much greater distance away from the actors. They will also place wireless microphones on actors when it is necessary. The boom operator is part of the sound crew, who manages to keep the microphone boom, near to the action, but away from the camera frame, so that it never appears on screen, but allows the microphone to pursue the actors as they move. They work closely with the production sound mixer, or sound recordist, to record all sound while filming including background noises, dialogue, sound effects, and silence.

Gaffer

The gaffer is the head electrician at the production set, and is in charge of lighting the stage in accordance with the direction of the cinematographer. In television, the term chief lighting director is often used instead of gaffer, and sometimes the technical director himself lights the studio set. The gaffer reports to the Director of Photography (DoP), Lighting Director (LD) or Lighting Designer, and will usually have an assistant called a Best Boy and a crew of rigging electricians.

Dolly Grip

In cinematography, the dolly grip is the individual who places and moves the dolly track were it is required, and then pushes and pulls the dolly along that track while filming. A dolly grip must work closely with the camera crew to perfect these complex movements during rehearsals. For moving shots, dolly grips may also push the wheeled platform holding the microphone and boom operator. The dolly is a cart on which the tripod and camera (and occasionally the camera crew) rest on. It makes the camera able to move without bumps and visual interruptions from start to finish while the camera is filming. It is commonly used to follow beside an actor to give the audience the sense of walking with the actor, or as the actor.

Key Grip

The key grip is the head grip on the production set. It is a grip's task to create shadow effects with lights and occasionally manoeuvre camera cranes, dollies and platforms while receiving direction from the cinematographer. The term grip is used in slightly different ways in American and British or Australian film making. In the British and Australian film industries, a grip is responsible for camera mounting and support, which can include anything beyond a basic tripod. Lighting in British and Australian film-making is headed by the gaffer, who is also part of the camera department. Grips can also be the people that do the laborious work on sets. These types of grips push, pull, roll, and lift various pieces of equipment under the watchful eye of the television director, producer, or art director.

Runner

Runners are the most junior members of a television crew. They are responsible for fetching and carrying and doing most of the donkey-work of a production.

Their role is usually to support anyone who needs help in a variety of ways, until such time as they have learned enough to assume more responsibilities.

Stunt Coordinator

Where the programme requires a stunt, and involves the use of stunt performers, the stunt coordinator will arrange the casting and performance of the stunt, working closely with the director.

Gallery/Control Room Team

The following crew positions are only utilised on a multi-camera production. The Gallery or 'Control Room' is a separate darkened area away from the studio floor where the action can be viewed across multiple monitors and controlled from a single source.

Television Director – Director

Unlike the film counterpart, a Director in television usually refers to the Gallery (or Control Room) Director, who is responsible for the creative look of a production through selecting which shots to use at any given moment. The Director views the action on the studio floor through a bank of screens, each one linked to one of the studio cameras, while issuing instructions down to the Floor Manager. They also control the Gallery area, calling for sound rolls, on-screen graphics (Astons) and video rolls (VT's). Some directors also work more closely with on-camera talent and others also act as both producer and director.

Production Assistant

Commonly referred to simply as the PA, the Production Assistant assumes a prompting role in the Gallery or Control Room. They are responsible for communication with the broadcasting channel during a live show, counting down the time before transmission aloud to the crew via the studio microphone. They also count down time remaining for sections of a programme, such as an interview or an advert break. Prior to a production, the PA is responsible for preparing and timing the script, noting pre-recorded inserts, sound effects and suchlike, and for clearing copyright and other administrative issues.

Vision Mixer or Switcher

The Vision Mixer is responsible for the actual switching between different video sources, such as camera shots and video inserts. They also maintain colour and contrast balance between the studio cameras. Vision mixer is, confusingly, also the name of the equipment which the Vision Mixer operates.

Aston, Chyron, or Graphics Operator

The Aston Operator prepares and displays on-screen graphics.

VT Operator

The VT Operator cues and prepares video inserts into a programme. Heavily used in sports programming, they are also responsible for action replays and quickly editing highlights while a show is in progress.

Post-production

Everything after the shooting of the film is post production. People involved in this stage of production include the editor, the publicist, the sound editor, the Foley artist, the composer, the title sequence designer, and the specialist editors.

Editor

The editor works in tandem with the director in editing the film that has been shot. The director has the ultimate accountability for editing choices, but often the editor has substantial contribution in the creative decisions concerned in piecing together a finalised product. Often, the editor commences their role whilst filming is still in process, by compiling initial takes of footage. It is an extremely long process to edit a television show, demonstrating the importance, and significance editing has on a production. Gradually more editors are beginning to work on a digital computerised editing system, limiting physical touching of the actual film, decreasing film corruption due to touch.

The editor follows the screenplay as the guide for establishing the structure of the story and then uses his/her talents to assemble the various shots and takes for greater, clearer artistic effect. There are several editing stages. In the first stage, the editor is supervised by the director, who spells their vision to the editor. Therefore, this first rough cut is often called the 'director's cut'. After the first stage, the following cuts are supervised by one or more producers, who represent the production company and its investors. Consequently, the final cut is the one that most closely represents what the studio wants from the film and not necessarily what the director wants.

Sound Editor

In television, the sound editor deals with the mixing, adjusting and fixing of the soundtrack. They usually have a major decision-making and creative role when it comes to sound and audio. A sound editor also decides what sound effects to use and what effects to achieve from the sound effects, edits and makes new sounds using filters and combining sounds, shaping sound with volume curves, and equalising. A sound editor takes the Foley artist's sounds and puts them in place so it works with the picture and sounds natural, even if the sound is unnatural. In many cases, a sound editor uses a sound effects library extensively, either self-compiled, bought or both, as many of the sounds don't get enough focus if they were taken straight from the shoot of the show.

Foley Artist

The Foley Artist on a film crew is the person who creates and records many of the sound effects. Foley artists, editors, and supervisors are highly specialised and are essential for producing a professional-sounding soundtrack, often reproducing commonplace yet essential sounds like footsteps or the rustle of clothing. The Foley Artist also fabricates sounds that can't be correctly recorded while filming, much like the sound editor does with digital sound effects.

Publicist

A publicist or advertiser has the task of raising public awareness of a production, and ultimately increase viewers and sales of it and its merchandise. The publicist's main task is to stimulate demand for a product through advertising and promotion. Advertisers use several recognisable techniques in order to better convince the public fo buy a product. These may include:

1. **Repetition**: Some advertisers concentrate on making sure their product is widely recognised. To that end, they simply attempt to make the name remembered through repetition.

2. **Bandwagon**: By implying that the product is widely viewed, advertisers hope to convince potential buyers to 'get on the bandwagon'.

3. **Testimonials**: Advertisers often attempt to promote the superior worth of their product through the testimony of ordinary users, experts, or both. For example, using film critics or media personalities. This approach often involves an appeal to authority such as a doctor of medical science.

4. **Pressure**: By attempting to make people choose quickly and without long consideration, some advertisers hope to make rapid sales, and a sense of urgency to watch or buy a product.

5. **Association**: Advertisers often attempt to associate their product with desirable things, in order to make it seem equally desirable. The use of attractive models, picturesque landscapes, and other similar imagery is common.

'Buzzwords' with desired associations are also used.

6. **Imagery**: Using advertising slogans, logos, or a common image increases familiarity, trust, and personality of a production, and the ability for the show to be remembered.

The publicist ensures the media are well aware of a project by distributing the show as a trial run, or a 'sneak preview', through press releases, interviews with members of the cast or crew, arranging exclusive public visits on set of the production, and creating media kits, which contain pictures, posters, clips, shorts, and trailers and brief descriptions on the show and the plot.

Composer

A composer is a person who writes the music for a production. They may also be the conductor of an orchestra who plays the music, or part of the orchestra. The composer is the originator of the music, and usually its first performer. The composer occasionally writes the theme music for a television show. A television programme's theme music is a melody closely associated with the show, and usually played during the title sequence. If it is accompanied by lyrics, it is a theme song.

Title Sequence Designer

A title sequence, in a television programme, is shown at the beginning of the show; which displays the show name and credits, usually including actors, producers and directors. A montage of selected images and a theme song are often included to suggest the essential tone of the series. A title sequence is essential in preparing the audience for the following programme, and gives them a sense of familiarity that makes them trust, and feel comfortable with the film. It is up to the title sequence designer to achieve this very goal, and make it catchy, entertaining, and appealing to increase the audiences feeling of positivity towards the show.

Post-Production Runner

A post-production runner, like a production runner, carries out tasks that are essential to the smooth running of a post-production house. They are the most junior members of a post-production team.

Specialist Editors – Special Effects Coordinator

Special effects (SPFX) are used in television to create effects that cannot be achieved by normal means, such as depicting travel to other star systems.

They are also used when creating the effect by normal means is prohibitively expensive, such as an enormous explosion. They are also used to enhance previously filmed elements, by adding, removing or enhancing objects within the scene. The special effects coordinator implicates these effects, and directs them with the help of the visual effects director. The task of the effects coordinator differs frequently, and can range from extensive over-the-top special effects to basic computer animation.

ADR Editor

Automatic Dialogue Replacement (ADR) is the process of replacing dialogue that was recorded incorrectly during filming, with the actors voices recorded and put into place during editing. The ADR editor oversees the procedure and takes the corrupted dialogue, and replaces it with newly recorded lines to the actor's mouth on film to make it lip sync correctly.

The Matte artist or Bluescreen Director

Bluescreen is the film technique of shooting foreground action against a blue background, which is then replaced by a separately shot 'background plate' scene by either optical effects or digital composting. This process is directed and coordinated by the blue screen director. The matte artist is a part of the special effects department who assists in making scenery and locations that don't exist. They assemble backgrounds using traditional techniques or computers that mix with the footage filmed to create a false set. Both are fairly alike, but bluescreen technology is more modern and more widely used.

Recording Studios and Radio Studios

- → Design and Equipment
- → Digital Audio Workstations
- → Project Studios
- → Isolation Booth
- → History
  - 1890s to 1930s
  - 1940s to 1970s
- → Radio Studios

Recording Studios and Radio Studios

Recording Studio

A recording studio is a facility for sound recording. Ideally, the space is specially designed by an acoustician to achieve the desired acoustic properties (sound diffusion, low level of reflections, adequate reverberation time for the size of the ambient, etc). Different types of studios record bands and artists, voiceovers and music for television shows, movies, cartoons, and commercials, and/or even record a full orchestra. The typical recording studio consists of a room called the 'studio', where instrumentalists and vocalists perform; and the 'control room', which houses the equipment for recording, routing and manipulating the sound. Often, there will be smaller rooms called 'isolation booths' present to accommodate loud instruments such as drums or electric guitar, to keep these sounds from being audible to the microphones that are capturing the sounds from other instruments or vocalists.

A Control Room with a Mixing Console, Monitor Speakers, and Computer-based 'DAW'

Design and Equipment

Recording studios generally consist of three rooms – the studio itself, where the sound for the recording is created (often referred to as the 'live room'), the control room, where the sound from the studio is recorded and manipulated, and the machine room, where noisier equipment that may interfere with the recording process is kept. Recording studios are carefully designed around the principles of room acoustics to create a set of spaces with the acoustical properties required for recording sound with precision and accuracy. This will

A Vocalist inside the 'studio', or 'live room' area of a Recording Studio

consist of both room treatment (through the use of absorption and diffusion materials on the surfaces of the room, and also consideration of the physical dimensions of the room itself in order to make the room respond to sound in a desired way) and soundproofing (to provide sonic isolation between the rooms). A recording studio may also include additional rooms, such as a vocal booth – a small room designed for voice recording, as well as one or more extra control rooms.

Equipment found in a recording studio commonly includes:

1. Mixing Console
2. Multitrack Recorder
3. Microphones
4. Reference monitors, which are loudspeakers with a flat frequency response

Equipment may also include:

1. Digital Audio Workstation
2. Music Workstation
3. Outboard Effects, such as compressors, reverbs, or equalisers

Digital Audio Workstations

General purpose computers have rapidly assumed a large role in the recording process, being able to replace the mixing consoles, recorders, synthesisers, samplers and sound effects devices. A computer thus outfitted is called a Digital Audio Workstation, or DAW. Popular audio-recording software includes Digidesign Pro Tools, Cubase and Nuendo also by Steinberg, MOTU Digital Performer, Ableton Live, Cakewalk SONAR, ACID Pro and Apple Logic Pro, Cool Edit Pro also known as Audition (after bought out by Adobe), Audacity, and ardour on Linux.

Current software applications are more reliant on the audio recording hardware than the computer they are running on, therefore typical high-end computer hardware is less of a priority. While Apple Macintosh is common for studio work, there is a breadth of software available for Microsoft Windows and Linux. A sizeable portion of both commercial and home studios can be seen running PC-based multitrack audio software.

If no mixing console is used and all mixing is done using only a keyboard and mouse, this is referred to as mixing in the box. There are also dedicated machines which integrate a recorder, preamps, effects, and a mixing console; these devices are frequently referred to as DAW's, generally in advertising.

Project Studios

A small, personal recording studio is sometimes called a project studio or home studio. Such studios often cater to specific needs of an individual artist, or are used as a non-commercial hobby. The first modern project studios came into being during the mid 1980s, with the advent of affordable multitrack recorders, synthesisers and microphones. The phenomenon has flourished with falling prices of MIDI equipment and accessories, as well as inexpensive digital hard-disk recording products.

Recording drums and electric guitar in a home studio is challenging, because they are usually the loudest instruments. Conventional drums require soundproofing in this scenario, unlike electronic or sampled drums. Getting an authentic electric guitar amp sound including power-tube distortion requires a power attenuator (either power-soak or power-supply based) or an isolation box or booth. A convenient compromise is amp simulation, whether a modelling amp, preamp/ processor, or software-based guitar amp simulator. Sometimes, musicians replace loud, inconvenient instruments such as drums, with keyboards, which today often provide highly realistic sampling.

Isolation Booth

An isolation booth is a standard small room in a recording studio, which is both soundproofed to keep out external sounds and keep in the internal sounds and like all the other recording rooms in sound industry it is designed for having a lesser amount of diffused reflections from walls to make a good sounding room. A drummer, vocalist, or guitar speaker cabinet, along with microphones, is acoustically isolated in the room. A professional recording studio has a control room, a large live room, and one or more small isolation booths. All rooms are soundproofed such as with double-layer walls with dead space and insulation in-between the two walls, forming a room-within-a-room.

There are variations of the same concept, including a portable standalone isolation booth, a compact guitar speaker isolation cabinet, or a larger guitar speaker cabinet isolation box.

A gobo panel achieves the same idea to a much more moderate extent; for example, a drum kit that is too loud in the live room or on stage can have acrylic glass see-through gobo panels placed around it to deflect the sound and keep it from bleeding into the other microphones, allowing more independent control of each instrument channel at the mixing board.

All rooms in a recording studio may have a reconfigurable combination of reflective and non-reflective surfaces, to control the amount of reverberation.

History

1890s to 1930s

In the era of acoustical recordings (prior to the introduction of microphones, electrical recording and amplification), the earliest recording studios had very basic facilities, being essentially soundproof rooms that isolated the performers from outside noise. During this era, it was not uncommon for recordings to be made in any available location, such as a local ballroom, using portable acoustic recording equipment.

In this period, master recordings were made by a direct-to-disc cutting process – performers were typically grouped around a large acoustic horn (an enlarged version of the familiar phonograph horn) and the acoustic energy from the voices and/or instruments was channelled through the horn's diaphragm to a mechanical cutting lathe located in the next room, which inscribed the signal as a modulated groove directly onto the surface of the master cylinder or disc.

Following the invention and commercial introduction of the microphone, the electronic amplifier, the mixing desk and the loudspeaker, the recording industry gradually converted to electric recording and this technology had replaced mechanical acoustic recording methods in 1925 for major labels like RCA Victor and Columbia, and by 1933 acoustic recording was completely disused.

1940s to 1970s

Siemens Sound Studio ca. 1956. Photo by William Alber

Electrical recording was common by the early 1930s, and mastering lathes were now electrically powered, but master recordings still had to be cut direct-to-disc. In line with the prevailing musical trends, studios in this period were primarily designed for the live recording of symphony orchestras and other large instrumental ensembles. Engineers soon found that large, reverberant spaces like concert halls created a vibrant acoustic signature that greatly enhanced the sound of the recording, and in this period large, acoustically 'live' halls were favoured, rather than the acoustically 'dead' booths and studio rooms that became common after the 1960s.

Because of the limits of the recording technology, studios of the mid-20th century were designed around the concept of grouping musicians and singers, rather than separating them, and placing the performers and the microphones strategically to capture the complex acoustic and harmonic interplay that emerged during the performance. Modern sound stages still sometimes use this approach for large film scoring projects today.

Because of their superb acoustics, many of the larger studios were converted churches. Examples include George Martin's AIR Studios in London, the famed Columbia Records 30th Street Studio in New York City (a converted Armenian church, with a ceiling over 100 feet high), and the equally famous Decca Records Pythian Temple studio in New York (where artists like Louis Jordan, Bill Haley and Buddy Holly were recorded) which was also a large converted church that featured a high, domed ceiling in the centre of the hall.

Electric recording studios in the mid-20th century often lacked isolation booths, baffles, and sometimes even speakers, and it was not until the 1960s, with the introduction of the high-fidelity headphones that it became common practice for performers to use headsets to monitor their performance during recording and listen to playbacks.

It was difficult to isolate all the performers – a major reason that this practice was not used was simply because recordings were usually made as live ensemble 'takes' and all the performers needed to be able to see each other and the ensemble leader while playing. The recording engineers who trained in this period learned to take advantage of the complex acoustic effects that could be created through 'leakage' between different microphones and groups of instruments, and these technicians became extremely skilled at capturing the unique acoustic properties of their studios and the musicians in performance.

Facilities like the Columbia Records 30th Street Studio in New York and EMI's Abbey Road Studio in London were renowned for their 'trademark' sound – which was (and still is) easily identifiable by audio professionals – and for the skill of their staff engineers.

The use of different kinds of microphones and their placement around the studio was a crucial part of the recording process, and particular brands of microphone were used by engineers for their specific audio characteristics. The smooth-toned ribbon microphones developed by the RCA Company in the 1930s were crucial to the 'crooning' style perfected by Bing Crosby, and the famous Neumann U47 condenser microphone was one of the most widely used from the 1950s. This model is still widely regarded by audio professionals as one of the best microphones of its type ever made.

Learning the correct placement of microphones was a major part of the training of young engineers, and many became extremely skilled in this craft. Well into the 1960s, in the classical field it was not uncommon for engineers to make high-quality orchestral recordings using only one or two microphones suspended above the orchestra.

In the 1960s, engineers began experimenting with placing microphones much closer to instruments than had previously been the norm. The distinctive rasping tone of the horn sections on the Beatles recordings 'Good Morning Good Morning' and 'Lady Madonna' were achieved by having the saxophone players position their instruments so that microphones were virtually inside the mouth of the horn.

The unique sonic characteristics of the major studios imparted a special character to many of the most famous popular recordings of the 1950s and 1960s, and the recording companies jealously guarded these facilities. According to sound historian, David Simons, after Columbia took over the 30th Street Studios in the late 1940s, A&R manager, Mitch Miller, issued a standing order that the drapes and other fittings left by the previous occupants were not to be touched, and the cleaners had specific orders never to mop the bare wooden floor for fear it might alter the acoustic properties of the hall.

There were several other features of studios in this period that contributed to their unique 'sonic signatures'. As well as the inherent sound of the large recording rooms, many of the best studios incorporated specially-designed echo chambers, purpose-built rooms which were often built beneath the main studio. These were typically long, low rectangular spaces constructed from hard, sound-reflective materials like concrete, fitted with a loudspeaker at one end and one or more microphones at the other. During a recording session, a signal from one or more of the microphones in the studio could be routed to the loudspeaker in the echo chamber; the sound from the speaker reverberated through the chamber and the enhanced signal was picked up by the microphone at the other end. This echo-enhanced signal – which was often used to 'sweeten' the sound of vocals – could then be blended in with the primary signal from the microphone in the studio and mixed into the track as the master recording was being made.

Special equipment was another notable feature of the 'classic' recording studio. The biggest studios were owned and operated by large media companies like RCA, Columbia and EMI, who typically had their own electronics research and development divisions that designed and built custom-made recording equipment and mixing consoles for their studios.

Likewise, the smaller independent studios were often owned by skilled electronics engineers who designed and built their own desks and other equipment. A good example of this is the famous Gold Star Studios in Los Angeles, the site of many famous American pop recordings of the 1960s. Co-owner David S Gold built the studio's main mixing desk and many additional pieces of equipment and he also designed the studio's unique trapezoidal echo chambers.

During the 1950s and 1960s, the sound of pop recordings was further defined by the introduction of proprietary sound processing devices such as equalisers and compressors, which were manufactured by specialist electronics companies. One of the best known of these was the famous Pultec equaliser, which was used by almost all the major commercial studios of the time.

With the introduction of multi-track recording, it became possible to record instruments and singers separately and at different times on different tracks on tape, although it was not until the 1970s that the large recording companies began to adopt this practice widely, and throughout the 1960s, many 'pop' classics were still recorded live in a single take.

After the 1960s, the emphasis shifted to isolation and sound-proofing, with treatments like echo and reverberation added separately during the mixing process, rather than being blended in during the recording. One regrettable outcome of this trend, which coincided with rising inner-city property values, was that many of the largest studios were either demolished or redeveloped for other uses.

In the 1960s, recordings were analog recordings made using ¼-inch or ½-inch two-track magnetic tape. By the early 1970s, the technology progressed to using various types of multi-track tape. The most common of which is the 2-inch analog tape, capable of containing up to 24 individual tracks. Generally, after an audio mix is set up on a 24-track tape machine, the signal is played back and sent to a different machine which records the combined signals (called printing) to a ½-inch 2-track stereo tape, called a master.

Prior to digital recording, the total number of available tracks onto which one could record was measured in multiples of 24, based on the number of 24-track tape machines being used. Presently, most recording studios now use digital recording equipment which only limits the number of available tracks based on the capacity of the mixing console or computer hardware interface.

Analog tape machines are still well sought after as some purists label digitally recorded audio as sounding too harsh, and the scarcity and age of analog tape machines greatly increases their value, as does the fact that many audio engineers still insist on recording only to analog tape. This harshness is widely attributed by them to the fact that digital recording will sample a sound wave many times per second allowing an illusion of solid sound waves to be created, where in contrast, analog tape captures a sound wave in its entirety.

However, others simply argue that the lack of high frequency noise and the higher fidelity of the digital medium make the recorded higher frequencies more prominent, which results in such perceived harshness in contrast to analog recording. Still others point to problems of early digital recordings caused by the inexperience of sound engineers with the new medium as the cause for critics to the digital systems. Finally, another possibly relevant effect derives from the fact that, since CD-quality audio uses a sampling rate of 44.1 kHz, no frequencies above the Nyquist frequency of 22050 Hz are acceptable for recording, otherwise aliasing occurs. Because of that, very steep low-pass filters are used on frequencies above 20 kHz (the theoretical limit for human hearing) that introduce slight distortions into the audible-range signal. This is one of the several reasons for the push on high-end equipment towards higher sampling rates, such as 48 kHz (used in video production), 88.2 kHz, 96 kHz and even 192 kHz.

Radio Studios

Radio studios are very similar to recording studios, particularly in the case of production studios which are not normally used on-air. This type of studio would normally have all of the same equipment that any other audio recording studio would have, particularly if it is at a large station, or at a combined facility that houses a station group.

Broadcast studios also use many of the same principles such as sound isolation, with adaptations suited to the live on-air nature of their use. Such equipment would commonly include a telephone hybrid for putting telephone calls on the air, a POTS codec for receiving remote broadcasts, a dead air alarm for detecting unexpected silence, and a broadcast delay for dropping anything from coughs to profanity. In the US, FCC-licensed stations also must have an Emergency Alert System decoder (typically in the studio), and in the case of full-power stations, an encoder that can interrupt programming on all channels which a station transmits in order to broadcast urgent warnings.

Computers are also used for playing ads, jingles, bumpers, sound bytes, phone calls, sound effects, traffic and weather reports, and now full broadcast automation when nobody is around. For talk shows, a producer and/or assistant in a control room runs the show, including screening calls and entering the callers' names and subject into a queue, which the show's host can see and make a proper introduction with. Radio contest winners can also be edited on the fly and put on the air within a minute or two after they have been recorded accepting their prize.

Additionally, digital mixing consoles can be interconnected via audio over Ethernet, or split into two parts, with inputs and outputs wired to a rackmount audio engine, and one or more control surfaces (mixing boards) and/or computers connected via serial port, allowing the producer or the talent to control the show from either point. With Ethernet and audio over IP (live) or FTP (recorded), this also allows remote access, so that DJs can do shows from a home studio via ISDN or Internet. Additional outside audio connections are required for the studio/transmitter link for over-the-air stations, satellite dishes for sending and receiving shows, and for webcasting or podcasting.

Radio Programming

- Old Time Radio/OTR
- Radio Theatre
- Audio Theatre Today
- Production
- Distribution
- Radio Drama
- History
  Early Years
- Widespread Popularity
- Radio Drama Today

Radio Programming

Radio programming is the content that is broadcast by radio stations. The original inventors of radio, such as Nikola Tesla and Guglielmo Marconi, expected it to be used for one-on-one communication tasks where telephones and telegraphs could not be used because of the impossibility of stringing wires from one point to another, such as in ship-to-shore communications. These inventors had no expectations whatever that radio would become a major mass entertainment and information medium earning many millions of dollars in revenues annually through commercial sponsorship. These latter uses were brought about after 1920 by business entrepreneurs such as David Sarnoff, who created the National Broadcasting Company (NBC), and later William S Paley, who built the Columbia Broadcasting System (CBS). These broadcasting (as opposed to narrowcasting) business organisations began to be called networks, because they consisted of loose chains of individual stations located in various cities, all transmitting the standard overall-system supplied fare, often at synchronised agreed-upon times. Some of these stations were owned by the networks, while others were owned by independent businessmen allied with the respective networks. By selling blocks of time to advertisers for commercial announcements, the medium was able to quickly become profitable and offer its products to listeners for free, provided they invested in a radio receiver set. The new medium grew extremely quickly through the 1920s, vastly increasing both the size of its audience and its profits.

In these early days, it was customary for a corporation to sponsor an entire half-an-hour radio programme, placing its commercials at the beginning and the end. This is in contrast to the pattern which developed late in the 20th century in both television and radio, where small slices of time were sold to many sponsors and no corporation claimed or wanted sponsorship of the entire show, except in rare cases. These later commercials also filled a much larger portion of the total programme time than they had in the earlier days.

In the early radio age, content typically included a balance of comedy, drama, news, music and sports reporting. US radio programmes included the most famous Hollywood talent of the day. Radio soap operas began in the US in 1930 with *Painted Dreams.* Despite the majority use of the radio being spoken entertainment, the Grand Ole Opry, as of 2006 being the longest-running radio programme, has been focused on broadcasting country music since it began in 1925.

In the late 1940s and early 1950s, television eroded the popularity of radio comedy, drama and variety shows. By the late 1950s, radio broadcasting took on much the form it has today – strongly focused on music, news and sports, though drama can still be heard, especially on the BBC.

In Britain, during the 1950s, radio broadcasting was dominated entirely by the BBC. Rock and pop music fans, dissatisfied with the BBC's output, often listened to Radio Luxembourg. During the post-1964 period, western Europe offshore radio (such as Radio Caroline broadcasting from ships at anchor or abandoned forts) helped to supply the demand for the pop and rock music. The BBC launched their own pop music station, BBC Radio 1 in 1967.

In South Asia, Radio Ceylon (the oldest radio station in the region) was the King of the Airwaves from the 1950s and 1960s. Broadcasting in Ceylon was lauhched by British Engineer, Edward Harper in 1925. Radio Ceylon became a public corporation in 1967 and was known as the Sri Lanka Broadcasting Corporation when the island turned into a republic in 1972.

Old Time Radio/OTR

There has been a recent resurgence of interest in what is now called old-time radio with surviving shows being traded and collected in reel-to-reel, cassette, CD, MP3 formats and Internet download. Some of the most popular shows were Honest Harold, Amos and Andy, Burns and Allen, Colgate Comedy classics. On Sunday January 1 1956 at 11 PM, there were plans to broadcast the final Comedy Hour both on radio and television. This was to be final show before format changed. The show planned to invite the three major teams in the world of comedy: Laurel and Hardy, Abbott and Costello, and Martin and Lewis for an hour (plus) special. 1956 was the last year those teams were together. All three teams had a radio show of their own in the late 1940s and early 1950s.

Radio Theatre

Radio Theatre or Audio Theatre is a dramatic performance written and performed specifically for audio presentation. It had its greatest popularity on radio, before television was introduced, during the period known as the Golden Age of Radio, and as a result has often been called 'Radio Theatre' or 'radio drama' although as a form, it is independent of its medium.

History

Audio theatre has deep roots, building on very old traditions of storytelling and stage presentation. In the 1880s, theatre performances were heard over the telephone. By the 1890s, sales of phonograph recordings were booming. For hot products, recording companies turned to well-known performers from Variety, Vaudeville, Chautauqua, Minstrel Shows, etc. Musical acts were obvious first choices, but the non-musical 'sketch' acts weren't far behind. Words were added to describe scenes, and set up sight—now sound-gags. Sound effects and music were adapted from stage technique, and audio theatre was born, years before sound was first broadcast over the radio. Called (and thought of) as 'Radio Theatre', it became the hottest mass-entertainment art form of the '20s, '30s, and '40s, now called the Golden Age of Radio.

In 1962, CBS suspended its last regular weekly series of network radio drama (until the advent of the CBS Radio Mystery Theatre), but today this Old-Time Radio (OTR) is popular again on recordings. In other countries, radio networks such as the Canadian Broadcasting Corporation and the BBC's Radio 7 continue to commission and broadcast radio plays. In the US, new productions are gaining popularity via XM Radio's 'Sonic Theatre' and on a growing number of community radio stations.

New technical developments in audio, including 'hi-fi' and stereo, have opened huge new possibilities. Creators like Stan Freberg, Cheech and Chong, Dick 'Chickenman' Orkin, and The Firesign Theatre made two major contributions to the development of the form:

1. They began to use the newly available tools of multitrack recording, overdubbing, and mixdown for convenience, efficiency, and precision control far beyond what is possible 'live'.

2. They accepted from the outset that this new material was intended to be heard primarily from recordings. Therefore, the listener had the opportunity to listen to part or all of the piece more than once. Significantly, the producer need not take pains to make certain the listener has followed every aspect and nuance before moving on: it's OK if the listener has something new to discover in repeated listenings.

The Midwest Radio Theatre Workshop, now the National Audio Theatre Festival, has trained and inspired hundreds of new young talents since 1980. By 2001, sales of audiobooks, OTR programmes, and the popularity of talk radio made it clear that there is a very large audience for spoken-word entertainment.

Audio Theatre Today

As the 21st Century begins, audio theatre appears to be growing and changing. Computer technology has made the audio engineering and production aspects easier and less expensive.

One result of this is the growth of fan-based audio dramas. An audio version of fanfic, these are original productions based on existing characters from literature, television, or movies. These are often, but not always, created without permission from creators or copyright holders of the works on which they are based. Such productions are often made available via podcasting.

Another result of new technology is the ability for experienced producers to do more with the medium than ever before. Advancements in microphones, mic techniques, and recorded media, allow subtlety in performance which could not be attempted during the 'golden age of radio', and advancements in computer-based audio production software allow for easier editing and post-production than previously available, allowing for a wider variety of sound design options.

Audio theatre also is gaining recognition in schools and universities around the world as an effective educational method. Several companies offer 'lesson plan' versions of audio theatre for use in teaching history, social science, or ethics. Some universities with broadcasting programmes have also begun to look to audio theatre as a method of training radio acting skills.

A drama CD is a form of audio theatre where a collection of audio files presented in one or more CDs consisting of voice actors who act out a set storyline by reading from a script and/or improvising. Much like the radio drama, a play is acted out simply with the use of sound and no visual stimuli to progress the story. Drama CDs are usually based on other series consisting mostly of TV shows and novels.

Drama CDs have effectively become well-known among Japanese anime and manga fans since many manga that become anime are later able to produce drama CDs using the seiyū, or voice actors that voiced the characters from the anime (see Radio drama in Japan). However, this is not always the case as there are examples of the drama CDs having an entirely different cast from the anime as in Ouran High School Host Club, DN Angel and Lucky Star. Additionally, drama CDs can be based on visual novels that have partial or full-voice acting associated with the video game.

Production

Four basic production methods are in use, singly or in combination, today:

Live Performance: where actors, sound effects performers, engineers and musicians gather and perform the script in real time, either in a sound studio or in a theatre with an audience.

Multitrack Studio: where voices are recorded separately, edited, and assembled in a multitrack environment in a sound studio or using computer-software. Music and other sounds are added on separate tracks, and all these elements are mixed and edited together to achieve the final result.

Location Production: where a single microphone is used as a movie camera, and the actors perform many of their own sound effects (footsteps, doors, telephones, etc) as they read the lines. Scenes are 'shot' in various locations outside the studio, capturing the characteristic acoustic responses and background ambience of different places.

Computer-based Production: This is a version of multitrack production. Computer technology has allowed performances to be recorded and edited entirely within the computer. This ranges from productions recorded with professional equipment (microphones, mic-pres or boards, and pro-sound cards) to productions with performances recorded with computer microphones, or over the phone, and assembled in the computer.

Distribution

Mostly, these days, the works are distributed as recordings, which allow the production to be enjoyed at a time and place of the listener's choosing. The Internet is creating new channels of distribution, and there is also a resurgence of broadcast audio theatre. Podcast audio theatre, especially, has been extremely popular, as the episodic nature of audio theatre conforms well to the podcast model.

Starting on the telephone and the wax cylinder, but achieving its biggest audience over radio broadcast, Audio Theatre returns to popularity on its original media: recordings and transmission wires.

Radio Drama

Radio drama is a form of audio storytelling broadcast on radio. With no visual component, radio drama depends on dialogue, music and sound effects to help the listener imagine the story.

Radio drama achieved widespread popularity within a decade of its initial development in the 1920s. By the 1940s, it was a leading international popular entertainment. With the advent of television in the 1950s, however, radio drama lost some of its popularity, and in some countries, has never regained large audiences. However, recordings of OTR (old-time radio) survive today in the audio archives of collectors and museums.

The single best-known episode of radio drama is probably the Orson Welles-directed adaptation of *The War of the Worlds* (1938), which some listeners believed to be real news broadcast about an invasion from Mars.

As of 2006, radio drama has a minimal presence in the United States. Much of American radio drama is restricted to rebroadcasts or podcasts of programmes from previous decades. However, other nations still have thriving traditions of radio drama. The BBC produces and broadcasts hundreds of new radio dramas per year on Radio 4, BBC 7 and Radio 3, - On Radio 4 as afternoon plays, Friday evenings, woman's hour daily short dramas, Saturday plays, Sunday classic serials and on Radio 3 Sunday evening drama on 3 and the once-monthly experimental wire slot. BBC7 output tends to be comedy, sci-fi, 7th dimension – and predominantly archived programmes. Podcasting has also offered a means to create new radio dramas in addition to the distribution of vintage programmes.

The terms 'audio drama' or 'audio theatre' are sometimes used synonymously with 'radio drama' with one notable distinction – audio drama or audio theatre is not intended specifically for broadcast on radio. Audio drama – whether newly produced or OTR classics – can be found on CDs, cassette tapes, podcasts, webcasts and conventional broadcast radio.

History

Early Years

English language radio drama seems to have started in the United States. '*A Rural Line on Education*', a brief sketch specifically written for radio, aired on Pittsburgh's KDKA in 1921, according to historian, Bill Jaker. Newspaper accounts of the era report on a number of other drama experiments by America's commercial radio stations: KYW broadcast a season of complete operas from Chicago starting in November 1921. In February 1922, entire Broadway musical comedies with the original casts aired from WJZ's Newark studios. Actors Grace George and Herbert Hayes performed an entire play from a San Francisco station in the summer of 1922.

An important turning point in radio drama came when Schenectady, New York's WGY, after a successful tryout on August 3, 1922, began weekly studio broadcasts of full-length stage plays in September 1922, using music, sound effects and a regular troupe of actors, The WGY Players. Aware of this series, the director of Cincinnati's WLW began regularly broadcasting one-acts (as well as excerpts from longer works) in November. The success of these projects led to imitators at other stations. By the spring of 1923, original dramatic pieces written especially for radio were airing on stations in Cincinnati (*When Love Wakens by WLW's Fred Smith*), Philadelphia (*The Secret Wave by Clyde A. Criswell*) and Los Angeles (*At Home over KHJ*). That same year, WLW (in May) and WGY (in September) sponsored scripting contests, inviting listeners to create original plays to be performed by those stations' dramatic troupes.

Listings in the *New York Times* and other sources for May 1923 reveal at least 20 dramatic offerings were scheduled (including one-acts, excerpts from longer dramas, complete three- and-four-act plays, operettas and a Moliére adaptation), either as in-studio productions or by remote broadcast from local theatres and opera houses.

Serious study of American radio drama of the 1920s and early 1930s is, at best, very limited. Unsung pioneers of the art include: WLW's Fred Smith, Freeman Gosden and Charles Correll (who popularised the dramatic serial), The Eveready Hour creative team (which began with one-act plays but was soon experimenting with hour-long combinations of drama and music on its weekly variety programme), the various acting troupes at stations like WLW, WGY, KGO and a number of others, frequently run by women like Helen Schuster Martin and Wilda Wilson Church, early network continuity writers like Henry Fisk Carlton,

William Ford Manley and Don Clark, producers and directors like Clarence Menser and Gerald Stopp, and a long list of others who were credited at the time with any number of innovations but who are largely forgotten or undiscussed today. Elizabeth McLeod's recent book on Gosden and Correll's early work is a major exception, as is Richard J Hand's 2006 study of horror radio, which examines some programmes from the late 1920s and early '30s.

Another notable early radio drama, one of the first especially written for the medium in the UK, was Danger by Richard Hughes, broadcast by the BBC on January 15, 1924, about a group of people trapped in a Welsh coal mine. One of the earliest and most influential French radio plays was the prize-winning Marémoto (Seaquake) by Gabriel Germinet and Pierre Cusy which presents a realistic account of a sinking ship before revealing that the characters are actually actors rehearsing for a broadcast. Translated and broadcast in Germany and England by 1925, the play was originally scheduled by Radio-Paris to air on October 23, 1924 but was instead banned from French radio until 1937 because the government feared that the dramatic SOS messages would be mistaken for genuine distress signals.

In 1951, American writer and producer Arch Oboler suggested that Wyllis Cooper's Lights Out (1934-1947) was the first true radio drama to make use of the unique qualities of radio:

Radio drama (as distinguished from theatre plays boiled down to kilocycle size) began at midnight, in the middle thirties, on one of the upper floors of Chicago's Merchandise Mart. The pappy was a rotund writer by the name of Wyllis Cooper. [1]

Though the series is often remembered solely for its gruesome stories and sound effects, Cooper's scripts for Lights Out were well-written and offered innovations seldom heard in early radio dramas, including multiple first person narrators, stream of consciousness monologues and scripts that contrasted a duplicitous character's internal monologue and his spoken words.

The question of who was the first to write stream-of-consciousness drama for radio is a difficult one to answer. By 1930, Tyrone Guthrie had written plays for the BBC like Matrimonial News (which consists entirely of the thoughts of a shopgirl awaiting a blind date) and The Flowers Are Not for You to Pick (which takes place inside the mind of a drowning man). After they were published in 1931, Guthrie's plays aired on the American networks. Around the same time, Guthrie himself also worked for the Canadian National Railway radio network, producing plays written by Merrill Denison that used similar techniques. A 1940 article in Variety credited a 1932 NBC play, Drink Deep by Don Johnson, as the first stream-of-consciousness play written for American radio. The climax of Lawrence Holcomb's 1931 NBC play Skyscraper also uses a variation of the technique (so that the listener can hear the final thoughts and relived memories of a man falling to his death from the title building).

There were probably earlier examples of stream-of-consciousness drama on the radio. For example, in December 1924, actor Paul Robeson, then appearing in a revival of Eugene O'Neill's "The Emperor Jones," performed a scene from the play over New York's WGBS to critical acclaim. Some of the many storytellers and monologists on early 1920s American radio might be able to claim even earlier dates.

Widespread Popularity

Perhaps America's most famous radio drama broadcast is Orson Welles's *The War of the Worlds*, a 1938 version of the HG Wells' novel, which convinced large numbers of listeners that an actual invasion from Mars was taking place.

By the late 1930s, radio drama was widely popular in the United States (and also in other parts of the world). There were dozens of programmes in many different genres, from mysteries and thrillers, to soap operas and comedies. There were occasional efforts at more 'literary' works, such as *Under Milk Wood* (1954) and Play for Voices by Dylan Thomas. Many playwrights, screenwriters and novelists got their start in radio drama, including Caryl Churchill, Rod Serling, Irwin Shaw and Tom Stoppard.

Decline in the United States

By the mid-1950s in the United States, television had achieved massive popularity, and radio drama was on the decline. Some successful radio programmes were able to make a successful transition to television (such as Gunsmoke, Dragnet, Guiding Light, and Jack Benny's programme), but radio drama never recovered its popularity in the US.

There have been some efforts at radio drama since the late 1950s. In the 1960s, Dick Orkin created the hugely popular syndicated comic adventure series *Chicken Man*. Inspired by The Goon Show, 'the four or five crazy guys' of the Firesign Theatre built a large following with their satirical plays on recordings exploring the dramatic possibilities inherent in stereo. A brief resurgence of production beginning in the early 1970s yielded veteran Himan Brown's CBS

Radio Mystery Theatre and works by a new generation of dramatists, notably Yuri Rasovsky, Tom Lopez of ZBS and the dramatic sketches heard on humorist Garrison Keillor's A Prairie Home Companion. Thanks in large part to the National Endowments for the Arts and Humanities, public radio continued to air a smattering of audio drama until the mid-1980s. From 1986 to 2002, National Public Radio's most consistent producer of radio drama was the idiosyncratic Joe Frank, working out of KCRW in Santa Monica.

Radio Drama Today

Radio drama remains popular in much of the world. Stations producing radio drama often commission a large number of scripts. The relatively low cost of producing a radio play enables them to take chances with works by unknown writers. Radio can be a good training ground for beginning drama writers as the words written form a much greater part of the finished product; bad lines cannot be obscured with stage business.

On the BBC there are two ongoing radio soap operas: The Archers on BBC Radio Four and Silver Street on the Asian Network. A third soap, Westway on the World Service was cancelled in October 2000 but continues in re-runs on BBC7.

The audio drama format exists side-by-side with books presented on radio, read by actors or by the author. In Britain and other countries there is also a quite a bit of radio comedy (both stand-up and sitcom). Together, these programmes provide entertainment where television is either not wanted or would be distracting (such as while driving or operating machinery).

The lack of visuals also enables fantastical settings and effects to be used in radio plays where the cost would be prohibitive for movies or television. The *Hitchhiker's Guide to the Galaxy* was first produced as radio drama, and was not adapted for television until much later, when its popularity would ensure an appropriate return for the high cost of the futuristic setting.

On occasion television series can be revived as radio series. For example, a long-running but no longer popular television series can be continued as a radio series because the reduced production costs make it cost-effective with a much smaller audience. When an organisation owns both television and radio channels, such as the BBC, the fact that no royalties have to be paid makes this even more attractive. Radio revivals can also use actors reprising their television roles even after decades as they still sound roughly the same. Series that have had this treatment include Doctor *Who, Dad's Army, Sapphire & Steel, The Tomorrow People, and Thunderbirds.*

Regular broadcasts of radio drama in English can be heard on the BBC's Radio 3, Radio 4 and BBC 7, on Radio 1 from the Canadian Broadcasting Corporation, and on RTÉ Radio 1 in Ireland. BBC Radio 4 in particular is noted for its radio drama, broadcasting hundreds of one-off plays per year in strands such as The Afternoon Play, in addition to serials and soap operas. The British commercial station Oneword, though broadcasting mostly book readings, also transmitted a number of radio plays in instalments until it closed in 2008.

In the US, radio drama can be found on ACB radio produced by the American Council of the Blind and on XM Radio. The networks sometime sell transcripts of their shows on cassette tapes or CDs or make the shows available for listening or downloading over the Internet. Transcription recordings of many pre-television shows have been preserved. They are collected, re-recorded onto audio CDs and/or MP3 files and traded by hobbyists today as old-time radio programmes. Meanwhile veterans such as Rasovsky and Lopez have gained new listeners on cassettes, CDs and downloads. In the mid-1980s, the non-profit LA Theatre Works launched its radio series recorded before live audience, which continues a tenuous hold in public radio, while marketing its productions on compact disk.

With 21st-century technology, modern radio drama, also known as audio theatre, has begun an exciting new movement. Local radio drama groups have kept the spirit of radio drama alive. The advent of inexpensive computerised production technology brought an explosion of activity. Not From Space (2003) on XM Satellite Radio was the first national radio play recorded exclusively through the Internet in which the voice actors were all in separate locations. As the podcasting phenomenon continues to grow, radio drama has found a new lease of life on the Internet. Podcasting provides a good alternative to mainstream television and radio because it has no restrictions regarding content.

Internet Ethics

What is the Internet?[99]

It is essential to start with some understanding of the history and the nature of the Internet.

So let's recapitulate!

•The Internet started life in 1969 as the US Department of Defence's Advanced Research Projects Agency network (known as ARPAnet). It was designed to provide a distributed, flexible and self-healing command network which would enable the US military to continue operating even if Soviet military missiles took out certain geographical locations on the network.

• Following its creation as a network for the American military, the Internet – as it became known as – evolved into a network for the American academic community, starting with universities and then spreading outwards.

• Newsgroups, where most child pornography on the Net is located, and chat rooms, where children are most vulnerable to approaches by paedophiles, followed the evolution of the ARPAnet into the Internet, but preceded and are independent of the World Wide Web.

• In 1989, what is now arguably the most popular feature of the Internet, the World Wide Web, was developed by the British scientist, Tim Berners-Lee, during his time at CERN in Switzerland.

---

99. Much of this chapter is inspired from a paper submitted by Professor Marc Le Menestrel and Professor Henri-Claude de Bettignies. The paper was titled – Individual, Business and Society – the Ethical dilemma.

• If there was one year in which the Web could be said to have taken off, it was in 1993, when the number of users doubled and the Internet really entered media consciousness and public debate. Today, there are more than 1 billion Internet users worldwide.

What are the Implications of this Evolution for the Ethics Debate?

• The distributed nature of the Internet, based on packet switching and the routing and rerouting of packets along multitudinous networks and nodes, makes any central control of the medium impossible, even if it was thought desirable.

• The Internet was developed originally for military and then academic purposes. As originally conceived and used, it was a closed network with specific uses and functions and therefore, initially at least, never provoked a debate about ethical issues in the way that cinema or radio or television, all immediately available to those who could afford it, immediately did.

• The Internet was originally designed for, and used by, the few and the intellectual. This gave it a particular set of values, such as tolerance of dissent and antipathy to control, that still pervades much of the debate about Internet content and regulation.

• The Internet was originally used exclusively by Americans and even today around two-fifths of all users reside in the USA. This means that the debate around the Internet has been influenced massively by American culture and values, notably the First Amendment of the US Constitution (which guarantees freedom of expression) and more generally hostility towards government intervention or control.

• The growth of the Internet has been exponential, more and more people are using it for longer and longer to do more things. This has at least three consequences:

• The Internet is no longer the preserve of the few and the intellectual. In many industrialised societies, a majority of citizens have access – whether at home or at work – and the user profile is increasingly approximating that of the citizenry as a whole.

• The Internet has ceased to be an American phenomenon. There are now almost as many users in Europe as there are in the USA and therefore much of the ethics debate now is a clash between American and European culture and values.

• As Internet growth continues especially as we see more users in Asia and South America, the ethics debate will not simply be an American vs European one. Increasingly we have to accommodate a wide diversity of cultures and value systems.

The Main Forms of Content are:

• Email which enables one to communicate almost instantly and at negligible cost with any of the other 400 million Internet users worldwide

• Internet Relay Chat (IRC) which enables people to converse either in groups or one on one in chat rooms – some 40,000 worldwide – focused on different subjects or different groups

• Usenet newsgroups – of which there are about 40,000 – which enable people to file articles or comments or pictures about a whole host of different subjects, ranging from the very technical to the sexually bizarre

• The World Wide Web which now consists of over one billion sites ranging from the ultra sophisticated like Amazon.com to the typical home page.

The types of activities which are taking place on the Net can be analysed as follows:

• Communications, previously through e-mail, but increasingly through telephony using the Internet Protocol (IP) networks

• The provision of information whether through data bases to which access is normally limited or through Web sites which are open to all Internet users with a suitable browser

• E-commerce whether it is business to customer (B2C) or – currently four times the size – business to business (B2B)

• E-Government whereby Government departments interact with citizens, from the simple provision of information to the completion of forms, through to various transactions.

What are the Implications of this Range of Services for the Ethics Debate?

• The Internet is not one network but many, indeed it is a network of networks. It does not provide one type of service offering but many, and this range will increase. These services have many different characteristics and the ethics debate has to take account of this, how we approach chat rooms and how we approach newsgroups, especially where children are concerned.

• The Internet has many actors with different interests. Infrastructure companies like Cisco or Oracle may have little or no involvement in content. Microsoft may start by 'simply' providing a browser (Explorer) and then go into the portal business (MSN). Not all Internet Service Providers (ISPs) provide access to all newsgroups and most chat rooms are not hosted by ISPs. If one is attempting to bring a sense of ethics to the Internet in any particular instance, it is essential to know who has the control and the responsibility.

• There is still a poor sense of understanding of the issues. On the one hand, those who campaign for more 'control' of the Internet often have little understanding of the technological complexities. Typically, they do not know how newsgroups and chat rooms are hosted and many politicians do not know the difference between a newsgroup and a website. On the other hand, many providers of Internet infrastructure and services have little understanding of, let alone sympathy for, the concerns of users. Frequently complaints about material or requests for meetings are dealt with in a cavalier fashion or even ignored.

• Increasingly the debate about the content of the Internet is not national but global, not by specialists but by the general populace. There is a real need for this debate to be stimulated and structured and for it to lead to 'solutions' which are focussed, practical and urgent.

Is there a Place for Ethics?

In considering whether there is a place for ethics on the Internet, we need to have understanding of what such a grand word as 'ethics' means in this context. I suggest that it means four things:

1. Acceptance that the internet is not a value-free zone

This means that the World Wide Web is not the Wild Wild Web, instead a place where values in the broadest sense should take a part in shaping content and services. This is recognition that the Internet is not something apart from civil society, but increasingly a fundamental component of it.

2. Application of off-line laws to the on-line world

This means that we do not invent a new set of values for the Internet but, for all the practical problems, endeavour to apply the law which we have evolved for the physical space to the world of cyberspace. These laws might cover issues like child pornography, race hate, libel, copyright and consumer protection.

3. Sensitivity to national and local cultures

This means recognising that, while originally most Internet users were white, male Americans, now the Internet belongs to all. As a pervasively global phenomenon, it cannot be subject to one set of values like a local newspaper or national television station; somehow we have to accommodate a multiplicity of value systems.

4. Responsiveness to customer or user opinion

This means recognising that users of the Internet, and even non-users, are entitled to have a view on how it works. At the technical level, this is well understood, bodies like the Internet Engineering Task Force (IETF), the Internet Corporation for Assigned Names and Numbers (ICANN) and the World Wide Web Consortium (W3C) endeavour to understand and reflect user views. However, at no level do we have similar mechanisms for capturing user opinions on content and access to it.

Now that we have a better understanding of what ethics means in the context of the Internet, we need to address the question: whose responsibility is ethics on the net? The answer is that responsibility should be widely spread.

- Government is the democratic mechanism for deciding what activity is unacceptable – and therefore should be criminalised – in a particular society. As far as practical, these same laws should be applied to the Internet. Not many new laws – hacking is one example – are necessary.

- Having made laws, they should be enforced – in cyberspace as much as in the real world – and, in many jurisdictions, the police themselves have too little technical expertise and resource.

- Internet service providers have to accept that they are not the same as the telecommunications operator or the postal service which deliver private one-to-one messages. Although, given the nature of the Internet, they cannot possibly be expected to pre-check content, once they receive a notification or a complaint about something they are carrying or hosting, they have to take a view.

- Equally, the operators of services on the Internet have to take account of how that service might reasonably be expected to be used. For instance, if a Web hosting company carries a site providing information on bomb making or suicide assistance, they cannot claim to have no responsibility if that information is used. Or, if a chat room is used by a paedophile to groom a young girl before he manages to meet and abuse her, the operator of the chat room cannot deny any responsibility. This is not a matter of legal liability but of moral responsibility.

• Of course, Governments, law enforcement, ISPs and service operators can only do so much, which is why we have to empower end users. Consumers should be given the knowledge and the tools to apply their own ethical codes to use of the Internet by themselves and their families. Parents and teachers have a special responsibility in this regard.

• Finally, we need a compelling recognition that children must have special protection. Use of the Internet is not like watching television: the device is not shared in real time with other members of the family in a public space like the living room and broadcasting conventions like the 'watershed' (no adult content before 9 pm) do not apply. We need new defence mechanisms.

In seeking to apply a sense of ethics to cyberspace, there are some major problems but also some useful solutions.

Among the problems are:

• Jurisdictional competence

Laws are nation-based but cyberspace is global. How does one apply up to 170 separate and different legal systems to the Internet?

• Technological complexities

The Internet is a complex technical network and one cannot simply apply 'old' regulatory conventions from the worlds of publishing or broadcasting.

• The 'geeks' vs the 'suits'

As many Internet-related companies have grown, there is now an internal tension between the old-timers, with their vast technical knowledge, and the new-comers who are more likely to be marketing people much more aware of consumer concerns.

• Populist campaigns

The Internet is still so new and so mysterious for many that it is still relatively easy for a populist campaign to be whipped up which exaggerates the dangers of Internet content and/or minimises the technical complexities of dealing with it. We must be sensitive to consumer concerns, but the agenda cannot be determined by ill-informed politicians looking for votes or newspapers seeking to boost circulation.

Among the solutions are:

• **Modernisation of laws**

Governments need to consider whether pre-Internet laws need up-dating to take account of new crimes such as cyber stalking or grooming in chat rooms.

• **More high tech crime fighters**

Law enforcement agencies need more people with greater technical training and resource to tackle increasingly sophisticated cyber criminals such as paedophile rings. One example is the recent creation of the National High Tech Crime Unit in the UK.

• **'Note and take down' mechanisms**

We need organisations to which Internet users can report allegedly criminal content in the confident knowledge that this hotline is equipped to judge the legality and identify the hosting of material so that, if it is illegal and if it is in their jurisdictional area, they can issue a notice to the relevant ISP to remove it. A good example of such an operation is the Internet Watch Foundation in the UK.

• **Labelling and filtering**

We can best empower end users by greater labelling or rating of Internet content and greater use of more sophisticated filtering software. The Internet Content Rating Association (ICRA) has made considerable progress in developing and promoting a genuinely global, culturally independent labelling system. A wide range of companies provide filtering software which operates on different principles. In this way, households can make their own decisions based on their own cultural or ethical values.

• **Walled gardens**

For young children or as a transitional stage to full Internet access, one could use a 'walled garden' which restricts access to those sites pre-selected by a particular provider, typically with a child-friendly brand.

• **Better supervision of children**

All those with responsibility for children – especially parents, guardians, teachers and carers– need to become better aware of some of the problems of Internet use by children and the range of solutions which are available. They cannot rely, though, on technical solutions – regular conversation with, and observation of, the child is essential.

So, how will all this come about?

We need to give Internet users more relevant information. This should start at the point at which one purchases a PC or other Internet-enabled device. There should then be further information in both appropriate physical places – like school rooms – and relevant cyberspaces – like child-focused chat rooms.

We need a more informed debate through education and awareness campaigns. We cannot leave the terrain to civil libertarian 'purists', who too often see the Internet as a value-free or (as they would put it) censorship-free zone, or to the scare merchants who would have us believe that the Internet has more filth than facts.

Ideally, there should be some sort of organisational focus for this debate and the promotion of advice, education and awareness. In the UK, the Home Office has recently established a Task Force chaired by Lord Bassam; there is the Internet Crime Forum which brings together law enforcement, children's organisations and others, and there is the Internet Watch foundation which started as a hotline to combat criminal content but is now developing a wide-ranging education and awareness programme.

In a sense, the passage of time and greater familiarity with the new Internet medium may – almost of itself – ease some of the difficulties. In some respects, we are experiencing the kind of reactions seen in the early days of the telegraph or television and we will learn to adjust to the new challenges and opportunities.

The Yahoo! Case Study

An excellent case study on Internet ethics – and one being developed by INSEAD in Fontainebleau – is the French legal case against the American company Yahoo!. What are the basic facts of the case?

• The legal action was brought in April 2000 by the French organisations the International League against Racism and Anti-semitism (ILCRA)] and the French Jewish students organisation (UEJF)].

• The case was brought against Yahoo! Inc as well as Yahoo! in France and charged that the American company was in breach of French law for allowing French users to access the company's American site where Nazi memorabilia was being auctioned, since the sale of such items in France is illegal.

• The case was heard in May 2000 in a Paris court by Judge Jean-Jacques Gomez.

• The judge convened a three-member technical panel to examine whether it was possible to block French users from accessing parts of an American site.

• The judge found – in an order talking of an ethical and moral imperative – that the company was guilty, ordered it to block access by French users to the relevant part of the American site, and threatened fines for non-compliance of 100,000 francs ($13,300) a day.

• In January 2001, Yahoo! Inc announced that it would no longer permit the sale of Nazi memorabilia on its American site, thereby removing access not just to French Internet users but all users.

• Yahoo! is now appealing in an American court against the right of a non-American court to impose penalties on an American company.

What issues are raised by the Yahoo! case?

1. Should the Internet raise issues of ethics and morality? Should a company like Yahoo! have any interest in, or concern about, what one of its users sells to another of its users?

2. Is there a fundamental clash between American and European values as applied to Internet content? If there is, how should a conflict be reconciled or accommodated?

3. Should the Internet be borderless or should there be geolocation checkpoints? If there are to be such checkpoints, how would they work?

4. Can the courts of one country apply penalties to a company based in another country? If so, how will Internet e-commerce cope with multiple jurisdictions?

5. At this stage, I prefer simply to pose these questions rather than attempt to answer them. However, I would offer some personal views on some of the lessons that could be drawn from the Yahoo! case.

1. Countries have very different cultures

The French understandably are acutely sensitive to issues concerning the Holocaust – it happened on European soil and was visited upon Europeans by Europeans – whereas, not withstanding the strong Jewish lobby in the United States, Americans appear less offended by the sale of Nazi memorabilia. Another cultural difference involves the trial itself: whereas it was comprehensively reported in the French media, the British and America media appeared to view it as a strangely Gallic affair that merited less attention.

2. Courts are blunt instruments for Internet regulation

Obviously, courts are legalistic, but they are also confrontational and costly. We need cheaper, faster, more flexible means of resolving Internet problems. Yahoo! would have saved itself a lot of trouble and opprobrium if it has engaged in a meaningful dialogue with LICRA and LICRA should have given the company more time to develop such a dialogue.

3. Public opinion can exert considerable influence

Yahoo! opposed a demand by the court that it block access by French users to parts of its action site and yet, only months later, voluntarily decided that no-one in the world should have access because the offending items are no longer for sale. Undoubtedly, it was the views of Yahoo! users around the globe that persuaded the company to make such a policy reversal or volte face.

4. There are often different technical or commercial opinions

Yahoo! told the French court that it was technically impossible to block French users from parts of its American site, but a technical panel appointed by the court argued that such geolocation blocking was possible. Yahoo! was originally 'happy' to see anyone auction anything on its site free of charge, but now it has a much more restrictive policy and a pricing requirement.

5. Where there is a will, there is usually a way

Commercial companies – especially new companies operating in very fast-changing and competitive environments – do not like people to query their methods of operation and are often very resistant to proposals that, at least at first sight, would appear to complicate further their already complicated lives. But the Yahoo! case has shown that, when companies engage with a problem, they can find a solution.

Conclusions

Some final thoughts about the Internet and ethics:

• Solutions do not have to be perfect to be useful. In other words, the best should not be the enemy of the good. All the time that we procrastinate, millions more are coming onto the Net

• At the moment, the debate is basically between the USA and Western Europe. However, as Internet use expands into every corner of the globe, we will have to take a broader view of ethics and values.

• This is not a Star Wars, like battle between good and evil. It is a difference in values which can and should be resolved by education and debate.

Glossary

a

Active Proceedings (sub judice) – These occur in a criminal court of law when a person has been arrested, a warrant for his or her arrest has been issued, there are bail conditions (including police bail), a summons has been issued or a person has been charged (with a criminal offence).

ABC – Audit Bureau of Circulations; a group that audits newspaper circulation figures.

ABCe – Audit Bureau of Circulations Electronic; division of the ABC that audits traffic figures for online publications.

ACAP – Automated Content Access Protocol; a platform that would allow search engines to recognise the terms and conditions of specific websites.

Add – Copy to be added to a story already written.

Adobe InDesign – Desktop publishing programme, now being used more widely in place of QuarkXPress.

Ad Impression – Term used to describe the number of times an advert is seen. Advertisers usually sell space based on the exposure per thousand impressions. This is called Cost per Impression (CPM). Alternatively, they might sell on a pay-per-click (CPC) basis (also known as Cost-per-Click – CPC).

ADSL – Asymmetric Digital Subscriber Line; high bandwidth web connection often just called broadband.

Advance – A story outlining a future event. Also means to raise the priority of a story or an upfront payment for written work, particularly long articles or text.

All Caps – A word or sentence written in all capital letters.

Advertorial – An advert in the form of a complementary editorial piece, usually labelled as an advert.

Analog Television – TV transmitted in radio waves as opposed to digital TV.

Angle – The approach or focus of a story. This is sometimes known as the peg.

AP – The abbreviation for the Associated Press.

Assignment – A job given to a journalist by an editor.

Astroturfing – A term used to describe fake grassroots support on websites and in blog comments. A method most usually employed by the public relations and advertising industry and political groups.

Attribute – To quote the original source of material, whether it be a quote of copyrighted work.

Audit – An independent assessment of the validity of statistics used in adverts, newspapers etc.

AOP – Formed in 2002, the Association of Online Publishers is an industry body for UK web publishers. The AOP represents the interests of 160 publishing companies.

Average Issue Readership – Number of people who have read the newspaper or magazine in the period that it was issued, also known as AIR.

B

B2B – Business to business; describes a business whose primary customers are other businesses.

B2C – Business to customer; describes a business whose primary customers are individuals.

Background – Information given to a reporter to explain more about the situation and details of a story. Sometimes shortened to BG.

Back Bench – Senior journalists on a newspaper.

Bandwidth – The amount of data that can be transferred through an Internet connection.

Banner Ad – Web advert, normally found at the top of a page. Typically around 468 by 60 pixels in size. Sometimes called a web banner.

BARB – Broadcasting Audience Research Board, measures TV audience numbers.

BBC – British Broadcasting Corporation.

Beat – The area or subject that a reporter regularly covers.

Best Boy – Broadcasting term for second-in-command of a lighting team.

Blawg – Weblog dealing with aspects of law.

Bliki – Combination of a blog and a wiki; a blog that can be edited by readers or an approved group of users.

Blind Interview – An interview with an unnamed source.

Blog – An online commentary or diary often written by individuals about hobbies or areas of specialist interest. Blogs commonly allow comments below entries and are published in reverse chronological order. Also known as a weblog.

Blogger – A person who writes a blog.

Blogosphere/Blogdom/Blogiverse/Blogmos/Blogostan – All things relating to blogs and blog communities.

Blurb – Brief introduction to the writer, usually following the headline.

BRAD – British Rate and Data; a company that logs every periodical that has to do with advertising in Britain.

Break – When a story is first published. Sometimes called breaking news.

Broadcast – Communicating using radio and/or TV.

Browser – A piece of software that allows users to view Internet pages. Popular browsers include Firefox, Internet Explorer and Safari.

Bulks – Copies distributed free, normally for promotion.

Bump – To move the position or timing of a story.

Button – A small web advertisement, usually around 165 by 90 pixels in size and commonly found in the right or left hand columns of a website.

Byline – A journalist's name at the beginning of a story.

C

Cable Television – TV delivered into the home through an underground cable.

Campaign – The various stages of an advertising project from beginning to end.

Caps – Upper case.

Caption – Text printed below a picture used to describe it and who took it. Sometimes called a cutline.

Cascading Stylesheets (CSS) – Technique used for designing web pages. One file that defines the style for a whole site.

Chat rooms – An interactive part of a website where visitors can write messages to each other people in real time. Also known as forums and message boards.

Churnalism – Bad journalism; journalists that churn out rewrites of press releases.

Centre of Visual Interest (CVI) – The prominent item on a page usually a headline, picture or graphic.

CIOJ – The Chartered Institute of Journalists.

Circulation – Number of copies sold by newspapers or magazines. In the UK these figures are monitored by ABC – The Audit Bureau of Circulations.

Citizen Journalism – Term used to describe the reporting of news events by members of the public most commonly on blogs and social networking websites. Other terms include participatory journalism and networked journalism though it should not be confused with civic journalism, which is practised by professional journalists.

Classified Advertising – Advertising placed by individuals in newspapers. Sometimes called small ads.

Clickthrough – When a reader clicks on an advert and is redirected to a new page. Advertisers sometimes buy adverts based on a rate per click called a Click-through rate or CTR.

Closed Question – A simple yes/no question that does little to encourage an interviewee to open up.

Column – A regular feature often on a specific topic, written by the same person who is known as a columnist.

Contempt of Court – The criminal offence of ignoring court rules.

Content Management System – CMS is a program for easily editing and placing content such as text, still images and videos on web sites.

Convergence – The term used to describe multimedia newsrooms producing news for different publishing platforms.

Cookie – Small text file that is downloaded to your computer when you visit a site. The next time you visit, the site can use the file to remember details such as your login information.

Copy – Main text of a story.

Copy Approval – A source or interviewer asking to see the text of an article prior to publication. (Always discouraged!)

Copywriting – Creating the text for an advertisement.

Coverline – Captions on a magazine cover.

Cover Story – Leading story used on front cover.

CPM – Cost per thousand impressions. This is the cost an advertiser pays for 1,000 page views. The M in CPM is the Roman numeral for 1,000.

Crosshead – A few words used to break up large amounts of text, normally taken from the main text. Typically used in interviews.

Cub – A trainee reporter. Also known as a rookie or junior reporter.

Cut – To remove text.

Cuttings – A journalist's collection of published print work. Also known as clips and sometimes presented as a portfolio.

Cuttings Job – An article which has been put together using research culled from a number of other articles or news items.

Cyber-journalist – A journalist that works on the Internet. An online journalist.

Dateline – A line at the beginning of a story stating the date and the location.

Deadline – The time at which an editor requests a journalists to finish an assignment.

Death-knock – Calling at the house of a bereaved relative or friend when reporting on the death. Also known as door-stepping.

Deck – Part of the headline which summarises the story. Also known as deck copy or bank.

Defamation – Information that is written by one person which damages another person reputation.

Digg – A community powered Internet link recommendation system. Furl offers a similar service.

Direct Quote – The exact reproduction of a verbatim quote in quotemarks and correctly attributed.

DHTML – Dynamic HTML. Allows exciting things to happen when you move your mouse over words.

Digital Television – TV transmitted in binary format, producing good picture quality.

Direct Marketing – Sending advertising material directly to potential customers either by post, fax, email or information by telephone.

Dogblogging – When the upkeep of a weblog becomes a hassle.

Dowdification – Deliberate omission of a term or terms to change the meaning of a quote. Refers to journalist Maureen Dowd.

Download – Copying a file from a website to your own computer.

Draft – The first version of an article before editing and submission to the editor.

Dropdown Menus – Name given to website menus that allow users to select from a list of options that drop down in a vertical menu.

DPS – Double-page spread; can also be referred to as a spread.

e – Often used to indicate an electronic version of something, for example eNews, for an electronic newsletter, or eGovernment, to describe electronic government.

Editor – Someone who prepares material for print or broadcast.

Editorialise – To write in an opinionated way.

Encryption – TV signals encoded so only paying subscribers can watch.

Endnote – Text written at the end of an article stating the authors' credentials.

eTail – Online or 'electronic' retail.

Exclusivity – When an advert appears exclusively on a page, rather than being in rotation with other ads.

Ezine – Specialised online magazines.

F

Feature – A longer, more in-depth article.

Fisk – Detailed word-by-word analysis and critique of an article. Refers to journalist Robert Fisk.

Flash – A programme used to display design-heavy, animated content.

Flash – Short news story on a new event.

Flatplan – A page plan that shows where the articles and adverts are laid out.

Follow-up – An update on a previous story.

Font – Typeface.

Freelancer – Someone that works alone, usually on a contract-to-contract basis.

Freesheet – A publication that is free to consumers and generates its revenue from advertising.

Free-to-air – TV service received without having to decode or pay.

Freeview – Commercial free-to-air digital service, between BBC, BSkyB and the transmission firm Crown Castle.

Frontline Club – A club in London that promotes "freedom of expression and support journalists, cameramen and photographers who risk their lives in the course of their work."

FTP – File Transfer Protocol. A method of moving files, usually used to transfer files from your computer to a web server.

FYI – An abbreviation meaning for your information.

G

Get – A very good or exclusive interview.

GIF – A type of picture file, often used for images that include text.

Glossite – The website of a glossy women's magazine.

Graf – Paragraph.

Grip – A person that looks after the equipment required to make a TV camera move.

H

Hard copy – When the article is printed out on paper.

Hits – Number of downloads of every element of a web page, rather than the page as a whole. A page of 20 images, text boxes, logos and menus will count as 20 hits, so hits are therefore not regarded as a reliable measurement of web traffic.

Headline – The main title of the article.

Homepage – The front page of a website.

House Style – A publication's guide to style, spelling and use of grammar, designed to help journalists write and present in a consistent way for their target audience. The Economist publishes a style guide as does The Guardian.

HTML – Hyper Text Mark-up Language. Basic programming code used for the design and display of web pages.

Hyperlink – A link that redirects the user to another web page.

I

Impressions – The number of times an advertising banner was viewed during a campaign.

An Internet – Any network of connected computers.

The Internet – The international network of interconnected computers. The World Wide Web, email, FTP and usenet are all part of the Internet.

Intranet – A private computer network inside a company or organisation for internal use only.

Intro – Very important first paragraph, known as a 'lead' in the US.

Inventory – The number of advertisement spaces for sale on a website at a given time.

Island position – An advert surrounded by editorial content in the middle of the page.

ITV Network – 15 regional franchises that make up ITV1. ITV is the Broadcaster that was formed by the merger of Carlton and Granada.

J

Javascript – A scripting language commonly used to add functionality to web sites beyond that which is achievable in HTML.

JPEG – Joint Photographic Expert Group. Common type of picture file used on the web.

Joost – Interactive television software produced by the makers of Skype and Kazaa.

Journalist – Someone who writes, researches and reports news, or works on the production of a publication. Sometimes shortened to journo, hack or scribe.

Kerning – Adjustment of horizontal space between two written characters.

Kicker – The first sentence or first few words of a story's lead, set in a font size larger than the body text of the story.

Kill – To cancel or delete a story.

Kill fee – A reduced fee paid to a journalist for a story that is not used.

Kittyblog – A pointless and boring weblog, possibly about the owner's cat.

Layout – (noun) How the page is designed and formatted.

Layout Sub-editor – A sub-editor who specialises in laying out pages.

Leader – An article that shows the opinion of a newspaper.

Leading – Adjustment of vertical space between two lines.

Leading Questions – A question that contains the predicted answer within the question.

Libel – A case for defamation. Defendant would need to show claims were true, fair comment or an accurate record of parliamentary or court proceedings.

Licence Fee – BBC funding system.

Lobster Shift – Working in the hours after a publication has gone to print. Also known as dog watch.

Long Tail – The effect of publishing content online and keeping it available in an archive. Unlike in a newspaper, old stories will continue to receive traffic long after publication date, hence the long tail.

m

Mark – Correction.

Martini Media – Media that is available "any time, any place, any where".

Mashup, Mashup, or Mash-up – a website or web application that seamlessly combines content from more than one source into an integrated experience.

Masthead – Main title section and name at the front of a publication.

Media Kit – Practical information available to potential advertisers regarding costs etc. See the *New York Times, San Francisco Chronicle* and the *Belfast Telegraph* for examples.

Microblogs – Blogs dealing with very specialised discussion.

Microblogging – Variant of traditional blogging in which users write brief text messages over the web. Popularised by web site Twitter, which limits users to 140-character updates.

Moblogging – Where individuals contribute to a blog using images or text sent from a mobile phone.

MPEG – Moving Pictures Experts Group. A file format used for digital video.

MPU – Known as a Messaging Plus Unit, a large square web advert usually in a central position below or inline with editorial. Typically around 350 by 250 pixels in size.

Multimedia – Term used to describe a range of different delivery formats such as video, audio, text and images, often presented simultaneously on the Internet.

Multiplex – Single digital terrestrial TV transmission comprising of several channels.

N

Navigation – Structure that helps web users move around the website.

NCTJ – National Council for Training of Journalists, official UK accreditation board for journalism courses.

Netiquette – Online etiquette, e.g. reciprocal links.

Networked journalism – Another term to describe participatory journalism or citizen journalism.

News Agency – Company that sells stories to newspapers or magazines.

Newspaper Society – Industry body representing the regional press & local press.

Newsreader – Software that helps receive and read RSS blog and news feeds.

NIB – News in brief – a quick summary of a story.

Nut graf – Paragraph containing the essential elements of a story.

NUJ – National Union of Journalists, a UK trade union.

O

Ofcom – Broadcasting industry regulator.

Off Diary – An unscheduled or unpredicted story.

Off the Record – Information that must not be disclosed.

On Diary – Scheduled story.

On Spec – Article that is written 'just in-case', but it will only be used if needed.

On the Record – Information given by a source that can be used in an article.

Op-ed – A feature, usually by a prominent journalist, presenting an opinionated story.

Open Source Software – Software with openly available code to allow developers or others to modify it.

Orphan – First line of a paragraph appearing on the last line of a column of text. Normally avoided.

P

PDF – Portable Document Format – a standard file format that allows web publishers to post documents viewable by any user who installs a copy of the free Acrobat Reader.

PACT – Industry body representing independent cinema and TV producers.

Pay-per-view – A single programme that the viewer has to pay for.

Pay TV – Paid subscription service for TV.

PDA – Personal Digital Assistant. A hand-held computer combining a phone, organiser and web client.

Photoblogging – Contributing photos to a blog.

Photoshop – (noun) Computer program used to edit photographs.

Pitch – Story idea sent to an editor by a reporter.

Pixel – An on-screen measurement. Most monitors display around 1024 pixels wide by 768 pixels high.

Podcasts – MP3 audio recordings that can automatically download to a user's computer as soon as they are published online.

Point size – Size of the type face.

Pop-under/pop-behind – A web advert that opens under the browser window.

Pop-up – A web advert that pops up on screen. These are commonly blocked with a pop-up blocker.

Post – To add a comment to a blog.

Pork – Material held for later use, if needed.

PPA – Periodical Publishers Association. Industry body representing UK magazine publishers.

Portal – A busy site often used as a starting point online through services such as messaging, news and searches.

Proof – Copy of a laid-out page ready to be corrected.

Prosumer – Marketing term used to describe professional consumers.

Puff Piece – A news story with editorialised, complimentary statements.

Pulldown – Web text that is activated by a down arrow on a web menu.

Pulitzer Prize – American journalism awards. There are fourteen prizes for journalism. The prizes have been awarded by Columbia University since 1917.

Pull-out quote – Selected quote from a story highlighted next to the main text. Often used in interviews.

Q

QuarkXPress – Desktop publishing programme.

Quote – Record of what a source or interviewee has said.

R

Radio Spectrum – Total capacity of radio frequencies that can be received.

Rate Card – A list of advertising rates provided by a publisher.

Recto – Right-hand page.

Redletter – Exclusive, breaking news coverage of a major news event, printed in red type.

Reporter – Someone who writes and researches news stories.

Reporters without Borders – An organisation founded in 1985 that fights for press freedom around the world.

Retraction – A withdrawal of a previously-published story or fact.

Revision – A re-written or improved story, often with additional quotes or facts.

Rich Media – Artwork formats such as Flash, Java and DHTML that allow interactive or multimedia content.

Roadblock – The sale of all the adverts on your home page to one advertiser.

RSS – This began life as Rich Site Summary in 1999, then mutated to Really/ Real Simple Simple Syndication in 2002, then Real Simple Synchronisation in 2005.

Run – To publish a story.

S

Sell – Short sentence promoting an article, often pulling out a quote or an interesting sentence. See also Pull-out quote.

Spider – Also known as a crawler or ant, a program that uses hyperlinks to make methodical searches of the web to provide information about pages for search engines.

Sacred Cow – News or promotional material which a publisher or editor demands be published, often for personal reasons.

Serif and Sans Serif – Plain font type with or without (sans) lines perpendicular to the ends of characters.

Satellite Television – TV received through a satellite dish.

Scoop – An exclusive or first-published story.

Scoopt – the world's first citizen journalism photograph agency owned by Getty Images.

Search Box – A tool that allows users to enter a word or phrase to search a database.

Server – A computer that hosts the pages of a web site.

Shockwave – Software that allows the user to play multimedia animations; published by Macromedia.

Skype – Popular free Internet telephony tool sometimes used to produce Skypecasts, or broadcast conference calls.

Skyscraper – A vertical banner advert, usually at one side of a web page and 60 x 468 pixels in size.

Social Bookmarking – A service that allows users to store interesting website addresses publicly on a web page and lets users network and pool recommendations.

Source – An individual who provides information for a story.

Spike – Not to publish a submitted article.

Splash – Front page story.

Standfirst – Line of text after the headline that gives more information about the article.

Stet – Proofreader's mark for 'restore to condition before mark up'.

Sticky Content – Content that encourages users to stay on one site for as long as possible.

Strapline – Similar to a subhead or standfirst, but used more as a marketing term.

Streaming – Watching or listening to video or audio in real time, rather than downloading files.

Sub-editor – The person that checksand edits a reporters' work and adds headlines and standfirsts.

Subhead – A smaller one-line headline for a story.

Superstitials – A type of rich media advert that downloads gradually without obscuring other content on the page; usually more popular than pop ups.

Tabloid – Smaller print newspaper size.

Technobabble – Confusing technical jargon.

Technorati – Powerful blog search engine.

Teeline – A form of shorthand.

Terrestrial Television – TV sent through a beam transmitter directly into the home.

Testimonial – Endorsement of a product, often by a celebrity or well-respected client.

TK – Proofreader's insertion mark for data to come. Sometimes written as TKTK.

Tie in – Placing the facts of a new story within the context of past events. Also known as a tie back.

Tip – A lead of piece of new information about a new story.

Top Heads – Headlines at the top of a column.

Traffic – Amount of users recorded by a website.

Twitter – A service that allows users to send 140 character messages to 'friends' via mobile SMS, website or Instant Messenger.

U

Unique Users – The number of individual users, as identified by unique computer addresses, that visit a web site.

Upload – To publish a file on the Internet.

URL – Uniform Resource Locator, technical name for a web address.

User – A visitor or reader on a web site.

User-generated content – Material created and submitted to sites by its **users** – such as photographs, video footage, comments, articles etc.

V

Verso – Left-hand page.

Video Blogger/Vlogger – A blogger who mainly uses video and publishes on the Internet.

Video Journalist – A journalist who publishes video reports on TV and/or on the Internet.

Vertical Search Engine – A search engine containing information on a specific subject area.

W

WAP – Wireless Application Protocol – an international standard for the application that enables access to a wireless Internet network using a mobile device.

Web Scraping – Automated process of finding content on web pages and converting it into another form for use on another web site.

Warblogs – Opinionated and political web logs.

Webcasting – Online visual and/or audio broadcasts, usually in real time.

Webmercials – Similar format to television adverts used online.

Webinar/Web Conference – A seminar, lecture or presentation delivered over the Internet.

Widow – Last line of paragraph appearing on the first line of a column of text.

Widget – Application available to download or embed on a desktop, homepage or social network. Allows you to share content, which will be automatically updated, e.g. journalism.co.uk's news headlines.

Wi-fi – Wireless Internet or network connection.

Wiki – An information site that can be edited and added to by readers. See **Wikipedia** – an online Wiki encyclopaedia.

Wires – Stories or photographs sent electrically to your desktop. Here is a list of wire news services.